T0272007

Bridges and Barriers

Language in African Education and Development

Eddie Williams

Routledge
Taylor & Francis Group

LONDON AND NEW YORK

First published 2006 by St. Jerome Publishing

Published 2014 by Routledge
2 Park Square, Milton Park, Abingdon, Oxon OX14 4RN
711 Third Avenue, New York, NY 10017, USA

Routledge is an imprint of the Taylor & Francis Group, an informa business

ISBN 13: 978-1-900650-97-7 (hbk)
ISSN 1471-0277 *(Encounters)*

Typeset by
Delta Typesetters, Cairo, Egypt

British Library Cataloguing in Publication Data
A catalogue record of this book is available from the British Library

Library of Congress Cataloguing in Publication Data
Williams, Eddie.
      Bridges and Barriers : language in African education and development /
by Eddie Williams.
        p. cm. -- (Encounters)
      Includes index.
      ISBN 1-900650-97-5 (alk. paper)
      1. Education--Africa. 2. Language and education--Africa. I. Title.
LA1501.W49 2006
370.96--dc22

                                                            2006020486

Encounters

A new series on language and diversity
Edited by Jan Blommaert, Marco Jacquemet and Ben Rampton

Diversity has come to be recognized as one of the central concerns in our thinking about society, culture and politics. At the same time, it has proved one of the most difficult issues to deal with on the basis of established theories and methods, particularly in the social sciences. Studying diversity not only challenges widespread views of who we are and what we do in social life; it also challenges the theories, models and methods by means of which we proceed in studying diversity. Diversity exposes the boundaries and limitations of our theoretical models, in the same way it exposes our social and political organizations.

Encounters sets out to explore diversity *in* language, diversity *through* language and diversity *about* language. Diversity *in* language covers topics such as intercultural, gender, class or age-based variations in language and linguistic behaviour. Diversity *through* language refers to the way in which language and linguistic behaviour can contribute to the construction or negotiation of such sociocultural and political differences. And diversity *about* language has to do with the various ways in which language and diversity are being perceived, conceptualized and treated, in professional as well as in lay knowledge – thus including the reflexive and critical study of scientific approaches alongside the study of language politics and language ideologies. In all this, mixedness, creolization, crossover phenomena and heterogeneity are privileged areas of study. The series title, *Encounters*, is intended to encourage a relatively neutral but interested stance towards diversity, moving away from the all too obvious 'cultures-collide' perspective that is dominant within the social sciences.

The target public of *Encounters* includes scholars and advanced students of linguistics, communication studies, anthropology, cultural studies, sociology, as well as students and scholars in neighbouring disciplines such as translation studies, gender studies, gay and lesbian studies, postcolonial studies.

Jan Blommaert is former Research Director of the IPrA Research Centre of the University of Antwerp and currently Professor of Languages in Education at the Institute of Education, University of London. He is author of *Discourse* (Cambridge University Press, 2005), co-author of *Debating Diversity: Analysing the Discourse of Tolerance* (Routledge, 1998), editor of *Language Ideological Debates* (Mouton de Gruyter 1999), and co-editor of the *Handbook of Pragmatics* (John Benjamins 1995-2003) and *The Pragmatics of Intercultural and International Communication* (John Benjamins 1991).

Marco Jacquemet is Assistant Professor of Communication Studies at the University of San Francisco. His work focuses on the complex interaction of different languages and communicative practices in a globalized world. His current research seeks to assess the communicative mutations resulting from the intersection in the Mediterranean area between mobile people (migrants, local and international aid workers, missionaries, businessmen, etc.) and electronic texts (content distributed by satellites, local television stations, Internet connectivity, cellular telephony). As part of this research, in the early 1990s he studied the communicative practices of criminal networks in Southern Italy and the emerging Italian cyberculture. In 1994 he conducted fieldwork in Morocco and Italy on migratory patterns between the two countries. Since 1998, he has been involved in multi-site ethnographic fieldwork in Albania and Italy, investigating the linguistic and socio-cultural consequences of Albania's entry into the global system of late-modern capitalism. Marco Jacquemet is author of *Credibility in Court: Communicative Practices in the Camorra Trials* (Cambridge University Press 1996).

Ben Rampton is Professor of Applied and Sociolinguistics at King's College London. His work involves ethnographic and interactional discourse analysis, frequently also drawing on anthropology, sociology and cultural studies. His publications cover urban multilingualism; language, youth, ethnicities and class; language education; second language learning; and research methodology. Ben Rampton is author of *Crossing: Language & Ethnicity among Adolescents* (St. Jerome 2004) and *Language and Late Modernity: Interaction in an Urban School* (Cambridge University Press, forthcoming), co-author of *Researching Language: Issues of Power & Method* (Routledge 1992), and co-editor of *The Language, Ethnicity & Race Reader* (Routledge 2003).

To the memory of Christopher Brumfit, Applied Linguist,
1940-2006.

Contents

List of Tables   xi
List of Figures   xiv
Abbreviations   xvi
Preface   xvii

1.   **Introduction**   **1**
     1.1 Africa: current preoccupations   1
     1.2 Education, language and development   6
     1.3 Concepts of development   8
     1.4 Education and development   10

2.   **Malawi and Zambia – The Background**   **16**
     2.1 Rationale for country selection   16
     2.2 Zambia   16
          2.2.1 General   16
          2.2.2 Language in Zambia   17
          2.2.3 Primary education in Zambia   21
     2.3 Malawi   24
          2.3.1 General   24
          2.3.2 Language in Malawi   25
          2.3.3 Primary education in Malawi   28
     2.4 Pedagogic approaches to reading in Malawi and Zambia   29
          2.4.1 Malawi   30
               2.4.1.1 Reading and English in the primary syllabus   30
               2.4.1.2 Reading in teacher training   32
               2.4.1.3 Classroom practice in reading   33
          2.4.2 Zambia   35
               2.4.2.1 Reading in the primary syllabus   35
               2.4.2.2 Reading in teacher training   36
               2.4.2.3 Classroom practice in reading   37
     2.5 Observations on classroom reading in Malawi and Zambia   39
     2.6 Previous research on reading in Zambia and Malawi   43

3.   **Reading in First and Additional Languages**   **48**
     3.1 Reading and literacy   48
     3.2 Language in reading   52
          3.2.1 Language and language levels   52
          3.2.2 First language, second language and mother tongue   52
          3.2.3 Language in models of the reading process   54

3.2.4 Grammar and reading   55
3.2.5 Vocabulary and reading   57
3.3 First language reading and second language proficiency.   61
3.3.1 Research evidence   61
3.3.2 Findings from educational surveys   62
3.3.3 Counter-evidence   64
3.3.4 Explanations for contradictory findings   65
3.4 Research Objectives   67
3.4.1 General aims   67
3.4.2 Research hypotheses   68

4. **The Reading Tests**   71
4.1 The schools   71
4.1.1 Selected schools in Malawi   72
4.1.2 Selected schools in Zambia   74
4.2 The students   75
4.3 The reading tests   79
4.3.1 Test construction   79
4.3.2 Rationale for modified cloze tests   82
4.3.3 African language tests   83
4.4 Test administration   86

5. **Results of the English Reading Tests**   87
5.1 General description   87
5.2 English reading test results, Malawi   90
5.2.1 National level   90
5.2.2 Differences between schools   91
5.2.3 Sex differences   93
5.2.4 Location (urban/rural) differences   96
5.2.5 Location and sex effects combined   97
5.3 English reading test results: Zambia   98
5.3.1 National level   98
5.3.2 Differences between schools   100
5.3.3 Sex differences   101
5.3.4 Location (urban/rural) differences   102
5.3.5 Location and sex effects combined   104
5.4 General comparison of the English test results in Malawi
    and Zambia   106
5.5 Testing of the hypotheses for English: Summary   108

6. **Results of the African Language Reading Tests**   111
6.1 General   111

6.2 Results of African language reading tests, Zambia   111
   6.2.1 National level   111
   6.2.2 School differences   112
   6.2.3 Sex differences   114
   6.2.4 Location (urban/rural) differences   115
   6.2.5 Sex and location differences combined   115
   6.2.6 Testees from Non-Nyanja Homes   116
   6.2.7 Comparison of English and Nyanja test results   117
6.3 Results of African language reading tests, Malawi   118
   6.3.1 National level   118
   6.3.2 School differences   120
   6.3.3 Sex differences   122
   6.3.4 Location (rural/urban) differences   123
   6.3.5 Sex and location differences combined   124
   6.3.6 Testees from non-Chichewa homes   125
   6.3.7 Comparison of English and Chichewa results   126
6.4 African language reading: Malawi and Zambia compared   129
6.5 Cross country comparison of English and African
   language results   131
6.6 Malawian performance on the Nyanja (Zambian) test   132
6.7 Testing of hypotheses for African language results:
   Summary   133
   6.7.1 Cross-country comparisons (Malawi and Zambia)   133
   6.7.2 Within-country African language comparisons   134
      6.7.2.1 Malawi   134
      6.7.2.2 Zambia   134

7. Individual Reading Sessions   **136**
7.1 The participants: assistants and students   136
7.2 The reading sessions   137
7.3 Techniques in the investigation of reading strategies   137
7.4 Individual reading of English   138
   7.4.1 The English reading text   138
   7.4.2 Findings for the English reading sessions   140
   7.4.3 Difficulties in the English text reported by
      students   145
   7.4.4 Strategies for assigning meaning in English   147
   7.4.5 The English reading sessions as validation
      for the test results   153
7.5 African Language Individual Reading Sessions   154
   7.5.1 The African language reading text   154
   7.5.2 Individual African language reading sessions, Malawi 155

7.5.3 Individual African language reading sessions,
     Zambia   157
7.5.4 Comparison of the African language reading sessions
     and the reading test results   162
7.5.5 Conclusion on African language reading   164

8.   The Language Dilemma in African Schools   168
8.1 General   168
8.2 Language in reading in Malawi and Zambia   169
8.3 Lexical competence in English   171
8.4 Explaining differential reading proficiencies   172
8.5 Learning in English across the curriculum   174
8.6 Possibilities for amelioration   178
     8.6.1 Reducing the dominance of English   178
     8.6.2 Improving teaching of English reading   181
     8.6.3 Comments on the possibilities   182

9.   Conclusion   186
9.1 Language Policy and Language Development   186
     9.1.1 English and unification   188
     9.1.2 English and development   192
9.2 Educational effectiveness and development   193
9.3 Politics, conditions, capitals and agencies   197

Envois   204

Appendices   205
1.   Map of Africa   205
2.   Text and Transcript for English Lesson, Malawi   206
3.   Text and Transcript for English Lesson, Zambia   212
4.   Test Type Exercizes from Course Books   218
5.   Year of Introduction of Lexical Items from English Test   219
6.   Extracts from Reading Tests   221
7.   Reliability Results for Tests   223
8.   Test Item Facility Values   227

Refrences   231

Index   252

List of Tables

Table 2.1   Main languages in Zambia by percentages   19
Table 2.2   Main languages in Malawi (used for household
            communication)   26
Table 3.1   Text coverage and word frequency   59
Table 4.1   Data Structure for Reading Tests (English and
            ChiChewa), Malawi   76
Table 4.2   Data Structure for Reading Tests (English and
            Nyanja), Zambia   76
Table 4.3   Pooled teacher estimates for English test scores   82
Table 4.4   Pooled teacher estimates for African language test
            scores   85
Table 5.1   Summary statistics for English test results, Malawi
            and Zambia   89
Table 5.2   Summary statistics for English test results, Malawi   90
Table 5.3   Summary statistics for English test results by school,
            Malawi   91
Table 5.4   Summary statistics for English test results
            by sex – Malawi   93
Table 5.5   Mean scores, English test of girls in single sex and
            mixed sex schools, by location, Malawi   95
Table 5.6   Mean scores, English test, of boys in single sex and
            mixed sex schools, by location, Malawi   95
Table 5.7   Summary statistics for English test results by location,
            Malawi   96
Table 5.8   Mean scores by location and sex, English test,
            Malawi   97
Table 5.9   Summary statistics for English test results, Zambia   98
Table 5.10 Summary statistics for English test results by school,
            Zambia   100
Table 5.11 Summary statistics for English test results by sex,
            Zambia   101
Table 5.12 Summary statistics for English test results
            by location, Zambia   102
Table 5.13 Summary statistics for English test results
            by location and sex, Zambia   104
Table 5.14 Summary statistics for Malawi and Zambia, English
            test results   106
Table 5.15 Malawi, significance tests for English test scores   109

Table 5.16 Zambia, significance tests for English test scores   110
Table 5.17 Malawi and Zambia combined, significance tests for
          English test scores   110
Table 6.1   Summary statistics for Nyanja test results, Zambia   111
Table 6.2   Summary statistics for Nyanja test results by school,
          Zambia   113
Table 6.3   Summary statistics for Nyanja test results by sex,
          Zambia   114
Table 6.4   Summary statistics for test score in Nyanja by location,
          Zambia   115
Table 6.5   Summary statistics for Nyanja results by location and
          sex, Zambia   116
Table 6.6   Summary statistics for Chichewa test results, Malawi   119
Table 6.7   Summary statistics for Chichewa test results by school,
          Malawi   120
Table 6.8   Significant differences by school means, ChiChewa,
          Malawi   121
Table 6.9   Summary statistics for Chichewa test results by sex,
          Malawi   122
Table 6.10 Summary statistics for test score in Chichewa by
          location, Malawi   123
Table 6.11 Summary statistics of test scores in Chichewa by sex
          and location, Malawi   124
Table 6.12 Spearman correlation coefficients between test
          score in English and in Chichewa, by school   127
Table 6.13 Frequency of pupils with English scores greater than,
          or equal to, ChiChewa scores, by school, Malawi   128
Table 6.14 Summary statistics for African language test results,
          Zambia and Malawi   129
Table 6.15 t-test of differences by language of instruction,
          Malawi and Zambia   131
Table 6.16 Statistical summary of results of Nyanja reading test
          for Malawian pupils   132
Table 6.17 Malawi and Zambia, significance tests for African
          language results   133
Table 6.18 Malawi, significance tests for Chichewa results   134
Table 6.19 Significance tests for Nyanja reading test results,
          Zambia   135
Table 7.1   Responses to Direct Reference Questions, Malawi   141
Table 7.2   Responses to Direct Reference Questions, Zambia   141
Table 7.3   Results of Text-based Inference Questions, Malawi   143

Table 7.4   Results of Text-based Inference Questions, Zambia   143
Table 7.5   Acceptable responses by Malawian students to prompts
            for unknown words   152
Table 7.6   Acceptable responses by Zambian students to prompts
            for unknown words   152
Table 7.7   Students who read Nyanja and claimed Nyanja as home
            language   161
Table 7.8   Mean Scores of High and Low Scoring Groups in
            English and Chichewa Reading Tests, Malawi   162
Table 7.9   Mean Scores of High and Low Scoring Groups in
            English and Nyanja Reading Tests, Zambia   163
Table 8.1   Pooled teacher estimates and actual scores, English
            test   174
Table 8.2   Pooled teacher estimates and actual scores, local
            language test   174

List of Figures

Figure 5.1   Facility values of items in English test,
             Malawi and Zambia   88
Figure 5.2   Histogram of total scores in English test,
             Malawi and Zambia   89
Figure 5.3   Frequency of total scores in English test, Malawi   91
Figure 5.4   Box plots of English test results by school, Malawi   92
Figure 5.5   Box plots of English test results by sex, Malawi   93
Figure 5.6   Mean scores in English, schools by sex, Malawi   94
Figure 5.7   Box plots of English test scores by location, Malawi   96
Figure 5.8   Distribution of English scores by location, Malawi   97
Figure 5.9   Box plots of English scores by location and sex,
             Malawi   98
Figure 5.10 Frequency of total scores of English Test, Zambia   99
Figure 5.11 Box plots of English scores by school, Zambia   101
Figure 5.12 Box plots of English scores by sex, Zambia   102
Figure 5.13 Box plots of English test scores by location, Zambia   103
Figure 5.14 Distribution of English scores by location, Zambia   104
Figure 5.15 Box plots, English test results by location and sex,
             Zambia   105
Figure 5.16 Histogram, mean English scores by sex and school,
             Zambia   106
Figure 5.17 Box plots of English test scores, Malawi and
             Zambia   107
Figure 5.18 Box plots of English test results by school,
             Malawi and Zambia   108
Figure 6.1   Histogram of frequency of scores for the Nyanja
             reading test, Zambia   112
Figure 6.2   Facility values of items in Nyanja test, Zambia   112
Figure 6.3   Box plots of Nyanja test results by school, Zambia   113
Figure 6.4   Box plot of Nyanja results by sex, Zambia   114
Figure 6.5   Box plots of Nyanja test scores by sex and location,
             Zambia   116
Figure 6.6   Mean scores in Nyanja and English by school,
             Zambia   117
Figure 6.7   Scatterplot of English and Nyanja scores   118
Figure 6.8   Histogram of frequency of total scores in ChiChewa,
             Malawi   119
Figure 6.9   Facility values, ChiChewa test, Malawi   120
Figure 6.10 Box plot of Chichewa test results by school, Malawi   121

Figure 6.11   Box plots of Chichewa scores by sex, Malawi   122
Figure 6.12   Distribution of ChiChewa scores (as percentages for
               each sex), Malawi   123
Figure 6.13   Box plot of Chichewa test scores by location,
               Malawi   124
Figure 6.14   Box plot of test scores in Chichewa by sex and
               location for Malawi   125
Figure 6.15   Mean scores by school in ChiChewa and English,
               Malawi   126
Figure 6.16   Scatterplot of scores in English and in ChiChewa,
               Malawi   128
Figure 6.17   Box plot of African language reading test results,
               Malawi and Zambia   129

Abbreviations

AIDS	Acquired Immune Deficiency Syndrome
CSO	Central Statistical Office
DFID	Department for International Development
ESP	English for special purposes
EU	European Union
GABLE	Girls' Attainment in Basic Literacy and Education
GDP	Gross Domestic Product
GLM	General Linear Model
IIEP	International Institute for Educational Planning
IMF	International Monetary Fund
LDC	Least developed countries
MDGs	Millennium Development Goals
MIITEP	Malawi Integrated Intensive Teacher Education Programme
MOE	Ministry of Education
NEPAD	New Partnership for Africa's Development
OAU	Organization of African Unity
SACMEQ	Southern African Consortium for Measuring Educational Quality
SAP	Structural Adjustment Programme
UK	United Kingdom
UN	United Nations
UNDP	United Nations Development Programme
UNESCO	United Nations Educational, Scientific and Cultural Organization
UNIP	United National Independence Party
US	United States
USAID	United States Agency for International Development
ZBEC	Zambia Basic Education Course
ZPC	Zambia Primary Course

Preface

"What's it got to do with you?" was my ungenerous reaction when years ago I came across a book written by an American about my home country, Wales. So I might well expect a similar response to this book. I am not from Africa. Indeed, for years I refused invitations to go to African countries. Flying visits by so-called "specialists" who know little of the country whose inhabitants they presume to address are usually unhelpful – and I certainly knew little of Africa.

However, in 1989 a workshop on curriculum renewal at the University of Rwanda took place, and I agreed to participate as one member in a larger team, where my experience of curriculum design in applied linguistics might complement the expertise of the Rwandan team. During this workshop I visited schools, and witnessed dual use of French and Kinyarwanda in classrooms, which faintly echoed my childhood experiences of English and Welsh. Encouraged by this African experience, I next worked on language achievement tests in Malawi and Zambia, where again I felt reasonably secure, for the tests were to be based strictly on existing syllabuses – I could focus on test construction, and African colleagues could ensure the appropriacy of our items. The series of visits provided an opportunity to study syllabuses, government pronouncements, the local press, school curricula, and teaching/learning materials, and to spend many hours observing life inside and outside classes, and talking to teachers, students, parents, and even people unconnected with education.

It soon became obvious that formal education in these countries was not in good heart. Buildings were inadequate, desks and books insufficient, teachers poorly rewarded, and parents unhappy. But such problems seemed relatively trivial compared with the fact that the vast majority of primary school children were sitting in their classes in a miasma of incomprehension, for the simple reason that the language which dominated the educational operation – English – was one in which they had little proficiency. This, of course, was through no fault of their own: most students, especially rural students, had little exposure to English other than a few brief periods in class, usually shared with a mass of others. Later in the 1990s, I seized the opportunity to return to Zambia and Malawi which I was now coming to know, to investigate in more depth the reading proficiency of students at year five, in both English and ChiChewa (an important language, also known as [Chi]Nyanja, and used in both countries). It is that research which provides the evidence basis for this book.

Simply to report on reading proficiencies in a vacuum would not be particularly illuminating. The book therefore puts this study in the context of human and economic development, as well as that of academic research. Chapter 1 looks at development in Africa, and the role that languages and education might play. Chapter 2 moves on to look at language and education in Malawi and Zambia, while Chapter 3 provides an overview of research into language and reading. In Chapter 4 we examine the rationale for the reading tests, and the settings for the administration of these tests. The results in English feature in Chapter 5, while Chapter 6 looks at the results in Nyanja (for Zambia) and ChiChewa (for Malawi). In Chapter 7 we hear the voices of students on reading in English, ChiChewa and Nyanja. Chapter 8 discusses the findings and the language dilemma in education – how to ensure adequate teaching of English, without damage to learning or to local languages. Chapter 9 tries to pull issues together by considering the educational language policies of the two countries from a political perspective, where unification and development are high priorities, and where economic, social and human capitals have a crucial role.

"What's it got do with me?" A difficult question, where one is tempted to appeal to Donne's "No man is an island" line. One might also suggest that academic research can be the richer for not observing national boundaries – new perspectives and fresh comparisons can illuminate, without, one hopes, putting the researcher at risk of a charge of "academic colonialism". More importantly, it seemed to me profoundly wrong that generations of African children were being short-changed by the experience of sitting for hours on end without the engagement and excitement that should occur in learning. Such is the hegemony of English, such the depth of the "education equals English" belief in Africa, that this stultifying experience was going largely unquestioned. I wanted to add my voice to those of the all too few who have for decades put forward the alarming proposal that it is probably a good thing if African children can understand what's going on in their classrooms (just as children in rich countries do), and further that if African children understand what's going on in their classrooms this is probably helpful to African development.

Moreover, this book is not entirely "to do with me", but has many contributors who have helped me to know Africa: in Malawi, Steve and Moira Chimombo, Alice Chimaliro, Sharon Chimaliro, and Wales Mwanza and his family were invaluable sources of cultural enlightenment; Hannock Mateche and Hartford Mchazime helped organize the research, while Rosemary Mkumba, Christon Moyo and Benson Zigona were indefatigable research assistants. In Zambia, Michael Kelly was an inspiration and constant source of reference, as he has been to so many newcomers to the country; I must also record my debt to the groundbreaking linguistic research of Mubanga Kashoki. Bridget Chipimo, Catherine Nakaanga, and Martin Phiri did sterling work as research assistants, while Rosetta Mulenga entered test data with speed and accuracy. Sadly there are four friends from Zambia who are not here to be thanked: Israel Chikalanga, who completed a PhD in the University of Reading before returning to Zambia where he helped set up the project; Dylan Aspinwall and Shati Sakala – rich mines of information on all things Zambian; Matthew Miti, who did so much to focus the attention of the MOE on reading in Zambian schools.

Crucial too, has been the assistance of the DfID who funded the field research on which this book draws, while individuals from its UK and African offices were generous with their personal support, among whom Terry Allsop, Cecilia Cruz, Myra Harrison, Steve Packer, Mike Reilly and Carew Treffgarne. No less crucial has been the support and forbearance of my family – Ann, Siôn, Mathew and Joe. Finally, the book would never have appeared without the encouragement of the Encounters series editors, Jan Blommaert and Ben Rampton, and the help of Ken Baker and his colleagues at St Jerome Publishing.

Needless to say, the main debt I have incurred in this research is to the head teachers, teachers and students of schools in Malawi and Zambia who graciously agreed to be tested, observed, interviewed and otherwise inconvenienced during my visits. They have remained anonymous, but they are not forgotten, nor the hard times which so many go through daily while they toil for the better lives that must one day come.

1. Introduction

1.1 Africa – current preoccupations

In a review of world poverty in 1995, Tabatabai commented that there was "an unmistakable trend towards the Africanization of poverty" (Tabatabai, 1995: 31). Ten years later, the UN Human Development Index Report of 2005 confirmed this gloomy prediction: sub-Saharan African countries showed a steady decline, and occupied 28 of the bottom 30 places in the world ranking of human development. Between 1990 and 2001 the proportion of very poor people in Africa, defined as those living on less than a dollar a day, increased from 44.6% to 46.4%. In terms of numbers this represented an increase of from 227 millions to 313 millions. At the same time the average income of these very poor people went down from $0.62 per day to $0.60 (UN, 2005: 6-7). The African Renaissance, envisioned by Nelson Mandela following the fall of apartheid in South Africa, and much heralded in the closing years of the 20th century, by such as Bill Clinton and Thabo Mbeki (Tikly, 2003), has not yet arrived.

This book argues that one reason, embedded in a complex of others, for this lack of improvement is the failure of the formal education sector. We explore the reasons behind that failure, and argue that an important factor is the dominant use, at all levels of African education, of ex-colonial languages as languages of instruction. The principal colonizers in sub-Saharan Africa (referred to from now on simply as Africa) were the British, French and Portuguese, each bringing with them their own language; we shall focus upon English, but other exoglossic languages have occupied similar positions in Africa. ("Exoglossic languages" refers to languages which are not the first language of the *majority* of the population e.g. English in Malawi.)

However, in addition to the dominant position English has occupied in African education since the colonial era, it has also in recent years become the language of choice of the global village (an ironic phrase given that villagers, especially those from Africa, are its least favoured denizens). African parents have accordingly become increasingly convinced of the value of English as a stepping stone to prosperity, and African governments increasingly reliant on it for international communication. The globalization of English has thus had the effect of consolidating its position within the African education sector, and buttressing the questionable language policies which prevail in many of the continent's "anglophone" states. While it would be misguided to attribute the lack of development in African countries solely to inappropriate language policies in education, it will be argued that significant responsibility does attach to the advocates of these policies. The prevailing language ideology in Africa has resulted in massive over-estimation of the value of English, while over-reliance on English in the educational domain has been a barrier, rather than a bridge, to development.

A variety of labels have been attached to countries which are economically poor, including *underdeveloped, developing, less developed* and *least developed countries* (LDCs – the fluent deployment of this acronym in the literature of poverty betokening the institutionalization of the condition). The labels may change over time, but sub-Saharan African countries have always featured prominently in the lists which they generate. Although development has long been a concern for Africans, it has in recent years loomed larger as an issue for those in the developed world. The motivations for this are various and contested (see, for example, Bond, 2001) and may include: an altruistic concern for humanity, an interest in reducing the number of economic migrants to rich countries, a wish to ensure access to huge mineral wealth, a desire for new markets for consumer goods and services, a fear that "failed states" may harbour "international terrorism", empire building by the "lords of poverty", or simply a quasi-missionary zeal to convert Africans to "our way of life".

Whatever the motivations, the view that amelioration in Africa is urgently needed has generated a number of initiatives from inside and outside the continent. The Millennium Development Goals (MDGs), proclaimed in 2000 by the United Nations, though global in their intended scope, are especially relevant to Africa. (The eight goals were irreproachable: to eradicate extreme poverty and hunger; to achieve universal primary education; to promote gender equality; to reduce child mortality; to improve maternal health; to combat disease; to ensure environmental sustainability; to develop a global partnership for development.) These MDGs underpin subsequent initiatives, such as the Blair-inspired Commission for Africa, established in 2004 with 17 members, 9 of whom were African, and which delivered its report in 2005. Within Africa, the Organization of African Unity (OAU) was in 2002 relaunched as the African Union (AU), the old organization having proved unable to galvanize development in the continent. The AU revived the New Partnership for Africa's Development (NEPAD, originally established by the OAU in 2001) the aim of which was that Africans should themselves take on as much responsibility as possible for the development of Africa.

Prominent in the Western media in 2005 (declared the "Year of Africa", Wickstead, 2005: 37) was the Make Poverty History campaign, which was led by a coalition of 540 aid organizations (Oxfam, ActionAid, etc.), and which gained massive publicity through the Live8 concerts held in five of the G8 countries (France, Italy, Germany, UK, US) in July of that year. The Live8 concerts, the initiative of Bob Geldof, which coincided with the G8 summit in the UK, were not without criticism. Some claimed Live8 was a vehicle to revive the careers of fading Western pop-stars (African musicians were largely absent); others that it was hijacked by the British government, who gave it enthusiastic public support in order to obscure the reality that the rich countries of the G8 were making few real concessions to poor countries.

Whatever may be the truth, this series of events generated huge publicity, further raising the rich world's awareness of poverty in Africa. Indeed the resulting construction of Africa has perpetuated a "development deficit" view of the continent, not unlike the "civilization deficit" view of the 19th century. Thus the World Summit Outcome of late 2005 notes that Africa is "the only continent not on track to meet any of the goals of the Millennium Declaration by 2015" (whether the goals were achievable by that date is not questioned). The development deficit story is not, of course, the whole of Africa's story, and the Western gaze may indeed be over-fixated on calamities and failures in the continent. However, while the 19th century British construction of Africa was arguably based on fragmented and unrepresentative evidence interpreted from a heavily Euro-centric perspective, the current view, albeit somewhat selective, is based on a significant accumulation of objective facts – relative to the rest of the world, malnutrition *is* widespread in Africa, infant mortality *is* high, and average life spans *are* short (UN, 2005). While much "received opinion" in the UK at the start of the 20th century held that the solution to Africa's problems lay in Christianity (e.g. Stewart, 1903), the consensus (at least at government level) in rich countries in the opening years of the 21st century is that these problems are now to be addressed through debt relief, aid and trade.

African debt stood in 2005 at £125 billion. Servicing the repayments is a huge financial burden for most African countries, leaving little to spare for development. Although in 2005 it was agreed that, for 15 heavily indebted poor countries in Africa, there would be relief for debts owed to the World Bank, to the International Monetary Fund, and to the African Development Bank, the implementation of this agreement made very slow progress. Furthermore, there was no relief for debts which Africa owed to other institutions, which, at £110 billion, constituted the bulk of Africa's debt, with repayments continuing to drain money from the continent (Smith, 2005: 29).

As far as aid is concerned, the G8 meeting in 2005 agreed the target of 0.7 per cent of GDP from each G8 country by 2010. A similar commitment was made by the established member states of the EU, to be achieved by 2015 (Wickstead, 2005: 37). Not all this aid, of course, is intended for Africa, and furthermore, within months of the G8 declaration it was acknowledged that their target would not be met (The Independent, December 2005). Irrespective of such targets, however, the term "aid" can be misleading if the amounts publicized are regarded as simple donations, for a large proportion of aid – estimated as from 10 to 70 per cent depending on the project – does not reach the intended recipients but goes into administrative costs, much of which "trickles back" to the donor countries. Again, while there are complaints that development aid is wasted, the 2004 world total of $79 billion spent on aid is less than one tenth of the $1 trillion spent on arms in the same year. Nonetheless, the value of even that relatively meager amount of aid is contested: some critics (e.g. Smith, 2005: 31) maintain that 50 years of aid (which coincidentally is also estimated at $1 trillion) have impoverished Africa by fostering a culture of dependency.

A further criticism (e.g. Easterby, 2005) is that large-scale aid plans are doomed to failure because of their very size and complexity: the UN's eight Millennium Development Goals are composed of 18 groups of targets, which in turn consist of 54 indicators, for which 449 separate interventions are proposed. Other aid agencies, of course, put forward their own separate plans. Thus in 1999 there was the Comprehensive Development Framework (World Bank), quickly superseded by the Poverty Reduction Strategy Paper (World Bank and International Monetary Fund), while the World Trade Organization proposed the Integrated Framework for Least Developed Countries. The integration and implementation of these plans requires planning "that would overwhelm the most sophisticated government bureaucracy anywhere, much less the under-skilled and under-paid government workers in the poorest countries" (Easterby, 2005: 4). Meantime, in 2005, the UN Secretary General's five-year progress report on the MDGs revealed that: "In sub-Saharan Africa, which already had the highest poverty rate in the world, the situation deteriorated further and millions more fell into poverty" (UN, 2005: 6). Easterby's conclusion is not that aid is useless, but that aid agencies should be "searchers", exploring problems on the ground through trial and error, adapting solutions to local demand, and expanding on those that work. This proposal is not without its own difficulties: What or who constitutes "local demand"? How are conflicts to be resolved if short term local demand (e.g. for borehole wells or chemical fertilizer) is predicted to cause longer term problems (reduction in the water table or leaching of the soil)?

Unlike debt relief and aid, the effects of which are a matter of dispute, there is a consensus that a key factor in African development is trade. The increased globalization of the world economy from the 1980s onwards is claimed by some (e.g. Bond, 2001) to have increased Africa's marginalization, and indeed the continent's share of world trade fell from 6% in the 1980s to 2% in 2005. Others (e.g. Khor, 2002) argue that globalization is a fact, and that African countries must inevitably engage with it. To raise Africa's share of world trade by only 1% would give Africa an extra $70 billion annually in export earnings, more than aid and debt relief combined. The reality, unfortunately, is that increasing trade is easier said than done: Europe, Japan and the US currently hand out more than £150 billion annually in subsidies to their own farmers. This keeps prices of agricultural produce from Africa artificially low; many African cotton farmers, for example, are put out of business because the price of American cotton is lower than the cost of production, thanks to US government subsidies. However, politicians from the rich countries dare not upset their agricultural lobbies by abolishing subsidies forthwith. Likewise in the short term there are unlikely to be significant changes in import tariffs, which make it difficult for Africa to export value-added products to rich countries. While it is true that African countries also impose their own import tariffs, to insist that they immediately be removed all round would expose African countries to competition that their fledgling industries would not be able to bear.

The effect of financial corruption in Africa on debt relief, aid and trade, estimated by the African Union in 2005 to cost at least $150 billion per year, is a matter of dispute. Jeffrey Sachs, Director of the UN Millennium Project, and a determined optimist with regard to African development (see especially Sachs, 2005), claims that many Asian countries with even greater corruption than that in African countries achieved rapid economic growth, suggesting that corruption alone is not the cause of poverty (Sachs, 2005: 23). On the other hand, other observers (e.g. Swain, 2005: 25; Mbeki, 2005: 31) consider the corruption of rulers as a prime cause of Africa's economic problems. Yet again, the French political scientist Bayart (1993: xviii) claims that the "condescending, sneering attitudes of the West towards politics in Africa are fuelled by misconceptions" and sees Western accusations of corruption as one such misunderstanding of the nature of African political life.

It is difficult to draw firm conclusions or make predictions from such ideologically disparate views – indeed to seek to make such generalizations would be presumptuous, given the variety of geography and of societies within the continent. Nonetheless two consistent themes do emerge: one is that the agency of Africans is key. The Commission for Africa (2005: 134) is typical "Unless Africa makes a concerted effort [to strengthen states] we believe that all other reforms, in international trade, debt and aid – essential though these reforms are – will have only limited impact". This view, commendable though it may be, by packaging the agents as "Africa", begs the question of who precisely are envisaged as the human actors.

The second theme is that there is no "quick fix" to be expected that will solve Africa's economic problems (King, 2005: 46). This acknowledges that not only do development process operate over the long term, but also that the application of Western-inspired remedies is not guaranteed to succeed (cf. Tikly, 2003: 4). Likewise, Ellerman (2005: 25) maintains that similar remedies for African problems have already failed in the 1980s. Ellerman is also not the only commentator to observe (*ibid.* 26) that "Where development has been most successful as in East Asia, they have taken their own path, and where countries have been mostly under the thumb of external advisors, lenders and donors (e.g. Africa) progress has been least."

1.2 Education, language and development

If African agency is crucial to African development, then it is reasonable to assume that African education has a role to play. Calls for educational improvements in the continent have grown more strident from the mid-1990s (cf. World Bank 1995a; DFID 1997). Moreover, given that the ability to read is of crucial importance in formal education, and further that education can contribute to development, then it follows that investigation into the reading capacities of learners, and into pedagogic practices relating to reading, may be of relevance to development and the alleviation of poverty in Africa. The wording of the preceding sentence is deliberately cautious, since the nature of the relationships is not one of cause and effect, but involves a variety of factors and interaction between them that are not clearly understood – indeed if they were, then poverty might long ago have been history.

The simple conception of the role of education in development, namely that it enables individuals to acquire knowledge and skills, which in turn promote national development, dates back at least as far as the industrial revolution, but developed as a science only in the late 1950s. Denison (1962), for example, concluded that, between 1930 and 1960, 23% of annual growth in the national income in the United States could be attributed to the increased educational level of the labour force[1]. There has, likewise, long been a belief that investment in education would have a similar effect in developing countries, and in some cases, such as Malaysia and Korea, this is what occurred. However, poverty in African countries remains both deeply rooted and widespread; it is also relevant to note that in African countries the medium of education in schools is usually a language that is not the first language of teachers and learners. In Malaysia, on the other hand, and indeed, all the "Asian tigers" (except for Singapore where special circumstances obtain), the language of schooling is for the most part, the language of the majority of the people.

Given the crucial role of language and communication in education, it is surprising that until the late 1990s, the issue of language received little attention in the literature dealing with development, with Arcand (1995) noting that the *Handbook of Economic Development* contains nothing on language, while the same is true of *An Introduction to Development Economics* (Elkan, 1993). Although there are volumes whose titles suggest a link between language and development, notably *Language and Development*, edited by Kenny and Savage (1997), and an identically entitled collection edited by Crooks and Crewes (1995), they are largely concerned with teaching language in developing countries, rather than exploring the links between language and development. Robinson (1996a: 6) speculating on the general neglect of the linkage, surmizes that for the developed world "development problems are not experienced first hand, but rather seen from a macro perspective, for instance as a matter of international trade, of large climatic regions, of disaster or famine"; he further suggests that governments in poor countries, with limited resources, may choose priorities other than communication. While the Commission for Africa Report (2005) is something of an exception in that it does contain a number of references to language, it is not seen as other than a peripheral and even a troublesome issue in Africa – the many languages of Africa yield problems of coping with diversity and ensuring access to information. On the other hand, the UN's Millennium Development Goals Report (2005) makes no mention of language, despite the fact that Goal Two is to achieve universal primary education by 2015.

Perhaps more surprising is that a large amount of educational research on developing countries, even that concerned with literacy and school

---

[1] Later studies (Denison 1967 and 1979, cited in Lewin 1993) put the contribution at 15% from 1950 to 1962, and 11% from 1948 to 1973, a pattern of diminishing returns over time, which supports the view that the potential returns to education are greater when the educational level of the labour force is low.

effectiveness, for long evinced little concern with language issues (e.g. Postlethwaite and Ross, 1992; Pennycuick, 1993), while *The Oxfam Education Report* (Watkins, 2000) devotes fewer than four pages out of 346 to language questions, and Machingaidze et al. (1998) less than 1 page in a 95 page report on education in Zimbabwe. Although there are exceptions (e.g. Treffgarne, 1986), the general impression is one of neglect. Watson (1999: 5) suggests this is because the field is dominated by educationists with a background in policy and planning, rather than language.

However, there are signs that interest in the links between language, education and development is beginning to take root: the 1990s saw an increasing number of papers with an agenda setting orientation, which make the case for the importance of language issues in development, some of a general nature (e.g. Arcand, 1995; Grin, 1996; Robinson, 1992; Watson, 1999), and some with an African orientation (e.g. Robinson,1996b; Bunyi, 1999; Heugh, 1999; Webb, 1999), while Tikly (2003) briefly raises the language and education issue in the context of the New Partnership for Africa's Development. Wagner (1995) raises a number of language education issues, although primarily focusing on adult literacy and development. This latter is a field which has inspired much research in recent years: Rassool (1999) looks at "literacy for sustainable development", and there has also been a great deal of work in ethnographic perspectives on literacy and development (e.g. Street, 2001). Language as a prime issue has, however, been slow to emerge in the ethnographic perspective (exceptions include Aikman, 2001; Herbert & Robinson, 2001), while the considerable difficulties that individuals may face in acquiring academic fluency in languages to which they have little exposure is largely neglected in development studies (although formal and informal second language acquisition has been a research topic in rich countries for decades, e.g. Cummins and Swain, 1986).

1.3 Concepts of development

Whether the word "development" conveys an agreed concept has long been questioned (e.g. George and Sabelli, 1994: 230). Likewise, the United Nations has "no established convention for the designation of "developed" and "developing" countries or areas" (UN, 2005: 43), while the view put forward in King (1998) is that categorizing countries as developed and developing is of doubtful validity, since all countries in the world face problems to do with "development". However, among the multiple interpretations of the term there are two which predominate in current usage: one sees development in terms of increased national economic growth, the second conceives of development as the meeting of human needs. The two interpretations, which are obviously not mutually exclusive, are the preferred perspectives of national governments and international development agencies. However, alternative perspectives on development may be projected by commercial interests, or by local grassroots organizations (Rogers, 2001: 213), while seeing development "principally as a spiritual phenomenon" as do the Nugunu of Cameroon (Robinson, 1966b: 167), is not uncommon in communities where the religious life is valued. In this book, however, the term development will be employed, as it has been thus far, in the two conventional senses, namely economic development and human development.

There are in turn two views on the preferred means of achieving development as economic growth: in the neo-liberal view the forces of supply and demand are seen as the most efficient way to set prices such that there is maximum "absolute gain". This is the capitalist "free market" – free of course in the sense of being relatively unfettered by state regulation. While it is generally acknowledged that much of the gain in a free market is accumulated by a minority of the population, neo-liberals have always claimed that wealth "trickles down" to benefit the poor, a view that has not gone unchallenged, and that we shall return to later.

The socialist view of achieving development as economic growth also recognizes the potential for growth of market capitalism, but here the intervention of the state in the market is valued, in order for wealth to be more equitably distributed, or to reduce the dependency of poor countries on rich countries. Intervention may be relatively low-key, for example setting import quotas, or erecting protective tariff barriers on goods produced by the country so as to protect local industries. Stronger examples of state intervention are the nationalization of services or industries deemed essential to national well-being, such as transport, communications, power supplies (gas and electricity) or mining.

The second conception of development in terms of the meeting of human needs, sees it as a process which enables the human personality to realize its potential (Thomas and Potter, 1992). Here development is seen not only as freeing individuals from economic poverty, and abolishing gross inequalities in the distribution of wealth, but also with increased participation in democratic processes, improvements in levels of health and education (particularly literacy), enhancing the status of women, achieving environmental sustainability, and reducing the vulnerability of relatively powerless groups. Vulnerability is invariably accompanied by lack of "voice" where people are unable to claim their rights, or hold to account those who in authority. Examples of vulnerability are legion:

forest peoples faced with well-armed ranchers, loggers or miners; ripar-
ian villagers whose land is threatened by damn construction; islanders
whose territory is required as a military base. Such "human poverty" is
often associated with "social exclusion" (a term long preferred in France
in preference to "poverty" because of the latter's association with charity
and liberal individualism, while French republicanism favours solidarity
and social integration (De Haan, 1999: 1-3)). "Development to meet human needs" is not, of course, incompatible with "development as economic
growth" (some holding that the former is inevitably contingent upon the
latter), but the human needs perspective pays particular attention to the
manner in which growth is achieved, in which the results are distributed,
and in which people and the environment are affected.

The human development view was given impetus by the realization
that simple increases in GDP do not necessarily "trickle down" to allevi-
ate poverty, particularly where populations are increasing rapidly. Thus
although a state's average per capita income may rise through economic
development, the benefits may be disproportionally allocated (DFID, 1997,
1.3). Economic development may therefore coincide with an increase in
the number of people in absolute poverty. In Uganda, for example, which
was regarded as an African economic success in the 1990s, Appleton (1996)
concludes that from 1992 to 1996, poverty actually increased for the poorest
20% in rural and urban areas. In Nigeria, despite the oil-boom of recent
years, the number of people below the poverty line rose from 19 million
in 1970 to 90 million in 2000 (Mbeki, 2005). In Africa overall, as mentioned above, the number of people living in poverty (less than $1 a day)
rose from 227 million in 1990 to 313 million in 2001 while at the same
time there was a marginal reduction in the average income of these very
poor people from $0.62 to $0.60 (UN, 2005: 7).

1.4 Education and development

Within the "development as economic growth" perspective, which dominated policy thinking until the early 1990s, there have been many studies
which demonstrate a positive correlation between national educational
levels and economic development (for a review, see Lewin, 1993). To find
whether education was actually a cause of economic development, as opposed to simply correlating with it, Hicks (1980) carried out a longitudinal
survey of 83 developing countries, and found that the twelve with the
fastest rates of growth had literacy rates 12% above average, suggesting
that that literacy does indeed make a causal contribution to growth. This
finding is supported by Wheeler (1980), who examined longitudinal data

from 88 countries and concluded that 20% to 30% increases in average literacy rates led to rises in GDP of 8% to 16%.

Education has been of particular relevance in human capital theory, which holds that the productivity of workers is increased by inputs such as education. Becker (1975) and Mincer (1976) (both cited in Woodhall 1987) recognize that these inputs comprize pre-school investments (e.g. informal learning from peers or adults) and post-school investments (training and learning by experience) as well as formal education itself. While the correlation between level of education and earnings is not in doubt, the mechanism of this relationship is disputed. Human capital theorists argue that education increases the cognitive abilities of individuals (abilities such as literacy and numeracy) thus raising their productivity so that they command higher earnings. There is also, however, a further suggestion that schooling does not simply affect cognitive abilities, but also the social attitudes and values of those who attend (children from lower socio-economic backgrounds developing values such as obedience, while children from higher social classes develop decision-making ability and independence) – which again means schooling contributes to productivity, albeit 'non-cognitively'.

On the other hand, screening theory threatens to completely undermine the human capital approach to education. Screening theory argues that schooling has no productivity-related impact on the student, either cognitive or non-cognitive, but instead acts as a 'screening device' for employers. Screening theorists maintain that it is the most *naturally* able students who will be the highest achievers in school, and that the superior credentials that they obtain from educational institutions serve as signals to employers of their natural ability and potential productivity[2]. The "hard" version of screening theory holds that education makes no contribution to this productivity.

Apart from the counter-intuitive nature of the "hard" position, a number of findings suggest that the productivity function of schooling is indeed significant. Colclough (Colclough with Lewin 1993) notes that any screening function of education can only operate in the formal sector – where educational credentials are issued – but that there is a considerable body of evidence from the non-formal sector which shows an effect of education

---

[2] Mincer (1980:125, cited in Woodhall 1987:217) points out that "the productivity and screening functions of schooling are not mutually exclusive". However, the difficulty of quantifying these two functions means that screening theory casts a shadow of doubt on any evidence of the impact of education on productivity where a direct relationship between productivity and earnings is assumed.

on productivity. Indeed, numerous studies (see below) have demonstrated this relationship using agricultural output as the measure of productivity. Colclough also points to the finding of Knight and Sabot (1990) that the predicted earnings of high achieving primary school leavers are nearly as much as those of low achieving secondary school leavers. High achievers at either level can expect to earn considerably more than low achievers at the same level, and Knight and Sabot conclude that the returns to high levels of cognitive achievement (literacy and numeracy abilities, etc.), are greater than the returns to simply the number of years of schooling. This meticulously documented "natural experiment" supports the human capital theory, which holds that increased cognitive abilities (which can be brought about by formal education) raises productivity, and results in higher earnings.

Other evidence correlating educational levels with productivity supports this view. Lockheed, Jamison and Lau (1980) concluded from studies of 13 developing countries that farmers with four years of education (compared with those with none) produced an average increase in productivity of 7.4%. Moock and Addou (1994) analysed a series of later studies from 12 countries in Asia, Africa and the Americas, and confirmed the findings that formal schooling is positively related to agricultural productivity. There is, moreover, evidence of a critical number of years of education (between 3 and 6 years according to different studies) below which the effect is negligible. Moock and Addou propose that this threshold represents a level of education where the degree of literacy and numeracy that learners attain is sufficient to be retained, and rewarded in later life. The Malawian Ministry of Economic Planning and Development (1995: 24), cited in Kadzamira and Rose (2003: 502) clearly adheres to the human capital view, holding that that basic education could contribute to "improved agricultural productivity and better prospects of employment, reduced infant and maternal mortality, lower incidence of diseases and fertility rates."

As far the human-needs approach to development is concerned, there is a widespread view that "education is a key factor in providing opportunities for healthier, more productive and more fulfilled lives" (Bermingham, 2005: 39). Much of the work has focussed on the role of women: in particular, it is claimed that the education of women yields 'externalities' of investment: externalities are those benefits which do not arise directly from an investment, but which nevertheless are of advantage to individuals and/or society. An externality of investment in education, for example, is that family planning programmes will be more effective, as educated women will be more likely to use the services. Although the precise pathways by which the effects operate are not always clear, there is a wealth of evidence demonstrating the impact of education of women in terms of improving their health and reducing the number of children they bear (e.g. Subbarao and Raney, 1993; DFID, 2000). Wheeler (1980, cited in Lewin 1993: 21) likewise concluded that literate women had fewer children after analysing data from 88 countries, while Cochrane (1989, cited in Puchner 1995) found mothers' education to be closely related to children's health.

Environmental benefits are claimed by Summers (1994) to be another externality of female education, a point that receives little attention elsewhere in the literature. Summers (1994: 13-14) proposes that: "Educating women contributes to reduced fertility. By raising the opportunity cost of women's time, it discourages them from clearing forests, and it increases their ability to manage natural resources efficiently." However, rather than discouraging women from clearing forests, perhaps a more significant effect of education is again through women having fewer children, and the consequent slowing of population growth, resulting in less pressure on the land. Large numbers of rural poor live on marginal land which is particularly vulnerable to degradation when under pressure from a growing population.

A number of major studies are reviewed by Hobcraft (1993), who confirms the claims that educating women has a significant effect on improving health and lowering the number of births. Hobcraft notes, however, that the effects of mothers' education on increased chances of child survival appear much weaker for countries in sub-Saharan Africa than in other countries. Hobcraft's method was to calculate the odds ratio for the "maternal education contrast" (an odds ratio of 0.5 means that the child of a mother with 7 or more years of education has a 50% probability of dying before age 2, compared with the child of a mother with no education). In all 9 American countries studied the ratio was below 0.5. On the other hand ratios in Kenya and Liberia were over 0.6, in Mali, Zimbabwe, Botswana and Uganda, 0.75 to 0.8, and in Ghana, 0.95. In short, 7 years of mothers' education in Ghana made little difference to a child's survival chances. Hobcraft says there is no convincing explanation for this finding, but it is a point which we shall revisit in the final chapter.

Research into economic development reported by Harbison and Myers (1964), Hicks (1980), and Wheeler (1980), all cited in Lewin (1993), concludes that education has a positive effect upon the alleviation of poverty at national level, while the DFID (2000: 16) claims that women's education has a significant effect upon economic, as well as human, development, and that countries in sub-Saharan Africa "that have not sent enough girls to school over the past 30 years now have GDPs 25% lower than if they had given them a better chance". In a particularly wide-ranging general review, Azariadis and Drazen (1990) examine the development history of 32 countries from 1940 to 1970 and from 1960 to 1980. They conclude that, while there was variation from country to country, for which clear reasons could not always be established, a threshold level for a number of factors, including the educational quality of the labour force, was a necessary, but not sufficient[3], condition for rapid economic growth. What they see as particularly significant is that *not one of the countries where the threshold level of labour force educational quality was not met, managed to achieve rapid growth.*

The 1960's view that mass literacy unsupported by other socio-economic change can be a causal factor in development, is now widely discredited (Rogers, 1990: 3), particularly following the failure of the Experimental World Literacy programme, supported by UNDP and UNESCO in 11 countries from 1967 to 1972, to generate development (Lind and Johnson, 1990: 71). In fact, the history of countries in western Europe suggests that industrialization preceded mass literacy (although Sweden is possibly an exception). However, although near universal literacy may not be essential for economic growth, it has long been held by development economists that a threshold level of education (including literacy) in an adequate proportion of the population is necessary for economic "take off" (see Azariadis and Drazen, 1990). As long ago as 1966, Anderson (1966: 347), estimated that "about 40% of adult literacy [...] is a threshold for economic development", although the claim begs many questions as to the degree and domains of competence, and is ironically dubbed the "magical figure of 40%" by Rogers (1990: 3; see also Street, 1984: 2; Rassool, 1999: 81). However, it should, in fairness to Anderson, be noted that he points out that: "that level of education would not be a sufficient condition in societies lacking other support systems" (*loc. cit.*). In short, while education does not have a direct causal effect on development and the alleviation of poverty, there are clear suggestions from the research that, in relationship with other factors, education does have a contribution to make.

In the case of sub-Saharan Africa, however, there is widespread acknowledgment that education is failing to make the requisite contribution because, particularly at primary level, it is of inadequate quality (Watkins,

---

[3] Azariadis and Drazen can offer no precise explanation for the failure of economic growth in countries where the threshold level of education obtained, mainly in Latin America, but speculate on the effects of "wasteful economic policies, wars and other political upheavals, natural disasters" (1990: 519), together with flaws in the working of credit markets.

2000: 103-110). Within the complex of factors that contribute to low quality of education, those commonly identified include curricula inappropriate to local practices and needs, teachers who are inadequately trained, poorly paid, or frequently absent, pupils who are hungry, in poor health, and whose attendance is sporadic, inadequate school buildings, grossly overcrowded classes and insufficient teaching materials. While it is highly likely that such factors do indeed play a part in the lack of educational achievement, an obvious and crucial factor in education is language, and in particular the language that is officially prescribed as the medium of instruction (sometimes referred to as the vehicular language) in which, of course, learners are expected to read.

This book will focus upon the effect of educational language policy in two very poor African countries, Malawi and Zambia, where an improvement in educational achievement may have the potential to improve lives. In particular, we investigate the effect of current English-oriented language education policies upon the reading proficiency of primary school children. Misgivings at the dominance of English, or indeed, the "English equals education" attitude prevalent in many developing countries have long been expressed (Serpell, 1989: 94). Likewise, at the level of pedagogic ideology, questions are now being asked of the consistency of education ministries which on the one hand espouse the rhetoric of child-centred education, and on the other hand persist in educating children through a language which the vast majority do not understand (Schmied, 1991: 102-104; Bamgbose, 1991: 81; Rubagumya, 1990: 2). Indeed, the efficacy of language education policies in countries throughout Africa has been called into question as a consequence of many damning reports on student learning (for Zambia, see Nkamba and Kanyika, 1998; for Zimbabwe, Machingaidze *et al*, 1998; for Zanzibar, Nassor and Mohammed, 1998; for Kenya, Bunyi, 1999; for Mauritius, Kulpoo, 1998; for Namibia, Voigts, 1998; for South Africa, Heugh, 1999 and Webb, 1999). The remainder of this book will, using Malawi and Zambia as exemplars, examine evidence for the disquiet that surrounds these language practices.

2.   Malawi and Zambia – The Background

2.1 Rationale for country selection

Isolating the effects of contrasting government education policies across
two different countries is of course not possible if the two countries have
variation in social, economic, and historical factors. However, the countries to be considered here, Malawi and Zambia, display considerable
background similarities. They are both southern African countries with a
common border of 837 kilometres (see map, Appendix 1), and a great deal
in common in their linguistic, historical, socio-economic and cultural backgrounds. They therefore provide a naturally occurring quasi-experimental
situation with reasonably similar contextual variables, which permit us not
only to use near identical research instruments to describe the differences
between children's reading performances, but also enable us to draw reasonable inferences as to effect of the policies.

2.2 Zambia

2.2.1 General

Zambia has a population estimated in 2005 at around eleven and a quarter
million[1], and is by African standards fairly heavily urbanized, with some
40% of the population inhabiting urban areas, in particular Lusaka (the
capital), Livingstone and the Copperbelt (as the name suggests a copper
mining area). The country was governed by the British South African
Company from 1890 to 1923, and then became, as Northern Rhodesia, a
British colony. It gained independence from the UK in 1964, under President Kenneth Kaunda, leader of UNIP (United National Independence
Party).

The Zambian economy suffered hugely during the 1970s as a result of
the decline in the price of copper; however, from 2004 the price of copper
increased, and new mines were opened. Nonetheless GDP per capita in
2005 was estimated at only US$900, i.e. less than $3 per day, and since
the poorest 10% of the population receive only 1.1% of total household

---

[1] Unless otherwise stated, all information on Zambia in this section is from the
World Factbook, [http://www.odci.gov.cia/publications/factbook/za.html] update
10/01/06.

income in 1998, it would seem that the very poor are in a state of considerable destitution. Kasonde-Ng'andu et al. (2000: 3) hold that the World Bank's Structural Adjustment Programme (SAP) "adopted vigorously by the government in the early 1990s", led to massive redundancies, and meant that "thousands of households" had problems supporting their families. Since SAP was implemented, declining government spending on education in the 1980s and 1990s affected that sector particularly badly. Over the four years 1993 to 1996 Zambia's spending on education was 2.5% of GDP, "among the lowest in the world" according to Kasonde-Ng'andu et al. (2000: 3). During the same period debt servicing amounted to 10.3% of GDP.

The rate of literacy – officially defined as those aged 15 and over who "can read and write English" – is 80.6%. Such a crude definition begs many questions: the research presented here suggests that the proportion of those who can read and write English well enough, for example, to have adequate comprehension of the local newspapers – which are entirely in English – is certainly lower. The population is for the most part highly religiously observant. Statistics on religious affiliation are not precise but it is estimated that from 50% to 75% of the population are Christian, and from 24% to 49% Muslim. Indigenous beliefs, however, are strong and there is a great deal of religious syncretism (of which the Mwana Lesa movement of the 1920s is one of the earliest and most striking cases[2]: see Ranger, 1975).

2.2.2 Language in Zambia

Precise information on the linguistic demography of Zambia is hard to obtain. As far as the total number of languages is concerned, a problem arises from the fact that each of the 72 different groups (also referred to as peoples, or tribes[3]) listed by the Zambian government, refers to the language they speak by adding a prefix (Ki-, Chi-, Ici-, Si-, etc.,) indicating "the language of", to their group name: thus the Chewa people speak ChiChewa, the Bemba people, IciBemba, the Lozi, SiLozi, etc.[4]). The 1990

---

[2] The Mwana Lesa movement, led by Tomo Nyirenda, combined elements of Christian and Lala beliefs. Unusually, the Lala account of the afterworld mentions not only language but also how it is acquired in that realm (see *Envois*).

[3] Kashoki (1990: 41) views the notion of "a culturally homogenous tribe" as an "artificial fossilisation" originating in colonial government (c.f. Bamgbose, 1991, 14).

[4] Zambians (e.g. Kashoki) writing in English usually drop the prefix. Malawians usually keep it, although Kayambazinthu (1999: 16) citing Bailey (1995: 34-35)

Census (CSO: 1995a: 34) says "it has been estimated that the country has 72 tribes, each with its own unique language or dialect". The claim for "uniqueness" is however dubious, and probably motivated by a political desire to avoid causing offence to the speakers of any variety, by suggesting their variety is less "unique". In contrast to these government accounts, the Zambian linguist Kashoki (1990: 109) claims that Zambia has "approximately 80 Bantu dialects" which are grouped into "slightly over 20 more or less mutually unintelligible clusters or 'languages' ". Grimes (1992: 433-8), on the other hand, lists 35 indigenous languages (many of which are of course also spoken outside Zambia). The discrepancies are partly attributable to the difficulties inherent in categorizing, by means of linguistic criteria, closely related varieties as "different" or "not different". Language is therefore variably defined in Zambia: according to socio-political perspectives the country has many languages; in terms of mutual comprehensibility or linguistic criteria there are fewer, although there is disagreement on how many fewer.

However, it is not only the lack of adequate identification of languages which complicates the attempt to describe the linguistic demography of Zambia: there has also been, in the official surveys and descriptions, a lack of consistency in the languages which are featured. While seven Zambian languages are officially designated by the government as subjects to be studied in the education system, and also as vehicles for local adult literacy programmes, these seven Zambian languages were selected partly on political grounds. The 1990 Census (CSO, 1995a: 34) notes that they do not correspond to the top seven most frequently spoken mother tongues, nor do they correspond to the seven "predominant languages of communication". A "predominant language of communication" is glossed as "the language most frequently spoken for day-to-day communication" (CSO, 1995b: 305). The 1990 Census also reports on the second language of communication "most frequently used after the predominant group" (CSO, 1995b: 305). Table 2.1 lists the predominant language groups, together with the predominant language of communication, and the second language of communication.

Despite the small numbers who speak English as a first language, it is the sole official language in Zambia, being "used in all government functions" (CSO, 1995a: 34), and would also would appear to be a significant

advocates dropping it. This book normally follows the Zambian usage for Zambia, and Malawian usage for Malawi. Likewise there is lack of agreement on whether the prefix should or should not be followed by a capital letter (ChiChewa or Chichewa).

second language of communication. Nkamba and Kanyika (1998: 24-25) report that 75.3% of their national sample of 2,558 year 6 students from 157 schools claimed to speak English "sometimes, often, or all the time" at home. There is no information on what degree of use could constitute "sometimes". In 1990 some 77,000 people in Zambia spoke English as a first language (CSO, 1995b: 305). The number in 1969 was about 41,000 (Kashoki, 1978a: 25). In neither census was information sought as to the number of English first language speakers who were expatriates or of British descent, so that it is not possible to assess whether language shift from Zambian languages to English is operating among the Zambian élite.

	Predominant Language Group	Languages of Communication	
		Predominant	Second
Bemba*	39.7	29.7	22.2
Chewa	n.a.	5.7	2.6
Kaonde*	n.a.	2.3	2.0
Lozi*	7.5	6.4	7.4
Lunda*	8.8	2.0	1.1
Luvale*	n.a	1.8	1.7
Mambwe	3.4	1.2	1.0
Nyanja*	20.1	7.8	18.6
Tonga*	14.8	11.0	4.0
Tumbuka	3.7	2.9	1.7
English	1.1	1.1	17.8
Other	0.9	28.1	19.9
Total	100.0	100.0	100.0
Size	7,001,936[5]	7,001,936	2,674,111

* one of the 7 officially designated languages
Source: CSO, 1990 Census of Population

Table 2.1 Main languages in Zambia by percentages

[5] Zambia's total population according to the 1990 Census was 7,383,097. "The dumb and the very young not able to speak" (CSO, 1995a: 305) do not feature in the language data.

The "big three" indigenous languages would appear to be Bemba, Nyanja and Tonga. A rather odd feature of Table 2.1 is the relatively small number of people who claim Nyanja as their predominant language of communication, compared with the number who claim Nyanja as their language group. The Census has no explanation of this, although the "confusion" of Nyanja and Chewa may be a partial explanation. Ethnic Chewa (who live on both sides of the Malawi-Zambia border) refer to their language as Chewa; ethnic Nyanja from Malawi and many Chewa-speaking urban dwellers in Zambia tend to refer to their language as Nyanja. However, it is widely agreed that the two languages are essentially one and the same (the entry for Chewa in Crystal, 1987: 452 says "See Nyanja"). The comment by Kayambazinthu (1999: 18) that "the linguistic affiliation between the Chewa and the Nyanja is still a matter of dispute as to who owns the language", again suggests that Chewa and Nyanja are the same language[6]. Under the label "Nyanja", the language was a *lingua franca* in the police and the civil service in colonial times in both Malawi and Zambia.

There are minor differences between the "ChiChewa language" of Malawi and the "Nyanja language" of Zambia in pronunciation, lexis, and spelling. However, it is claimed that both ChiChewa and Nyanja have intralanguage geographic varieties which may well display greater differences than do the two standard versions of the languages (see Kashoki, 1990:75 for Nyanja; Kayambazinthu, 1999:50 for ChiChewa). In particular the "Town Nyanja" of Zambia is reported to contain lexical borrowings from English (as well as other Zambian languages, notably Bemba); thus *flowers* in town Nyanja is *mafulowas* (English *flowers*, but with Nyanja morphology and phonology, rather than standard Nyanja *maluwa*).

All indigenous Zambian languages (with a couple of very minor exceptions to be considered later) are part of the Bantu language family, and share a degree of mutual comprehensibility, acknowledged by Kashoki's use above of the phrase "more or less"; Bemba and Nyanja are said to share slightly over one third of their "basic words" (Lehmann, 1978: 108) although such a claim begs many questions, pronunciation and meaning being but two areas where questions could be asked. Furthermore, attitudes to language can affect use and comprehension: Wolff (1964), for example, documents one-way comprehensibility for two closely related varieties, Nembe and Kalabari, in West Africa, which he attributes to

---

[6] The Nyanja ("people of the lake" Kayambazinthu, 1999: 18) live around the south west of Lake Malawi and the Shire River; the Chewa live in central Malawi and eastern Zambia.

attitude. Many Zambians, however, agree that they have some degree of comprehension of most Zambian languages, although those who are not of the Lozi group tend to regard Lozi as the most "difficult" of the Zambian languages. There may be an attitudinal dimension to this perception: according to Carter (1969) "the rest of Zambia still regards Barotseland as a remote 'bush' backwater". Barotseland is the land of the Rotse, an older spelling of Lozi. The Lozi people historically tended to regard themselves as a group apart, and had hoped to establish Barotseland as an independent state with the decolonization of Northern Rhodesia in 1964. Indeed, the British government at the time had given the Lozi reason to believe this would be the case, but *real politik* carried the day, and the British did not grant separate independence to the Lozi.

The only non-Bantu African languages said to occur in Zambia are Hukwe and Kwengo, which are Khoisan (the so-called "click") languages spoken, according to Kashoki (1978a: 15), on the fringes of the Western province by "small scattered nomadic groups". Khoisan languages are generally associated with more southern parts of Africa (especially Botswana, which shares a border with Zambia). Kashoki further notes that they "were apparently not enumerated in the 1969 census", while Zambians generally are quite unaware of them. This neglect is not untypical for highly marginalized groups in developing countries, although it is possible that the Hukwe and Kwengo people no longer travel within Zambia.

2.2.3 Primary education in Zambia

Students in Zambia officially start school aged 7, and follow a 7 year primary course. The school year coincides with the chronological year (starting in January, finishing in December). Education is not compulsory. Although shoes and uniforms are no longer an official requirement for school attendance, many families and even teachers believe that they are, and providing these can constitute a significant household expense. The MOE allows schools to charge various fees, including a registration fee, a PTA (Parent Teacher Association) fee, a general purpose fund, and various examination fees. The average annual fees in 1998 varied from around $4.00 to around $10.00 (Kasonde-Ng'andu et al., 2000: 50). Kelly (1998) suggests that the high costs for poor quality education, which low-income households increasingly believe will result in little direct gain, discourage them from sending their children to school.

Classes in urban areas are limited to 50, and the limit generally enforced. This enforcement meant that in the capital Lusaka, schools in the 1990s could admit only two thirds of the school age population. Durstan

(1996: 5) put the Zambia-wide figure of school age students who did not attend school at 656,000. The position of those who cannot attend government schools is to some extent addressed by non-government "community schools"; however, only a very small proportion of children have access to such schools, which in any case offer only a very restricted basic curriculum. To cope with the numbers wishing to attend urban government schools while observing the limit of 50 students per class, schools may run two, or even three teaching shifts a day.

Despite the rates of enrolment in schools being restricted to 50, the numbers actually physically present in classes are often lower, and sometimes very much lower. This is due to a high rate of school drop out and chronic absenteeism. In some classes fewer than a third of registered students are present at any given time, although this varies depending on the time of year (rural children may be absent to help with harvesting), and the day of the week (many children, for example, are absent on market days). Cultural activities and initiation ceremonies for boys and girls may also affect attendance. The Nyau cult is particularly important for many Chewa people, and has been a means of resisting colonialism and Christian proselytizing (Linden, 1975): induction into the cult and social activities related to it (e.g. the Nyau dance at the funeral of a chief) can be time-consuming for boys, while Chewa girls cite the Chimuthali dance as being a reason for missing school (Kasonde-Ng'andu et al., 2000: 66). As far as drop-out rates are concerned, accurate data are difficult to come by, partly because some students drop out only to re-enrol the following year, yielding "negative drop out", reported for the first three years of primary school in Zambia in 1996 (Kasonde-Ng'andu et al., 2000: 13). Some three-quarters of drop-outs are due to lack of money to meet the costs of schooling (*ibid.* 49).

Most of the annual recurrent education budget for primary education is spent on teachers' salaries (97% in 1991, MOE, Zambia, 1992: v, and 93% in 1996, Kasonde-Ng'andu et al., 2000: 15). This has left many schools in an extremely dilapidated condition, with doors, windows, and even roof sheeting missing. There is usually a shortage of books, shelves, cupboards and desks. Many classes in both urban and rural areas are held in the open, with students sitting on the ground.

The 1966 Education Act in Zambia enshrined English as the medium of instruction from the beginning of schooling. This decision was in accordance with the 1965 Hardman report[7] which was itself an endorsement

[7] Hardman was a language officer seconded to Zambia to investigate the teaching of English.

of a 1964 UNESCO review in Zambia which recommended that "The medium of instruction should be English, from the beginning of schooling" (UNESCO, 1964: 105, cited in Linehan, 2004: 1)[8]. Despite subsequent reviews which made the case for local languages, English has since been the official language of instruction from year one for all subjects apart from spiritual instruction and Zambian language instruction. English has since 1965 had strong institutional support within the education system, since "each student must pass [English] to obtain a full certificate" at both primary and secondary levels (CSO, 1995a: 34).

The situation changed slightly after 1999, with the implementation of the Primary Reading Programme, on a seven-year timescale, from 1999 to 2005 (Linehan, 2004). The programme provides for the teaching of initial literacy in local languages (but only during the first year of primary school), although this is again restricted to the seven "officially designated" Zambian languages. Prior to 1999, there had been in theory a few lessons per week on one of these seven languages, the language depending on the area where the school was located. In reality, little importance had been accorded to teaching local languages, largely because they did not feature in the selection examinations for secondary schools (MOE, Zambia, 1992: 45), a neglect confirmed by students (see Chapter 7). However, in order to support the Primary Reading Programme, local languages may now be counted towards selection (Linehan, 2004: 4). Although initial literacy is, according to the Primary Reading Programme, to be in one of the seven "official languages of education", the language of instruction is – even in the first year – still officially English, and textbooks are still in English, while "basic literacy in English" is to be achieved by the end of year two (Linehan, 2004: 4). The current situation is "untidy" (Linehan, 2004: 8) and "confused to say the least" (Manchisi, 2004: 6). One obstacle to the teaching of Zambian languages is that a number of teachers teach outside their home areas, and may therefore lack fluency in the language of the area where they teach. The practice of placing teachers outside their own language area was official policy in the 1960s and 1970s during the Kaunda government in Zambia, as part of the move towards national unification and "de-ethnicization". The research reported on in chapters five to seven in this book took place pre-1999, when English was the official medium from day one of primary school, and Zambian languages had a very low profile.

---

[8] In contradiction of UNESCO's well-known pronouncement ten years earlier: "we take it as axiomatic that the best medium for teaching is the mother tongue of the pupil" (UNESCO, 1953: 6).

The supply of books in primary schools has been a problem since the mid-seventies. New English course books (the New Zambia Basic Education series) were published and distributed in the 1990s (starting with grade 1 in 1991 ending with grade 7 in 1997). The government's target in the distribution of these new books was to provide one book per two students; however, an accurate estimate of how many usable books are actually in schools at any given point in time is difficult to arrive at, partly because books may not be distributed properly in the first instance, or because they become unusable fairly quickly, book life in Zambian schools being estimated at 3 years. This relatively brief life-span means that in the case of the abovementioned New Zambia Basic Education project, by the time the books for year 7 were being distributed in 1997, those in the preceding years were already past their book life.

2.3 Malawi

2.3.1 General

The borders of what is now Malawi were established in 1891, when it became the British Central Africa Protectorate, under British rule, in the wake of the "Arab War". This "war" was a series of skirmishes between the Arab slave trader Mlozi, and the African Lakes Company (set up by the Free Church Mission), contemporary press reports of which generated "an emotional response" in the British public (Williams, 1978: 49). While the Atlantic slave trade had ended by 1870 (Thomas, 1997: 784), the Indian Ocean trade had continued. Moslem slavers raided deep into the hinterland of the east African coast, with the notorious slaver Tippu Tib (Hamed bin Muhammad), sending expeditions as far west as the Congo, where, in 1876, he helped the explorer Stanley (Pakenham, 1991: 29-31). These African slaves were taken to work in the spice industry of Zanzibar and as domestic servants in the Arabian Gulf. In Malawi the Islamicized Yao acted as middlemen (Kayambazinthu, 1999: 25), and Lake Malawi had major staging posts in the trade (Williams, 1978: 32-36). Although the aforementioned Mlozi and his slavers were defeated in what was to be Malawi, it was judged necessary to maintain British forces in the area to prevent a revival of the slave raids. In 1907 the British Central Africa Protectorate became the Nyasaland Protectorate (more generally referred to as Nyasaland), and continued to be governed by Britain until 1964 when, a few months before Zambia, it gained its independence under the late President Hastings Banda, also known as Kamuzu Banda.

Malawi today is a predominantly rural country with a population of approximately ten million of whom about 11% live in four main urban areas (Lilongwe, the capital city; Blantyre, the commercial centre; Zomba, the seat of government, and Mzuzu, capital of the Northern Region). Population density is 105 per square kilometre (National Statistics Office, 2000: xii), and 78% of the population are subsistence farmers (*ibid.* xviii). By any definition of poverty, Malawi[9] is among the poorest countries in the world, and depends on aid from various external donors "for almost 50% of its entire recurrent budget" (King, K. 2005b: 52), with Bernbaum et al. (1998) estimating that 40% of the primary education budget was provided by external donors. Indeed Finlayson (2005: 49) notes "The Commission for Africa Report reads as if it were written specifically with Malawi in mind." The GDP per capita, estimated at US$600 for 2005 (US$1.64 per day), was slightly better than Zambia's but still low, and conceals considerable inequities; the real growth rate of 1% (2005 estimate) is not only low, but from a very low base, and is concentrated in the hands of a small proportion of the population (World Bank, 1996: 24). The principal foreign exchange earnings come from tobacco (over 50%), and tea. There is a limited amount of tourism in the national parks, and around Lake Malawi.

The literacy rate (defined as those aged "15 and over who can read and write" – no mention is made of how this is established) was estimated in 2003 at 62.7% (World Factbook, 2006). Other estimates vary from 42% to 64.9%, but again no criteria are provided (Rogers, 2003: 49). As in Zambia, the population in general is very religiously observant. Some 80% of the population is Christian, and some 13% Muslim (World Factbook, 2006). However, indigenous religious beliefs are strong, and there has been, again as in Zambia, considerable syncretism (see Linden, 1975) with indigenous cultural practices (e.g. the initiation rituals of the Chewa who are a major group in Malawi, as well as eastern Zambia) claimed to affect both attendance and drop-out rates in primary schools (see below; also Colclough et al., 2000).

2.3.2 Language in Malawi

The 1998 Census of Malawi (National Statistical Office, 2000) lists 12 indigenous spoken languages for the country, plus English, Portuguese, and an unspecified number of "other" languages. This Census, unlike the previous Census of 1966, does not list languages by L1 speakers, but by the "type of language mostly used for communication in the household".

---

[9] Unless otherwise stated, economic information on Malawi is from the World Factbook [http://www.odci.gov.cia/publications/factbook/mi.html], update 10/01/06.

Language	Total	Urban	Rural	Total %
Chichewa	5,679,482	1,016,152	4,663,330	57.2
Chinyanja	1,272,205	94,225	1,177,980	12.8
Chiyao	999,024	77,319	921,705	10.1
Chitumbuka	939,109	126,179	812,930	9.5
Chilomwe	241,576	17,239	224,337	2.4
Chinkhonde	84,000	17,914	66,086	0.8
Chingoni	74,198	17,699	56,499	0.7
Chisena	264,172	21,526	242,646	2.7
Chitonga	165,654	17,302	148,352	1.7
Chinyakyusa	24,824	1,868	22,956	0.2
Chilambya	44,385	5,242	39,143	0.4
Chisenga	19,959	1,405	18,554	0.2
English	17,479	11,165	6,314	0.2
Portuguese	2,458	789	1,669	0.02
Other	105,343	9,412	95,931	1.1
Grand Total	**9,933,868**	**1,435,436**	**8,498,432**	

Table 2.2 Main languages in Malawi (used for household communication)
(Percentage total > 100 due to rounding)

Although there is more agreement as to the identification of languages in Malawi than in Zambia, there is no unanimity: the Census of 1966 listed "about 16 languages. The criteria for determining languages and dialects were not clear" (Kayambazinthu, 1999: 28); Grimes (1992: 295-7) lists 12 indigenous languages; Sichinga (1994) has 35; Kayambazinthu (1999: 15) speaks of "13 Malawian languages and their numerous dialects". As is the case in Zambia, the discrepancies are due to difficulties in classifying varieties that may be closely genetically related, but spoken by different groups.

It is of course highly likely that the fact that the census asked for "the language mostly used for communication" in households boosts the numbers for the "larger" languages, at the expense of the "smaller" languages, as compared with the technique of the previous census which simply asked for the respondent's "first language". The reason for this is that in cross-linguistic partnerships where a locally dominant language is the first language of just one of the partners, then it is very likely to become the language of communication for the whole household. However, given the difficulties which may arise in establishing one's "first language" in contexts of multiple language contact, a census based on household use has merit. It might also be argued that it better indicates the dynamics of language shift.

Table 2.2 shows that 70.0% of the population use Chichewa/Chinyanja in 1998, compared with 50.2% that claimed the two languages (lumped together as Chichewa) as a first language in 1966. The dominance of Chichewa was boosted by the late President Hastings Banda, himself a Chewa, and a strong supporter of the language. In 1968, the Malawi Congress Party under President Banda had recommended that "the name Chinyanja henceforth be known as Chichewa" (Kayambazinthu, 1999: 49; the Chewa and Nyanja people have a virtually identical language; see 2.2.2). Not surprisingly, given the absolute power of the President, the recommendation took effect. Following the demise of Banda, political opponents felt linguistic re-labelling was called for, and Kayambazinthu (1999: 61) notes that in the late 1990s:

> The name of the language also became a contentious issue. Some [...] felt that ChiChewa was too closely identified with Dr. Banda and wanted to revert to the old name ChiNyanja for neutrality.

Such pressures notwithstanding, the current situation is generally agreed to be as follows:

- Chichewa is the *de facto* lingua franca in the central and southern regions (the 1998 census shows it as the numerically dominant language in both regions)
- Chitumbuka is the *de facto* lingua franca in the northern region (and also the numerically dominant language. Chitumbuka, together with Chichewa, are also significant languages in Zambia: see Table 2.1)
- Chiyao, and more so Chilomwe, both found mainly in the southern region, have been declining since the 1960s

In Malawi, as in Zambia, there is much language contact in urban areas, generating non-standard contact varieties, especially of ChiChewa. These have generally met with disapproval, and President Banda excoriated the "anglicized 'Chi-mission' or 'Chi-heaven' or 'Chi-planter' which was currently in the town" (Hansard [Zomba], 1963: 844, cited in Kayambazinthu, 1999:50).

2.3.3 Primary education in Malawi

Students in Malawi officially start school at age 6 (but in practice often much later), and follow an 8 year primary course. The school year has since 1997 coincided with the chronological year, bringing Malawi into line with Zambia, and neighboring countries. As in Zambia, material provision in schools is extremely poor, especially in rural areas. A particular feature of Malawi is the enormous class sizes, with over 100 students being frequent in urban areas, and over 200 not unknown. The teacher/ student ratio for qualified teachers in 1997 was 1:119 and 1:61 for all teachers (Milner et al., 2001: 3). As in Zambia, there is a much higher proportion of qualified teachers in urban schools (75%) than in rural schools (51%) (Kadzamira et al, 2003: 511); here we should bear in mind that about 90% of the population in Malawi is rural. Another striking feature in Malawian primary schools is the very wide variation in age within classes, with Milner et al (2001: 20) reporting student ages ranging from 9 to 24 years at year 6 (when they should all be 11 or 12 years), while Kadzamira et al (2003: 512) report the age range in year one of 4 to 18, with even some 30 year olds enrolled in primary school.

As in Zambia, many primary schools are in poor material condition, with leaking roofs, broken or missing doors and windows, and inadequate provision of desks and books. Very few schools have electricity: Kadzamira et al (2000: 97) report that none of the 20 schools surveyed for their research had it. From 1990 to 1997 expenditure per student fell in real terms by 26%, while the proportion of the recurrent budget spent on wages (85% in 1997) leaves little room for improving learning conditions (Kadzamira et al, 2000: xv). Many classes are held out of doors or in temporary bamboo and grass classrooms, which often become unusable in the rainy season (September to March).

Until 1994 primary education in Malawi was not free; fees varied according to year of schooling and urban/rural location but did not exceed the equivalent of US$3 per year in the upper years of urban schools, and was less in lower primary school and in rural areas. With the introduction of free primary education in 1994 enrolments went up from 1.9 million to almost 3 million in 1997 – a gross enrolment of 138% reflecting the large numbers of over-age children in the system (Kadzamira et al, 2000: xiii). However, drop-out rates are high, with one third of girls and boys dropping out between years 1 and 2, while some 15% of children in 1997 were repeating years. The combined effects of drop-out and repetition means that "very few children complete primary school [while] about one fifth of the children who enter primary school complete it within the prescribed eight-year period" (Kadzamira et al,, 2000: xiv). Again as in the case of Zambia many parents/carers are under the false impression that shoes and uniform are compulsory for school attendance, and in some cases this belief is encouraged by teachers. Kadzamira et al (2005: 50), notes that "Children, particularly girls, may simply withdraw due to lack of clothes socially deemed 'presentable' to wear to school." As in Zambia, absentee-ism because of seasonal labour in rural areas, and street vending in urban areas, is frequent (Devereux, 1999).

The language of instruction for the first 4 years, throughout most schools in the country, is ChiChewa, with English as a curriculum subject. This is despite the fact that in March 1996 a government directive indicated that: "The Ministry of Education would like to inform all that with immediate effect, all standards 1, 2, 3 and 4 classes in all our schools be taught in their own mother tongue [...]. English and ChiChewa will however, con-tinue to be offered as subjects [...] However, English will be used as a medium of instruction beginning in Standard 5" (MOE cited in Kayambazinthu, 1999: 58). In June 1996 the MOE acknowledged that "although other languages were banned as mediums of instruction in stand-ard 1-4 [..] many teachers [...] have used and are still using the commonly spoken languages in their schools [..] The new policy is to grant teachers the freedom to use languages commonly spoken in the area" (MOE cited in Kayambazinthu (1999: 77). However, in practice ChiChewa has con-tinued to be used as a medium, primarily because course books are currently only available in that language. The exception is some schools in the Northern Province where ChiTumbuka is reported to be used (how-ever, it should be recalled that the languages of Malawi belong to the same Bantu family, and have a considerable degree of similarity).

From year 5 until year 8 the medium is English, with ChiChewa as a curriculum subject. However, there is in practice some language "seep-age" in both directions: the primary course *New Malawi Arithmetic* is in English from year 3 onwards (Mchazime, 1989: 3), while the year 4 book contains English that seems much more difficult than that presented at year 4 in the English course (see Chapter 7); conversely many teachers continue to use ChiChewa or other local languages "unofficially" in the classroom beyond year 5.

2.4 Pedagogic approaches to reading in Malawi and Zambia

In both Zambia and Malawi materials and methods for teaching English generally, and teaching reading in English in particular, have always had a great deal in common. After independence in the mid-sixties both countries favoured a rather narrow structuralist approach to the English language syllabus, with a behaviorist approach to methodology, which relied very much on repetition, manifested in the teaching of reading through heavy dependence on "look and say" techniques. In the early nineties both countries began to introduce new rather more "communicative" courses.

2.4.1 Malawi

2.4.1.1 Reading and English in the primary syllabus

In the first year of primary schools, children throughout Malawi are taught to read in ChiChewa, mainly through the syllabic approach. This is widely known in Malawi and Zambia, but seems to be used exclusively to teach initial reading African languages, rather than English[10]. It is based on "consonant-vowel" sequences e.g. *ba, be, bi, bo, bu; ka, ke, ki, ko, ku,* etc. From these, teachers prepare written "syllable charts", as in the following example (from Ms Bernadette Zulu, Kabwata Open School, Lusaka):

a	*e*	*i*	*o*	*u*
la	*le*	*li*	*lo*	*lu*
sa	*se*	*si*	*so*	*su*
ma	*me*	*mi*	*mo*	*mu*
ta	*te*	*ti*	*to*	*tu*
ka	*ke*	*ki*	*ko*	*ku*

Far from being, as some critics claim, the basis for mindless repetition, such charts provide the basis for various cognitively engaging activities, particularly making up different words by combining the syllables from the chart (e.g. *ka-lu-lu (kalulu:* hare); *su-ku-lu (sukulu:* school); *a-ma-i (amai:* mother)). Such word play activity is very popular with learners, and alerts them to the fact that words are composed of sounds, and sounds are (albeit not always in a perfect one-to-one relationship) represented by letters.

This syllabic approach is well suited to ChiChewa/Nyanja, since, in common with other languages of the Bantu family, it is a CV language, with the syllabic structure being predominantly an optional consonant followed by a vowel, which may be symbolically represented as SYLL = {C}V . This phonological structure yields words such as: *ka+lu+lu = kalulu (hare); ma+lu+ba = maluba (flowers); a+ma+i = mother.* (There

---

[10] A similar method for initial reading in English was advocated by Coote (1596) cited in Baynham (1995: 169).

are consonant digraphs such as *ch, mb, ts* or *ns* but these are regarded as representing single consonant sounds.) The syllabic method of initial reading instruction does not of course lend itself as readily to English (which allows for consonant clusters at syllable initial and final position), but the "onset and rime" approach is analogous.

Reading in English effectively starts in year 2, employing the "look and say" method which is the only method used in the first term. It would seem likely, however, that the year 2 students would have acquired, from learning to read in ChiChewa, a reasonable idea of the sound value in English of letters, among other things. It is not clear why this knowledge is not, at least in official advice, capitalized upon. In the second term of year 2 the phonic approach (often referred to as the "phonetic" approach in Malawi) is introduced. Although Teacher's Book 2 of the course *English in Malawi,* (MOE, 1965-68) gives attention to the presentation of meaning, it is clear that the correct pronunciation of written words is an important aspect of reading in Malawi, and the unqualified term "reading" in the Teacher's Books seem normally to refer to "reading aloud". There are a number of examples where this is implied: "the children will imitate whatever sounds you make, good or bad, so the quality of your reading and pronunciation is of the greatest importance". Elsewhere the fact that reading will consist largely of "reading aloud" is made overt: "much of the reading will be oral reading – 'reading aloud' – so that the pronunciation and meaning of the words (sic) become surely fixed in the children's minds" (Teacher's Book 2: 20). Silent reading is suggested as a supplement to "look and say" from about half-way through Book 2. In Teachers' Books 3 and 4 more attention is given to silent reading, although reading aloud is still retained. In the upper primary school (Year 5 onwards) the official approach is that silent reading of a text should be the norm, followed by oral questions and answers.

For the period relevant to the research reported here, the English syllabus in Malawi primary schools was embodied in the *English in Malawi* series together with the associated teacher's books. The series was first published in the mid-sixties. It is a structurally organized course, and the linguistic complexity increases sharply from Book 3 onwards. A new English language course *Activities with English* was introduced in the 1990s, Book 1 in 1992-93, with the others following in successive years. The approach to beginning reading in English in the new course is broadly in line with that of the old, while the basic approach to reading, for the vast majority of teachers, is reported to be no different with the new material. The reasons may be deficient teacher education, or teachers' lack of confidence in the new approaches (see Kadzamira et al, 2003: 511), or simply a tendency, when faced with daily pressure, to teach according to familiar routines.

The official weekly time allocation to English is:

Standard 1 and 2: 5 x 30 minutes
Standards 3 and 4: 7 x 35 minutes
Standards 5 to 8: 8 x 35 minutes

2.4.1.2 Reading in teacher training

Until 1995, the principal route for achieving trained teacher status in Malawi was a two-year full-time course in one of the seven teacher training colleges (TTCs). From 1995 onwards there were a number of changes in teacher training, the most significant being the introduction of the Malawi Integrated Intensive Teacher Education Programme (MIITEP), which was devised to cope with the rapid in-service training of large numbers of teachers who were needed following the introduction of universal free primary education (around 18,000 temporary teachers and 2,000 retired teachers were recruited to cope with the increase). MIITEP replaced the standard teacher training programs which were to be suspended until the backlog of untrained teachers had been dealt with. However, since the average annual primary teacher requirement in Malawi is over 5,600 teachers, and the "traditional" pre-1995 two-year training programme produces only 1,500 graduates per year, an in-service training programme similar to MIITEP "will probably be necessary for the foreseeable future" (Kadzamira et al, 2000: 150).

The various teacher syllabuses, however, give little overt attention to reading English with understanding in the first two years of primary school. The view of teacher trainers is that much reading in standard 2 is "pattern reading", not necessarily accompanied by comprehension. "Pattern reading" refers to the behaviorist repetition, through reading aloud, of selected grammatical structures. Trainers feel that this results in a great deal of reading aloud with little understanding of the text, a view supported by observation. They also claim that a greater emphasis on comprehension comes in year 3 (although observation suggests that reading aloud without comprehension seems to extend well beyond that year).

As concerns teacher training for the teaching of reading in ChiChewa, there is relatively little information available. The Student Teacher's Handbook 2 (MOE, Teacher Development Unit [n.d.]), which is used for the above-mentioned MIITEP courses has 22 of its 389 pages devoted to ChiChewa and 47 to English. The same principles are advocated for ChiChewa as for English.

2.4.1.3 Classroom practice in reading

Observation of over 100 English reading lessons during the 1990s, and reports from other sources suggest that there is a similarity of practice throughout Malawi from years 2 and 3 onwards, with many English reading lessons falling into the following pattern:

(i)   The lesson begins with the teacher writing various words on the blackboard; the words are read aloud by the teacher, and repeated by the class, as a whole and/or in various combinations (e.g. boys, girls, front row, back row etc.), or by individuals.

(ii) The text is read out from the book or from the blackboard by the teacher (or by students known to be competent readers), sentence by sentence, and each sentence repeated, as for (i), before proceeding to the next sentence.

(iii) The whole text is read by the teacher from beginning to end, and sections of it then read again by students, as for (i).

(iv) Oral questions are asked by the teacher. These are normally direct reference questions. The questions often follow the sequence of sentences in the text, in which case the questions can be answered by students reading the sentences in sequence.

(v)   The students may be asked to write the answers in their exercize books.

(Variation to this pattern occurs, and often the lesson starts with step (ii).)

The following partial transcript of a lesson at Year 2 (from Williams, 1993a: 45) is representative of this approach. The teacher of the class observed was a woman with full two-year TTC training. She was teaching a class of 128 children, and was the only person in the room with the course book. It was open at the relevant page, and the teacher showed the illustration to the class from time to time (see Appendix 2).

The classroom had no desks, except one for the teacher. It also had, as is normal in Malawi, a very wide (some 15 feet) wall-painted blackboard. The children sat close together in rows on the floor. (One advantage to the lack of desks is that rooms can accommodate such large numbers relatively easily.) The text of the lesson had been copied onto the board, and the teacher added a number of individual words in the course of the lesson. The transcript of the first part of the lesson, with translation from ChiChewa indicated by italics, is as follows (for the transcript of the whole lesson, see Appendix 2):

Teacher: Now it's time for English. Class, who can remember to read this word? ... Yes?

Student:	Any.
Teacher:	Very good. Clap hands for him. (*Students clap*.)
Student:	What about this word? What does it say?
Student:	Tins.
Teacher:	Very good. Clap hands for ... her. (*Students clap*) And everybody say "tins".
Class:	Tins.
Teacher:	Tins.
Class:	Tins.
Teacher:	(writes "bottles") Who can read this word? ... Yes?
Student:	Bottle (*sic*)
Teacher:	Bottles. Very good. Clap hands for her. (*Students clap*)
Teacher:	Now everybody read.
Class:	Bottles.
Teacher:	Again.
Class:	Bottles.
Teacher:	(writes "matches") What does this say? Yes, Donald?
Student:	Matches.
Teacher:	Matches. Very good. Clap hands for him. (*Students clap*) Everybody say after Donald.
Class:	Matches.
Teacher:	Again.
Class:	Matches.
Teacher:	Now look here. Look on page forty six. Everybody can see it? *Can everybody see it?*
Class:	*Yes.*
Teacher:	*Right.* Now, what can you see? What can you see? Yes, Kenneth?
Student:	I can see Timve.
Teacher:	You can see Timve. Yes, now where is Timve? Where is Timve? Yes, Makanso?
Student:	(unintelligible)
Teacher:	No, no. Yes, you.
Student:	Timve is wearing a shirt and shoes.
Teacher:	I said, I said, where is Timve? *Where is Timve?* Where is Timve? Yes?
Student:	Timve is in the store.
Teacher:	Yes, Timve is in the store.
Teacher:	Yes, Timve is in the store. Clap hands for her. (*Students clap*)

This is a typical opening to an English reading lesson. The most striking feature, given that it is a foreign/second language situation, is the almost complete neglect of the presentation of meaning, or of the checking of understanding of meaning. This applies at the level of both sentences, and individual words (although many of the content words in the text have been borrowed into ChiChewa e.g. *store* as *sitolo*, there is no guarantee that the children have made the connection). The repetition sequence whereby the class repeat twice a word that has already been read aloud by the teacher or a "model" student is also characteristic. However, it would not be correct to say that understanding is not involved at all in this extract. Most students appear to understand the instructions, and the two questions asked towards the end of the extract (*What can you see? Where is Timve?*) also require comprehension. The second question is initially misunderstood, possibly through the students confusing "where" and "wear". It is noticeable, however, that the teacher makes no attempt to probe or disentangle this misunderstanding, but simply repeats in ChiChewa, and seeks an answer from a different student. This somewhat dismissive attitude is a frequent response to students who commit errors, and again suggests a reluctance to deviate from the "plan" by grappling with issues of meaning and comprehension. The remainder of the lesson proceeds along similar lines, going on to reading aloud of the sentences, then the whole text.

2.4.2 Zambia

2.4.2.1 Reading in the primary syllabus

The new *Zambia Primary Course* (ZPC) for English (see McAdam, 1978) which was the relevant course at the time of this research, was rather cumbersome, consisting of separate teacher handbooks for *Language*, *Reading* and *Writing* for each term, together with a students' reader for each term, plus 3 or 4 supplementary readers for each year. The course also included an audio tape recorder and cassettes (which have long since become unusable). The ZPC English course could be characterized as a text-based, and structurally organized, moving from simple to complex language structure. The methodology outlined in the teachers' guides is largely behaviorist, with a considerable emphasis on repetition.

The principal approach to reading in the ZPC is the "look and say" method, applied to "whole words" and "whole sentences". Phonics are introduced in grade 2, but the phonic approach is given little prominence. The class readers for grades 1 and 2 are "taught" through the whole sentence method. "The children are drilled in the story sentence by sentence, and children memories these sentences by heart" (Kapembwa, 1990: 27). The sentences in the readers are structurally graded and overwhelmingly consist of descriptive language e.g. *"The ball is green" "Mulenga is kick-ing the ball"*.

Beyond year 2 the methodology of reading follows much the same pattern as in Malawi, namely questions by the teacher on the picture accompanying the text, a list of new words for the text, reading aloud by the teacher and students, followed by oral and possibly written comprehension questions. Reading aloud by the teacher is officially phased out in grade 4, while discussion of the picture is phased out in grade 5. The texts increase in terms of language complexity and length with each year, but the basic teaching approach of reading the text and answering the questions remains the same.

The ZPC course was replaced from 1991 to 1997 by the new *Zambia Basic Education Course* (ZBEC) in primary English, starting with Year 1 books in 1991. The new course consists of one teacher's guide, and two or three students' books, per year. ZBEC English integrates the oral skills, reading and writing to a greater extent than the previous course, and is generally felt to be more "communicative" although the principle of linguistic grading has still been observed. The amount of time per week devoted to teaching English (MOE, Examinations Council of Zambia, 1986: 1) was:

Grades 1 to 4: 4 hours 30 minutes
Grades 5 to 7: 4 hours 40 minutes

However, as previously mentioned, all subjects apart from Zambian languages and spiritual education are taught through the medium of English, so that the students' exposure to English is in theory considerable.

2.4.2.2 *Reading in teacher training*
Primary school teachers are trained in one of the 10 teacher training colleges. Trainees follow a very heavy taught programme (typically forty-five 40 minute periods per week) which lasts for two years, and is devoted largely to rehearsing the contents and the methods of the Teacher's Handbooks for the relevant subjects. In 1991 about 15% of primary school teachers were untrained (MOE, Zambia, 1992: 163), a proportion that had risen to "approximately one-quarter" in 1996 (Kasonde-Ng'andu et al. 2000: 92), with these untrained teachers being concentrated in rural areas. In 1998 it was estimated that average teacher salaries were below the poverty line, while subsequent increases have had little real effect (Kasonde-Ng'andu et al. 2000: 92). As a result, many teachers have supplementary occupations. (In fact, low salaries throughout much of the

continent mean that many African primary school teachers have become "virtually part-time in their service" (Williams, P., 1986: 97)).

The *Primary Teacher Training Colleges: English Syllabus* (MOE, Curriculum Development Centre, 1991) states that its general objectives with respect to reading in English are that are that trainees should by the end of their course "be able to explain the methods and conduct effectively the reading activities set out in the ZPC English component and other methods and activities suggested by the colleges" (MOE, Curriculum Development Centre, 1991: 5). It goes on to say that the trainees should also be able to:

- define the nature and processes of reading
- explain the psychology and physiology (sic) of reading
- list the aims and purposes of reading
- interpret and apply the principles of reading readiness

In practice however, the lecturers in the teacher training colleges report that relatively little attention is given to general principles (i.e. reading processes and background theory) in the teacher training courses. The main emphasis in their view is upon imparting the specific techniques prescribed for the course books. Such rigid preparation means, according to the Zambian Ministry of Education (1992: 10.4), that "the development of problem-solving skills, essential to the student who is to cope with difficult and diverse classroom conditions, is neglected".

2.4.2.3 Classroom practice in reading

As in the case of Malawi, most reading in English proceeds on the basis of "look and say" using the whole word and whole sentence approach. The following is a transcript of the first part of a lesson in a school in a rural school some 20 kilometres from Lusaka. It is of a third year class, with 45 students present (20 boys, 25 girls), taught by a male teacher with full two-year TTC training. The teacher was the only person with a book, and had copied the text (see Appendix 3) onto the blackboard.

Teacher:	English reading. We are going to read the story that is Chuma and the Rhino. That is paragraph three and four, which has been written on the board. Who can read the first sentence in paragraph three? Yes?
Student:	Look at that hippo's mouth father.
Teacher:	Read aloud.
Student:	Look at that hippo's mouth father.
Teacher:	Once more.

Student:	Look at that hippo's mouth father.
Teacher:	Yes. The sentence is "Look at that hippo's mouth father".
Class:	Look at that hippo's mouth father.
Teacher:	Look at that hippo's mouth father.
Class:	Look at that hippo's mouth father.
Teacher:	Yes. (Points) What is that sentence? Who can read the next sentence? Simon?
Student:	It is very big isn't ... isn't it, said Chuma.
Teacher:	Again.
Student:	It is very big isn't it, said Chuma.
Teacher:	Thank you. The sentence is "It is very big isn't it, said Chuma". Read.
Class:	It is very big isn't it, said Chuma.
Teacher:	It is very big isn't it, said Chuma.
Class:	It is very big isn't it, said Chuma.
Teacher:	Big.
Class:	Big.
Teacher:	Big.
Class:	Big.
Teacher:	It is very big isn't it, said Chuma.
Class:	It is very big isn't it, said Chuma.
Teacher:	OK. Who can read the next sentence? Navis?
Student:	Now, hippos have very -
Teacher:	Is this word "now"?
Student:	Now -
Teacher:	No, no, no, no...
Student:	Yes, hippos have very big ... Yes, hippos have very big mouths, said his mother.
Teacher:	Thank you. Uh, what's that word?
Student:	Father.
Teacher:	OK. Yes, hippos have very big mouths said his father. Read.
Class:	Yes, hippos have very big mouths, said his father.
Teacher:	Yes, hippos have very big mouths, said his father.
Class:	Yes, hippos have very big mouths said his father.
Teacher:	Say mouths.
Class:	Mouths.
Teacher:	Don't say "mouths", say "mouths".
Student:	Mouths.

As in the case of Malawi, there appears to be little attention to the presentation or checking of meaning. Informal assessment at the end of this lesson suggested that very few students of the 45 present appeared to know the meanings of key words in the passage; 4 claimed to know *river* in their own language, 4 *hippo*, and 6 *crocodile*. The teacher's focus is on pronunciation rather than comprehension, exemplified by his insistence on the pronunciation of "mouths". As in the Malawian lesson, the "model reading" was presented by students known by the teacher to be competent. The complete transcript and text for the lesson appear in Appendix 3.

2.5 Observations on classroom reading in Malawi and Zambia

Although it is easy to condemn these lessons in terms of their apparent failure to engage students on a cognitive level, it should be appreciated from the outset that the social, economic and material context in which the teachers are operating is extremely difficult. In the two schools where the above lessons were recorded, there was no electricity, no running water, no books (other than the one which the teacher was using), no desks in the Malawian case, and desks for only about half the students in the Zambian case. Teachers lived in cramped accommodation, sharing with other teachers, in houses which lacked running water or electricity. Their monthly salaries were the equivalent of some £25 to £30, with no certainty that they would even receive that amount at the end of the month. In such conditions, that the fact that so many teachers deal constructively with the situation is remarkable.

Nonetheless, such lessons constitute the "point of delivery" of education systems that are, in terms of their avowed goals, failing to "deliver" (see Chapters 4-7), and some reflection on that is appropriate. Two features emerge from both lessons. One is the "text-bound" nature of the interactions, with a focus upon reading aloud, and the concomitant lack of attention to meaning[11]. There is no attempt in these lessons to link the text to the students' experiences, and the lesson "proceeds" by "proceeding through the text", and by constant reference to, and repetition of, the text.

"Safetalk" is the term coined by Chick (1996), to refer to this situation in South African schools where the "co-ordinated chorusing prompts and responses enabled the teacher and students [...] to hide their poor command of English; to obscure their inadequate understanding of academic content; and to maintain a façade of effective learning taking place" (Chick, 1996: 238). The result of "safe-talk" according to Hornberger and Chick

---

[11] Most Malawian and Zambian primary school teachers see reading as "reading aloud", with the aim of improving pronunciation, and report the poor pronunciation of students to be a major reading problem (Williams, 1998).

(1998) is that "teachers and learners know more or less what to expect and how to behave in class, but where a high price is paid in terms of (a lack of) learning, e.g. [...] chorusing, reading as repeating, writing as copying." The two lessons from Malawi and Zambia present examples of "reading-like" behaviour, where appropriate vocal responses are made as repetitions, or in response to a seen pattern, rather than reading that proceeds from recognition of written words. "Safe-talk" may also be motivated by a desire to "get through the lesson" without being "sidetracked" by individual student concerns. This desire is not confined to Malawian and Zambian teachers: Bernhardt (1991b) notes that the primary concern of teachers in the USA is maintaining the ongoing flow of classroom activities rather than interrupting them to accommodate students' immediate concerns.

A more positive view of this classroom approach to reading is that it allows students the opportunity to practice "saying things" in English, and that whole-class choral reading maximizes the opportunity for students to participate, in what might be termed a "structured participatory" approach. Reading the text aloud also permits students who cannot read, or do not have access to a book, to participate actively in the lesson, by volunteering answers to comprehension questions put to the whole class. Likewise, in making choral responses to questions, as opposed to choral reading aloud, teachers expect the students will be learning from their friends (Croft, 2000). Wright (2001: 62) contends that similar chanting in Eritrean schools results from teachers:

> [C]*hoosing to interpret* the L2 curriculum in their own ways, and that these choices are based on their own concerns about what is best for the students, what is possible given the constraints of the material circumstances, their beliefs about students and their families, and in some cases awareness of their capabilities and limitations as teachers" (italics in original).

From a practical point of view, the practice of choral repetition is also encouraged by the fact that, as Wright implies, the teacher is often the only person in the class with a book; the text must therefore be written on a blackboard; there are limits to how much can be written on the board, and if the text is only read once, then it will have been dispensed with in a matter of moments. In order to make the effort of writing the text on the board worthwhile, teachers have to exploit them over time – and repetition offers one way of achieving this[12]. Here we might note that in both les-

---

[12] Croft (2002) suggests a number of techniques whereby teachers manage the material constraints of their classrooms in Malawi.

sons, what was being read (words in the case of the Malawian lesson, a paragraph in the case of the Zambian one), had been written on the blackboard.

A "negative" view of the practice of choral repetition of text without understanding is that classroom lessons have become a ritualized behavioural routine, one characteristic of such a routine being that it is an activity periodically carried out, and accorded value within a given cultural setting. Serpell (1989: 99) likewise refers to "ritualized performance" in Zambian classrooms. Although a certain value might attach to this literacy practice, it could hardly be maintained that this is sufficient justification for requiring students to be submitted to it on a daily basis for most of their school careers. For most students, there is no doubt that classes consisting largely of choral repetition in English are a process of mystification in the sense that they do not understand the meaning of what they are repeating.

However, the fact that choral repetition occurs in Malawian classrooms when the medium of instruction is ChiChewa (and common to teacher and students) suggests that it is not necessarily simply a function of teachers' lack of confidence in their own proficiency in English, but may equally be rooted in social practice. Williams et al (2001) analysed a total of 26 social science lessons, thirteen conducted through the medium of English in Year 5, and thirteen through ChiChewa in Year 4, and found that the degree of repetition by teachers is roughly similar for both English and ChiChewa medium, which suggests that the high degree of repetition in English results from a "teaching style" rather than reluctance to engage in complex concepts through English. However, although repetition is roughly the same in both languages, the teacher talk in lessons conducted through English is more text bound than those conducted through ChiChewa. In effect the English social science texts are "re-discoursified" through oral repetition to generate a classroom literacy practice that is "safe", since it consists of predictable language, similar to that described in the English reading lessons.

Discussions with students, teachers, teacher trainers, Ministry advisors, and staff of the University of Malawi (reported in Williams et al., 2001b) reveal that many regarded repetition as having pedagogic value. Students' views on choral repetition included (italics again indicating translation) include:

So that we learn
So that we remember what we learn.
We help one another by learning from fast learners.

While teachers claimed:

> The purpose of repetition is to have good pronunciation, to make students master a word [...] to make pupils get it [...] for points to stick in their heads.

as well as:

> When you say "Repeat" and they are getting it right, you feel that "My lesson is going well"

On the other hand, some teachers attribute repetition to inefficient teaching:

> The teacher doesn't know what to do, and as a result he is always repeating.
> It is a teaching technique of the teacher – the pupils just recite, and for them it is teaching.

While a district advisor harshly observes:

> There is teaching but no learning in Malawian schools.

Strangely no teacher mentioned the severe shortage of books which, until the late 1990s, had been a feature of most Malawian classrooms, as a contributory factor in repetition.

However, in life outside the classroom in Malawi, there are a range of situations in which choral repetition occurs. Examples include: political rallies, traditional Chewa rites of passage (e.g. the Chinamwali ceremony, where boys returning from their initiation camp give choral responses to the cues of the elders), Christian church services, funeral processions and traditional story telling. Although choral repetition may in these cases serve the purposes of focusing the audience's attention, as is claimed for the classroom, it seems to have additional social functions. First it establishes "horizontal" solidarity among the members of the group (made overt when audiences to story telling make the choral response *Tili tonse* – We are together). Secondly, it indicates "vertical" solidarity in acknowledging the authority of the group principal (political leader, story-teller, preacher or teacher; see Chimombo, 1988: 88). Thirdly, there is a more subtle process where the group response also binds in the leader, who receives assurance from the audience that the solidarity "extends upwards", as indicated by these comments from two teachers:

> Teacher 1:   So [if the students] don't respect – respond – it means they are not interested.

Teacher 2:   They are not part of you.
Teacher 1:   Yes. You are not together with them.

The last two sentences indicate powerfully that the teacher should be "with" the students, as well as the students being "with" the teacher.

That the practice of choral repetition in classrooms is culturally gener- ated, rather than a response to a pedagogic situation, emerges from the remarks by several teachers that they are not aware of "doing" repetition.

Teacher 1:   We don't see this thing [*sci.* repetition]
Teacher 2:   You don't realize that you are doing that.

Such lack of realization is a sure sign of culturally normal behaviour which participants are unaware of precisely because it is unmarked routine. Given that choral repetition pervades so much of social life in Malawi, what would be surprising would be its absence, rather than its presence, in the classroom. Beyond demonstrating solidarity, however, repetition in Eng- lish is largely superficial in the sense that it reproduces a surface sequence of sounds, rather than transmits meaning. The majority of these English sequences are not understood by the majority of the students, and so can be of no value in terms of cognitive growth. However, one would not wish to suggest that there are cultural styles that *of themselves* contribute to educational failure. Historically, there has been a cultural confluence whereby a language practice from Malawian culture, namely choral rep- etition, takes place in a language of British culture, namely English, with resultant lack of understanding for most Malawian students. Classroom practices such as choral repetition, illustrate "the elusiveness of cultural capital for the disenfranchized" (May, 1994: 25), and its prevalence casts doubt over official pronouncements that the purpose of education in Ma- lawi is to "develop the child's communicative skills" and "develop the individual child's potential abilities to their maximum through a variety of creative learning experiences" (Ministry of Education [Malawi] n.d.).

2.6 Previous research on reading in Zambia and Malawi

Until relatively recently, little research on reading in primary schools had been carried out in Zambia and Malawi. Overall the results from the research (much of which is in the so-called "grey literature", i.e. that available only as government and agency reports, and generally difficult to obtain) yields rather discouraging findings. In Zambia, Sharma (1973) ad- ministered a 40 word recognition test in English to 3,298 grade 3 children (a 5% sample of the national grade 3 population). The words were drawn from Zambian course books at years 1, 2 and 3. Only 4.14% could read all the words correctly, while 5.16% could not read any of the words. Of the year 3 children, 17% could read all the year 1 words correctly, while only 7.2 % could read all year 1 and 2 words correctly. However, it seems clear that by "read" Sharma means simply "read aloud". The assessment of a response as "correct" or otherwise must therefore be problematic in some instances.

Chikalanga (1990: 69) reports a 1973 study in Zambia which tested 583 grade 5 children and concluded that "there is a very large group of very poor readers in most classes and they are unlikely to be able to cope with the English course of the New Zambia Primary Course nor be able to do much of the work in other subjects".

Between 1980 and 1992 Chifwa, a Zambian school inspector, carried out informal assessment in 11 schools in the Southern Province of Zambia, and 6 schools in the Eastern Province at all years except year 1. He classified students in terms of a 4 point scale as "good readers" "average readers" "poor readers" and "can't read". His results are reported separately for each class in each school and are not consolidated. It appears that from about one tenth to one third of the students in years 2 to 5 in each of the 17 schools are in the "can't read" category (Chifwa, n.d.).

Kapembwa (1990) surveys primary school reading methodology and materials in Zambia, but has no assessment of reading. Her conclusion (Kapembwa, 1990: 66) is that:

> … until the child uses English with reasonable fluency ... there is little point in making them start to learn to read (sc. in English), and as such, time spent teaching her to read English will be better used teaching them to speak it. (sic).

Williams (1993b) reports on the results of modified cloze testing at years 3, 4 and 6 in 5 schools in Zambia (452 students). The tests were carried out in English and Nyanja and the conclusions were that there was inadequate comprehension of material in English judged to be at their level on the part of approximately 85% of year 3 students, 88% of year 4 students, and 74% of year 6 students. On the positive side there were large and statistically significant mean improvements on the whole test between years, suggesting that overall students improve year on year (although there is a possibility that this improvement is enhanced by weaker students dropping out). As far as reading in Nyanja is concerned, Zambia students achieved very low scores, with means of 3.3, 7.5 and 21.6 out of 60 at years 3, 4 and 6 respectively.

In 1994, the International Institute for Educational Planning (IIEP), and the Zambian Ministry of Education carried out, as part of a programme set up by the Southern African Consortium for Measuring Educational Quality (SACMEQ), a national survey of year 6 students in Zambia. The survey included reading in English, but not local languages. A sample of 2,558 students from a sample of 157 schools were tested: the conclusions were that 74.2 % of year 6 students did not reach a "minimum level of mastery" in reading in English (Nkamba and Kanyika, 1998: 64-65). The finding for year 6 coincides closely with that of Williams (1993b) reported above, that there was inadequate comprehension of material in English judged to be at their level on the part of approximately 74% of year 6 students. Nkamba and Kanyika (1998: 65) conclude that the results present "an extremely gloomy picture concerning the reading performance of grade 6 students in Zambia". Kasonde-Ng'andu et al (1999: xvii) somewhat harshly conclude that "from the results of the SACMEQ survey, three-quarters of grade 6 pupils are judged to be illiterate, according to standards set by the MOE"

Prior to the mid-1990s there is little published research available on reading in Malawi. Mchazime (1989) carried out an analysis of primary school reading materials in English, but did not examine student proficiency. The 1990s, however, saw a considerable increase in educational research in Malawi. Williams (1993b) reports on the results of a reading test (using modified cloze) at years 3, 4 and 6 in 5 schools (480 students). The tests were carried out in English and ChiChewa, and it was concluded that there was inadequate comprehension of material in English judged to be at their level on the part of approximately 65% of year 3 students, 89% of year 4 students, and 78% of year 6 students. As in the Zambia, there were statistically significant mean improvements on the whole test between years, suggesting that students improve year on year (although again this may well be enhanced by weaker students dropping out). In the ChiChewa reading tests, the mean scores out of 60 were 16.0, 29.1 and 45.7, at years 3, 4 and 6 respectively, a much stronger performance than that of the Zambian students (on a virtually identical test).

A great deal of subsequent research in Malawian schools focused on gender (reviewed by Kadzamira et al, 2000: 31-43). Much of the impetus for this came from the GABLE (Girls' Attainment in Basic Literacy and Education) initiative funded by USAID. In the field of reading, Chimombo (1994) has a general survey of the teaching of initial literacy with particular reference to English, while qualitatively-oriented research on the learning and teaching of literacy is reported by Johnson, et al. (2000), through a project that had "the aim of developing a methodology for assessing and monitoring children's learning" (p.iii), in 10 schools in and around Lusaka. To assess reading in English and Chichewa "teachers were asked to select six to ten children in their classes on the basis of whom they thought were 'good', 'average' and 'weak' communicators" (*sic*) (Johnson et al; 2000: 19). These children were then asked to read aloud, and assigned to one of four levels. Level descriptors include the "dramatic quality" of reading (e.g. Level 3: "shows understanding [....] through expression, volume and emphasis" Level 4: "shows understanding by reading through expression" (Johnson et al, 2000: 34). Such descriptors (despite the fact they are said to have been generated by teachers themselves) seem inappropriate to Malawian children who are not coached in "expressive" reading. Furthermore, while reading "with expression" might indicate comprehension, there is no evidence that Malawian children who read without expression necessarily fail to comprehend. Johnson et al., (2000: iii) concluded that "32.4% of children achieved the expected level of reading texts in English and 34.4% in the reading of texts in ChiChewa". However, since this project, was primarily an attempt to help teachers generate activity-based interventions so as to develop insights into teaching, their conclusions on student comprehension might not be representative of Malawi. Rose (2002, cited in Kadzamira et al, 2003: 511) found that 10% of a sample of year 3 children could not write their names, and "fewer than half of the children interviewed could read common words in English or ChiChewa which appear frequently in textbooks."

Milner et al. (2001) report on the IIEP/SACMEQ project in Malawi (a project very similar to the Zambian IIEP/SACMEQ project mentioned above). Because of lack of transport, poor roads, and student absence, data in Malawi were only obtained from 1,938 students (around two thirds of the very carefully planned sample of 3,100 students from 155 schools), and their report is therefore classed as "interim". These "interim" results suggest that "only 21.6% of Standard 6 pupils in Malawi reached the minimum level of mastery on the reading test [...] in other words 78.4% of pupils did not reach the minimum level prescribed by the reading specialists in Malawi [...] This is indeed a deplorable state of affairs" (Milner et al, 2001: 60). Remarkably, this conclusion (like that from Zambia) is again almost identical to the conclusion reported by Williams (1993b) who found inadequate comprehension of material in English judged to be at their level on the part of approximately 78% of year 6 students.

Such research from Zambia and Malawi added to the awareness of the Ministries of Education in both countries that the situation in their primary schools gave cause for concern. The Ministry of Education of Zambia (1996: 40) noted that:

Zambia has had almost thirty years of using English as the medium of instruction from Grade 1 onwards. Children who have had very little contact with English outside school have been required to learn how to read and write through and in this language which is quite alien to them. They have also been required to learn content subjects through this medium. The experience has not been altogether satisfactory.

3. Reading in First and Additional Languages

3.1 Reading and literacy

"We all know what reading is" proclaim Urquhart and Weir (1998: 13). True, but we do not all agree on exactly what we "know". To tease out the differing concepts of reading, it is useful to start by considering reading within the broader framework of literacy. Work in literacy may be divided into two traditions, the "narrow" and the "broad". The narrow tradition is typified by the standard dictionary definition of literacy as "the ability to read and write". This definition is implicit in much public discourse, and focuses upon the capacities of the individual, generating studies of initial reading and writing, reading as comprehension, and writing as composition, in both first and additional languages.

Literacy in the broad interpretation, on the other hand, examines the deployment of literacy practices in society, and has its origins in sociology and anthropology. It is part of an intellectual movement which came to the fore from the 1980s, and which turned away from a focus on the individual, characteristic of the previous psychological approaches, and towards a focus on the social. The broad approach concentrates upon describing literate behaviour in social contexts, and analysing its meanings and values in those contexts. It is compatible with the general notion of communicative competence (Hymes, 1972), and, much as early work in communicative competence addressed the ethnography of speaking, so the broad approach to literacy addresses the ethnography of literacy.

Within the narrow psycholinguistic view of literacy, reading may be defined as the process of perceiving and understanding written language, a definition in line with that put forward by many applied linguists and language educationists in recent decades (e.g. Widdowson, 1984: 39; Nuttall 1996: 3). Reading research in this tradition has been preoccupied with characterizing what knowledge and competencies readers need, and how these are deployed in the construction of meaning, the central concept for this view. Reader proficiency in the language of the text is therefore seen as crucial, and a great deal of research attention has been devoted to the relative importance of "reading ability" and "language proficiency" in second/foreign language reading.

Reading within the broad interpretation of literacy is viewed as a social practice, occurring in a variety of contexts, the possibilities being mediated by text type, social context and the purposes and capacities of the reader. While it may be tempting to see the narrow and broad approaches to reading as complementary, with the former investigating how the individual makes sense of marks on paper, and the latter investigating the role of the activity in social contexts, this would be misleading: one reason – among many – is that while understanding is central to "reading" in the narrow definition, "reading" in the broad approach does not necessarily involve understanding of the text.

Thus in traditional Arabic literacy, a non-Arab speaker might memorize and recite the Quran "even though he might not actually comprehend the sense of what he has read" (Wagner, 1998: 175). Street (1984: 132) refers to this as "maktab literacy", described by Wallace (1992: 21) as the ability "to recite relevant sections of the religious texts without necessarily having decoding ability, let alone the ability to read for meaning". In a similar context in Pakistan, Farah (1998: 253; see also Rassool, 1999: 31) suggests that the majority of non-Arabic speakers do not understand the Quran in a linguistic sense, and comments:

> For members of the community, reading the Quran is a blessing and an honor. The meaning of Quranic literacy for members of this community lies not entirely in the interpretation (literal message of the text), but rather it is symbolically related to the Quran being the word of God.

In its reliance on memory, and the fact that children do not understand the meaning of what they are repeating, the "chanting" of text by Malawian and Zambian children in English classes is comparable, although of course the social value attached to the activities is quite different. Clammer (1976, cited in Street, 1995: 78) similarly points out that 19th century Fijians chanted their geography lessons, but did not derive much meaning from the activity. Street's (*ibid.*), criticism of Clammer on the grounds that Fijians were adapting imported procedures to their own cultural practices, is reasonable, but does not invalidate Clammer's point. In similar vein, Baynham, who also views reading as situated social practice, holds that "What 'counts' as reading may vary from culture to culture to culture" (1995: 171) and observes "From a reading for meaning perspective it might seem that reading as the memorization and recitation of a text might not even count as reading". Baynham is correct in his suspicion – from the reading for meaning perspective, recitation without understanding is indeed not reading.[1] The absence of a "meaning making" perspective may

---

[1] 'Reading for meaning' and 'reading by memorisation' are not, of course, mutually

also explain the lack of attention to language in the broad approach to literacy, other than in a general sense, exemplified in Street's claim (2001: 97) that "each time a literacy is embedded in another language its meanings alter – new literacy practices are involved, not just translations from one language to another." True enough, and as Blommaert (cited in Kell, 2005) points out "language is context" but all the more reason for not ignoring language proficiency as a barrier to the generation of meaning in written texts. Multiple-language literacies (e.g. of the Ghanaians described by Herbert and Robinson (2001)) are enabled precisely because the exponents are proficient in, among other things, the various languages of their literacy practices.

Rather than focus on literacy practices this study will focus on the psycholinguistic perspective of "reading for meaning". The reason for this is the "cognitive imperative" in contemporary education. Much formal education depends on the student's ability to create meaning from text, to accommodate that meaning within existing knowledge structures, and thus to grow as a student. Such academic reading is overwhelmingly an individual process[2], often self-accessed, inevitably self-monitored, with the outcome dependent on the student's competence in the skill of reading and in the language of the text (and, of course, appropriate knowledge schemata). Rote repetition without understanding, while it is certainly a literacy practice in schools, and while social value may be attached to it, cannot contribute to a student's academic growth, since such a contribution must be grounded in cognitive engagement. The observation of reading as a literacy practice in African communities is instructive, but such studies yield information that is local and contingent. The aim of this study, on the other hand, is too seek relevant information on the extent to which the educational operations in Zambia and Malawi are meeting their self-imposed targets, and whether those targets are reasonable.

Of course, one would hope that the reading and writing targets of the educational operation have social relevance, as well as cognitive value.

---

exclusive. Muslims who recite the Quran without understanding Arabic, also read for meaning in other languages (e.g. the London Bangladeshis described in Gregory and Williams [2000: 167-179]).

[2] One may of course object that the individuality of the academic reading mode is incompatible with the more collective ethos of African society. Such an objection would speak to the need for radical educational reform. This research, however, is examining reading proficiencies in the light of the current educational practices in Africa (which attach great weight to individual examination performance, for example).

However, whether the analysis of social practices can provide a sufficient basis for literacy pedagogy is uncertain, since the social view of literacy lacks any theory of learning. As Street (in Martin Jones, 2000: 29) says of social literacy studies their "sternest test [is] that of practical applications in the field of mainstream education". Street (2003: 84) in a paper entitled "The Implications of the 'New Literacy Studies' for Literacy Education" has a "provisional check list of principles" for these implications (e.g. "Literacy is more complex than current curriculum and assessment allows"), but continues "Specific proposals for curriculum, pedagogy and assessment would follow".[3] It seems that while the social view of literacy has delivered an energizing critique from an anthropological perspective, it is not an appropriate basis for answering questions such as "how well do students understand their textbooks?".

The psycholinguistic model is valid in the banal sense that if one cannot read, then one cannot read anything. Equally, the ideological literacy model is valid in the sense that the converse proposition "If one can read, then one can read everything" is wrong. We all have varying degrees of illiteracy, but they do not flow from the inability to read. However, even if we restrict the discussion of reading to the psycholinguistic model, there are still a number of other issues which arise from the definition of reading as "a process of perceiving and understanding written language": these concern the nature of perception, the nature of understanding and the nature of written language. The reader's perception, for example, may not correspond to what is actually on the page, while the term "understanding" raises the question of whether we are dealing with the reader's or the writer's understanding of the text (c.f. Urquhart, 1987): such considerations need to be kept in mind in any assessment of reading. Since we shall be concerned with investigating reading outcomes of educational policies in contexts of a home-school language switch, not only is the construct of "reading proficiency" crucial, but also the place of language in this construct.

---

[3] Describing unsuccessful attempts in Africa to implement social literacy approaches, Papen (2005: 9), notes that in one adult literacy programme "Neither learners nor facilitators agreed with the rather negative view of school education […] that is widespread among those who adhere to the social view of literacy". She further observes that literacy needs of adults are not necessarily tied to the practices of their current livelihoods; indeed, people may seek literacy classes so that they can escape their existing lives. Proponents of social literacies are well aware of this criticism (e.g. Rogers, 2003: 25), but the proposal of transformational programmes based on ethnographic approaches (Street, 2001: 12-14) likewise faces the stern test of practical application (see Kell, 2005: 86).

3.2 Language in reading

3.2.1 Language and language levels

A language, in the sense in which it will be used in this book refers to a
rule-governed human system, the operation of which enables the generation of meanings. Thus in terms of the grammatical rules of English *Charles
has hurt June* is has a different meaning from *June has hurt Charles* while
Abi plays a mean game of pool is different from *Abi played a mean game
of pool.* In terms of the English lexicon *cabbage* does not mean the same
as *king.* Different rules obviously result in different languages. The term
"language" may also be used to refer to realizations of these systems in
the form of spoken or written utterances. This is a well-known distinction
originating in de Saussure's *langue* versus *parole* dichotomy, and Chom-
sky's separation of competence and performance. While "performing one's
competence" suggests a focus on individual psycholinguistic capacity, it
is of course clear that a language is a social phenomenon in the sense that
its ontogeny and ontogenesis are socially determined, and also in the sense
that rules for use (i.e. the deployment and interpretation of utterances, in
both spoken and written modes), are social rules.

3.2.2 First language, second language and mother tongue

The reference of the terms "first language" (L1), and "second language"
(L2), are often taken as unproblematic in much of the psycholinguistically-
oriented literature. However, it may be misleading to suppose that a reader
is reading in his or her "first language" simply because the same language
label is applied to the reader's language and the text language.

   One reason for this is that whereas most texts are written in a standard
language variety, for example standard Arabic, standard Welsh, standard
English, etc., most speakers of Arabic, Welsh, or English do not have the
standard variety as their first language. Non-standard languages are a common feature of social, ethnic or geographic groups in every country; like
standard varieties, they are rule-governed systems, although social attitudes towards them differ. Cases of diglossia, which one might roughly
describe as institutionalized alternation of standard and non-standard varieties, have been amply documented since Ferguson's seminal work in
1959: one of the defining features of Ferguson's "high" varieties (which
for present purposes roughly correspond to "standard") is that they are
normally learned through formal education, and used especially in written
mode, while "low" varieties are normally acquired "naturally" and used

in oral mode with family and friends. The difference between the standard and non-standard varieties may vary from slight differences in pronunciation up to comprehensive lexical and syntactic differences, where readers may understand little of their putative "first language". In reading research, the possibility of such variety mismatch must always be borne in mind lest one attribute reading difficulties to readers who simply have a language difficulty with the standard variety of their language.

A crucial assumption concerning diglossia for Ferguson was that social consensus underpinned the functional differentiation of language varieties, a view followed by Fishman (1970) and especially Gumperz (1968). Such a view accorded well with mainstream American and British sociology which was consensus-oriented. On the other hand many in Europe (e.g. Ninyoles, 1972; Williams, 1992) see diglossia precisely as an indication of structural conflict between groups, with the "high" variety being that of the dominant group, or one to which they have ready access, and which was used in statusful and powerful domains (education, politics, law, religion), while the "low" variety is used by relatively powerless groups for less prestigious domains (and survives through its value as a marker of group solidarity). Thus while one may subscribe to the commonplace that all languages are equal "linguistically" they are not, for a given context, equal "socially" and ideologies of language have built up over time (if unequal power relations remain stable), whereby differing varieties are imbued with intrinsic qualities. Such developments have not been without effects upon the language policies of once-colonized countries.

It is also, of course, possible that a person's first language may be one which has no written form. There are also languages which do have a written form, but where very little is written in them; there are still other cases where a language has written material but many speakers have little or no exposure to that written material. Thus in some communities very little reading in the community language may occur, and this would have to be appreciated if one were to investigate the relationship between "first" and "second" language reading.

Finally, we also need to take into account the context of acquisition of the "second" language. Some children are exposed to two or more languages from early childhood, and have "bilingualism as a first language". Serpell (1989: 99) documents this in the case of Zambian children in Lusaka (for other contexts, see Pearson *et al.*, 1993; Vihman and McLaughlin, 1982; Zentella, 1997). Although the languages may have been differentiated by interlocutor or domain, the result is that such a person's "first" or "second" language may not be readily identifiable. In other cases the chronological "first language" may have atrophied and the chronological "second language" may have become dominant. (Here it may be noted that the term "mother tongue" is normally used in the research literature to refer to what may be termed "chronological first language".) "Mother tongue" is also used in sub-Saharan Africa to refer to the language of the group of which a person is a member but which he or she did not acquire (normally as a result of family migration); this gives rise to apparently anomalous claims such as "I have never learned my mother tongue". (It goes without saying that the term "second", especially with respect to English, may not be correct in cases of those who already know two or more languages, where the adjective "additional" would be more appropriate.)

Such circumstances as those outlined above should counsel caution in discussions of reading performance in "first" or the "second" languages, or indeed the "mother tongue" of bilinguals (see also Davies, 1986: 9). Likewise at the sociolinguistic level the distinction between contexts where English is a "second language" and plays an official role in the country, as opposed to those countries where English is a "foreign language" and is far less visible, means that one has to be wary of attributing exclusively to curricular interventions differences that students display in L1 or L2 reading proficiency. (Moreover, the rise of English as an international language in global communication, means that the second language/foreign language distinction with respect to English has increasingly to be treated with caution.)

3.2.3 Language in models of the reading process

Readers who "know the language" which they are reading, are able to, indeed must, make use of (among other competences) their competence in vocabulary and grammar. Conversely, readers with inadequate competence in vocabulary and grammar experience difficulties. Psycholinguistic models of the reading process assume a reader who is competent in the language being read. Issues of linguistic comprehension are therefore, for those models, not as salient as they might be in the case of readers reading in a less familiar language.

In terms of language levels and reading, the question of whether vocabulary poses greater problems than grammar, is one that can only be answered in specific cases, rather than in a general sense. For example, ESP (English for special purposes) students who are familiar with the technical English vocabulary of their specialization might find syntax a greater problem than vocabulary. Likewise a speaker of a Latin-based language such as Spanish, when reading a formal English text with a high proportion of Latinate words might find it easier than a text that contains the corresponding "Anglo-Saxon" terms. Thus Haynes (1993) points out that *radiant* and *splendid* were not a problem for her Spanish and French speakers, since their languages contain similar cognates; however, the same words were a problem for Japanese and Arabic students. In that English and African languages do not share any cognates in that sense, then speakers of African languages do not have those lexical supports. On the other hand, African languages in ex-British colonies have borrowed a large number of words from English (see Kashoki, 1990 for borrowings into Zambian languages).

3.2.4 Grammar and reading

Studies of the relationship between grammar (or syntactic competence), and reading for L1 readers are relatively scarce (c.f. Urquhart and Weir, 1998: 58). The reason for this neglect would seem to be that, as Fries (1963: 70) had pointed out some years previously, those learning to read in their first language already have syntactic competence. Syntax therefore, unlike vocabulary or spelling, does not feature as a major problem, and there was, claims Fries, a general assumption that "grammatical meanings are intuitive" (*ibid.* 70). Schlesinger (1968) likewise concluded after a series of experiments that for first language subjects, syntax did not significantly affect the reading process.

On the other hand, a number of child psychologists working with young readers of varying proficiency, have found evidence suggesting that syntax is important in first language reading. Vellutino and Scanlon (1982: 236) reviewing the work of a number of specialists, conclude that competence in syntax facilitates the process of identifying written language, in that it can provide immediate feedback if a "reading" is at variance with the grammatical context; it can also limit "readings" of words in terms of particular grammatical classes (e.g. nouns cannot substitute for verbs), and finally it can limit the contexts in which a particular word may be employed. They also (*ibid.*: 237) report on a study by Goldman (1976) who found that, faced with sentences such as *John promised Mary to shovel the driveway*, poor readers tended to see *Mary* as doing the shovelling. The explanation adduced for such misinterpretation is the so-called "minimum distance principle" (Rosenbaum, 1967), where the noun phrase in closest preceding proximity to an infinitive is judged as the implicit subject, possibly generalized from sentences such as *John told/wanted/asked Mary to shovel the driveway*. A decade later Rayner and Pollatsek (1989) likewise concluded from their studies that syntax does play a part in L1 reading, and introduced the similar "garden path" explanation. This claims that readers structure written sentences in the most "economic" manner, by trying to relate new items syntactically to preceding items. If the original "path" does not lead to a satisfactory meaning, they "re-route" as needed. Their approach is illustrated by the responses of many readers to sentences such as: (1) *Because Tim always eats a whole chicken this doesn't seem much to him,* as opposed to (2) *Because Tim always eats a whole chicken is just a snack for him.* Here it is predicted that the first sentence is easier to process than the second, since the "default" path is to attach "a whole chicken" to "eats" as the object of a transitive verb.

Although the review of research by Vellutino and Scanlon (1982) finds correlations between syntactic proficiency and reading ability, they point out that "cause and effect relationships are not necessarily entailed" and suggest that syntactic weaknesses could be "secondary manifestations of more basic problems in other domains of language" (*ibid.*: 242). However, we should bear in mind that Vellutino and Scanlon are dealing with readers reading in their L1. Were such findings to be discovered in the reading of English as an additional language by those who are competent first language readers, then we would probably be more inclined to the view that the proficiency in the syntax of the additional language is causal, rather than attribute their difficulties to "basic problems of processing language".

In fact, despite the small number of L2 studies, there is near universal acceptance of the view that a certain degree of second language syntactic competence is necessary in second language reading. Among the research studies investigating syntax in second language reading, Berman (1984: 139), claims that "efficient FL readers must rely – in part, though not exclusively – on syntactic devices to get at text meaning". Further evidence for the view that syntax comes into play in the process of reading, is the strong positive correlations between test results in grammar and reading (e.g. Alderson, 1993). The opposite view of Strother and Ulijn (1987) that syntactic processing is not necessary in reading, is, as Urquhart and Weir (1998: 60) say "frankly unbelievable".

However, a note of reserve is in order. Reading is a receptive (though not necessarily a passive) process, and accordingly it may well be the case, as Urquhart and Weir (1998: 61) point out, that successful processing of text may be achieved with less than native-speaker competence in syntax, through a combination of lexical knowledge and background knowledge. In other words, readers may "guess" at a structural meaning, as they may "guess" at a word meaning. This is possibly an explanation as to why children in Fiji could read with understanding unfamiliar English structures in the context of meaningful sentences (Elley, 1984: 295).

3.2.5   *Vocabulary and reading*

The importance of the relationship between lexical development and reading ability is supported by a great deal of work with mainstream (L1) English primary school readers, largely from the USA. A number of such studies are cited by Vellutino and Scanlon (1982), including Fry (1967) and Schulte (1967) who claimed that poor readers' vocabulary levels were below those of "normal readers" and less well elaborated. In addition, early work on readability (Chall, 1958; Klare, 1974) as well as research into L2 academic reading (Saville-Troike, 1984) have indicated the importance of vocabulary in reading. Subsequent surveys among second language learners (e.g. Leki and Carson, 1994) invariably yield vocabulary as a reading concern.

Unlike syntax, vocabulary is an area that L1 speakers are aware of as a source of difficulty. That competence in vocabulary is not "intuitive" is generally accepted: L1 monolingual dictionaries are regularly used by L1 speakers if they "don't know a word". However, although research and reports from readers attest the strong relationship between lexical proficiency and reading ability, the direction of causality cannot necessarily be inferred. Indeed it is likely that the direction of causality varies according to circumstance: thus having a well developed vocabulary would probably help an initial reader reading in L1, while fluent readers might improve their lexical proficiency through extensive reading.

One obvious problem in vocabulary research is what constitutes a "word": we shall not pursue this point, but for present purposes the orthographic definition will be employed, namely that a word is a sequence of letters "bounded on either side by a space or punctuation mark" (Carter, 1987: 4). There remain, of course, a number of problems in deciding what counts as a "different word", notably:

1. words that are formally identical but with clearly different meanings, such as *(savings) bank* and *(river) bank*. These are generally counted as different words.
2. different inflectional forms within the same grammatical category (*play,* plays, *played, playing* – as verb forms). Such forms are counted by applied linguists as "the same word".
3. different forms in different grammatical categories (*beauty* – noun; *beautiful* – adjective; *beautifully* adverb; *beautify* – verb). Such different derivational forms are normally counted by applied linguists as "different words" (e.g. Carter, 1987: 10).
4. different forms resulting from simple prefixation, in the same

grammatical category (e.g. *true/untrue* – adjectives; *tie/untie* – verbs). These are not considered to be inflections, but derivations, and as such different lexemes.

5. "multi-word" items such as phrasal verbs. A phrasal verb such as *put off (an appointment),* may be regarded as a single lexeme from a semantic perspective, whereas in our orthographic definition it would be two words. Likewise *put up with (an inconvenience)* would be a different lexeme. However, the orthographic definition would count *put* as the same word in both examples. Moreover, some phrasal verbs are very frequent: while *give up* only constitutes some 5% of the occurrences of give, it is still a frequent item (Moon, 1997: 45).

A basic distinction that has been implied in the above discussion is that between structural or grammatical words on the one hand (which are regarded as part of grammar or syntax), and lexical words (also known as "full words" or "content words"), on the other. Discussions of "vocabulary" usually focus, as we do here, on lexical words. However, many word frequency counts or dictionary compilations use the terms "head word" and/or "word family". While the definitions and uses of these two terms are unfortunately not always consistent, generally accepted current usage is that "head word" refers to a single word lexeme which is the stem or base form of the word (c.f. Coxhead, 1998: 1), while "word family" refers to "a base word, its inflected forms, and a small number of reasonably derived forms" (Nation and Waring, 1997: 8).

Apart from problems of defining the coverage of head words and word families, there are two other important vocabulary issues is second language learning contexts: one is what constitutes knowing a word, and a second is what words are likely to be most useful. From the language production perspective we might suggest that knowing a word implies knowledge of meaning, pronunciation, grammatical association, collocations, and association (c.f. Laufer, 1997: 141); from a reading point of view what is crucial is being able to recognize the word in written form, and knowing the meaning in the given context (c.f. Nation, 1990: 31).

As concerns which words are likely to be most useful, one criterion, in terms of general language use, as opposed to domain specific language use, is frequency. Over the years of research into lexis, one fairly consistent finding is that the 2,000 most common words (including grammatical function words) account for approximately 80% of the total number of words in most prose texts. Nation and Waring (1997) cite the Francis and Kuchera (1982) analysis of the Brown corpus, which has the 2,000 most frequent words accounting for 79.7% of the 500 written texts which they analysed. Table 3.1 shows the proportion of these texts covered by high frequency vocabulary (in this instance lemmas, not word families, plus grammatical words):

Vocabulary size	Text coverage (%)
1,000	72.0
2,000	79.7
3,000	84.0
4,000	86.8
5,000	88.7
6,000	89.9
15, 851	97.8

Table 3.1 Text coverage and word frequency
(Source: Francis and Kuchera, 1982, cited in Nation and Waring, 1997: 9)

While knowing the 2,000 most frequent words is obviously helpful, and one response to this is to attempt to ensure that the learners know these 2,000 most common words, we should be aware that "ease" and "frequency" do not necessarily correlate. We should also not lose sight of the fact that the remaining 20% of these texts is made up of the remainder of the words of the English language (of which there are several hundred thousand, although as McArthur (1992: 1091) says "the overall vocabulary of English is beyond strict statistical assessment"[4]). When language learners learn more and more vocabulary items which are increasingly infrequent, and therefore account for less and less text, they are moving into an area of diminishing returns. There is also, as Richards (1974) observed, a paradox here: the 2,000 most frequent words are common to

---

[4] McArthur (*ibid.*) goes on to note that "The *Oxford English Dictionary* (1989) defines over 500,000 items described as 'words' [...] Specialist dictionaries contain vast lists of words and word-like items [...]When printed material of this kind is taken into account [...] the crude but credible total for words and word-like forms in present day English is somewhere over a billion items". Nation (1990: 16) says "The large Webster's dictionary contains about 128,000 headwords" while according to Nation and Waring (1997: 7) *"Webster's Third* has a vocabulary of around 54,000 word families."

most texts. It must therefore be the case that what contributes to making texts different from each other, what contributes, in other words, to the "message uniqueness" of texts, is not the 2,000 most common words, but the words that constitute the remaining 20%, which can come from any of the other several hundred thousand or so words in English.

Most native-English speaking individuals have a vocabulary far smaller than several hundred thousand words; an educated adult knows some 60,000 head words or 156,000 including derivatives (Seashore and Eckerson, 1940 cited in Krashen 1989: 452). Nation and Waring (1997: 7), however, propose a smaller figure of 20,000 word families. The differences are said to stem from how "head words" and "word families" are defined.

It is to be expected that English language learners in a formal second language learning situation will know a relatively small number of English words, since they have little exposure to English outside the classroom, and the amount of vocabulary to which they are exposed through the English course book is restricted. Thus the Zambian *Teaching Syllabus: Functional Objectives* (MOE [Zambia], n.d.) recommends that by the end of grade 7 Zambian pupils should have a vocabulary of "*at least 2500-3000 words*", while the associated *Writer's Guide Word List* (MOE [Zambia], n.d.: 1) lists 2,735 headwords to be taught. (This, however, is with reference to the English language syllabus, and seems to ignore the fact that the pupils, most of whom will at this point be over the age of 13, are studying all their other subjects through the medium of English.) However, many adult foreign learners of English, even those who have learned English for several years (in a non-English environment), have acquired, according to Nation and Waring (1997: 8) a vocabulary of only around 5,000 word families.

These differences in vocabulary knowledge typically found between native speakers and second language learners have implications for the advice given to second language readers that they should guess the meanings of words from context. It may well be a strategy to be taught, along with the strategy of tolerating uncertainty in the meaning of some words, or even tolerating the unknown. However, in order to be able to guess unknown words from context, Hirsh and Nation (1992) estimate that readers need to know approximately 95% of the other words in a text. Such estimates are rather crude, and the reader's background knowledge may well play a part, while the nature of the context of the unknown word is crucial. Haynes (1993) showed that, as one might expect, local context (where the "clues" are in the same clause or sentence) is more helpful in identifying unknown words than is global context (where the clues are not so located, but dispersed throughout the text). Likewise, as Haynes (1993) also points out, not all learners, particularly those at a low level, can use context clues, either because they do not have enough language to understand the context, or because the word form seems to be more psycholinguistically salient than the context. Huckin and Bloch (1993) also found that poorly understood context was of limited value: using protocol analysis on a translation activity involving three Chinese ESL students, their subjects made successful guesses only 25 times out of 44 opportunities.

3.3 First language reading versus second language proficiency.

3.3.1 Research evidence

While the view that language proficiency is important for reading is generally accepted (e.g. Alderson, 1984; Connor, 1978; Favreau and Segalowitz, 1982), there has been considerable debate about the relative contributions to effective second language reading of, on the one hand, reading ability, as manifested in first language reading, and on the other, proficiency in the second language (c.f. Alderson, 1984). Some have argued that L2 reading depends crucially on L1 reading, that "reading is only learned once" and that poor L2 reading is in part due to poor L1 reading skills or failure to transfer such skills (e.g. Hudson, 1982). However, it is a matter of simple observation that many people *only* learn to read in their chronological L2 or learn to read in L2 *first* (both common occurrences with minority groups whether indigenous or migrant). The view that L2 reading depends on L1 reading therefore cannot be taken too literally. The converse view is that reading ability in L2 is largely a function of proficiency in that language, and that a minimal level of proficiency in L2 is needed before L1 reading skills will transfer (the so-called "language threshold" hypothesis of second language reading; see Clarke, 1979; Devine, 1987). A number of studies have examined these views.

Bernhardt and Kamil (1995) administered reading tests in English and Spanish to 187 English L1 US Air Force cadets at 3 levels of Spanish instruction. Their general conclusion (*ibid*: 25) is that "reading variables account for between 10 and 16 per cent [of the variance] in second language reading; language proficiency accounts for 30 to 38 per cent. In other words, while language proficiency accounts for a greater proportion of the variance, first language reading also makes a significant contribution".

Rather more subtly, Carrell (1991) compared Spanish and English students, and concluded that both first language reading ability and second language proficiency level are significant predictors of second language reading ability. However, the relative importance of each of the two factors varies: at high levels of second language proficiency, first language reading ability has a positive effect (the case of her Spanish students, who knew English well); however at low levels of second language proficiency, the degree of language proficiency has an effect (the case of the English students who were relatively weak in Spanish). Thus the results of the Spanish group tend to support the transfer of skills hypothesis, while the results of the English group support the "language threshold" hypothesis.

The effect of differential language proficiency was further explored by Lee and Schallert (1997). They investigated 809 Korean middle-school students at five different levels of English, and confirmed both their hypotheses: firstly that the contribution of L2 proficiency is greater than the contribution of L1 reading ability in predicting L2 reading ability, and secondly that a threshold level of language proficiency exists such that L1 reading ability has little effect on learners with low levels of L2 proficiency when they read in L2 whereas learners with higher levels of L2 proficiency show a positive relationship between their L1 and L2 reading performance.

3.3.2 Findings from educational surveys

In addition to the above small scale research, there is evidence of a rather different nature coming from relatively uncontrolled surveys of school populations. UNESCO's 1953 monograph states a widely held view: "we take it as axiomatic that the best medium for teaching is the mother tongue of the pupil" (UNESCO, 1953: 6). Survey research carried out since supports the axiom (one which naturally has implications for reading): thus the World Bank (1995b: 33) in a survey of bilingual programmes in eight countries concludes that "the first language is essential for the initial teaching of reading, and for comprehension of subject matter" while Greaney (1996: 24) claims that "Research findings suggest that initial instruction should be offered in a child's first language." Elley (1994) reports on a survey of 32 countries, which found that pupils whose home language differed from the school language performed less well on reading tests than those who were tested in their home language.

Positive findings for use of the mother tongue is supported, although in some cases weakly, due almost certainly to differences in contextual factors, by research from other parts of Africa. Evaluation of the Ife-Ife project in Nigeria whereby Yoruba was used as a medium of instruction for the first 6 years, with English as a subject, found positive results for academic achievement (Bamgbose: 1991: 85), confirmed by Afolayan (1999) who found literacy more easily acquired through Yoruba than English. A report by the Association for the Development of African Education (1996) finds positive academic results from a study of mother tongue medium rather than French in Mali, although the Association suggests that the findings are flawed by methodological factors (*ibid*.: 10). In Tanzania, students at secondary level "clearly show that teaching in Swahili has a cognitive advantage over teaching in English" (*ibid*: 11). Eisemon *et al.* (1993), in a carefully sampled study of nearly 2,000 rural sixth-grade students in Burundi, found from tests of reading comprehension, composition and science/agriculture, that scores were significantly higher for students tested in Kirundi versions rather than in French versions[5].

Conversely using a second or unfamiliar language as the medium of instruction tends to be associated with negative academic achievement, with the situation in sub-Saharan Africa giving particular cause for concern: in Zambia there is ample evidence that the vast majority of primary school pupils are not able to read adequately in the official language of instruction, English (Chikalanga, 1990; Nkamba and Kanyika, 1998; Serpell, 1978); in Tanzania, Criper and Dodd (1984, cited in Yahya-Othman, 1990: 49) estimated that only 29% of pupils had English good enough to follow studies at their level, while in Zimbabwe, Machingaidze *et al.* (1998: 71) conclude that at Grade 6 between 60% and 66% of pupils did not reach "the desirable levels" of reading in English. Even in the many African countries (e.g. Kenya, Malawi, Nigeria, and some South African schools) where local languages are used to varying degrees as media of instruction their role is largely "transitional", intended to facilitate the pupils' introduction to formal schooling and to academic skills, with the switch to English generally occurring between years 3 and 5. Inadequate second language proficiency at the point of change is widely identified as one cause of lack of effectiveness of such transitional programmes. Research supporting this includes Luckett's work on a transitional programme in South Africa (Luckett, 1994) which suggests that shifting from mother-tongue to English at year 3 was not successful, possibly because 2 years was insufficient to establish the necessary threshold aca-

---

[5] Only in mathematics were the test results similar for the two language versions, and the authors' explanation is that the concepts of computation have already been assimilated into Kirundi from French, and taught to pupils from the lower primary grades onwards as part of Kirundi.

demic competence in the mother-tongue. Chick (1992), also in South Africa, reports considerable language problems on the part of pupils after the transition from local language instruction to English. Likewise Roller (1988) suggests that it would be more appropriate to delay the introduction of reading in English to rural Shona speaking children in Zimbabwe from the first year to an unspecified later year, since transfer from L1 reading ability (Shona) does not appear to be occurring, probably because of lack of proficiency in L2 (English).

3.3.3 Counter-evidence

There is, however, some claimed counter-evidence to the view that children will only succeed in reading if they are taught in their mother tongue. One example is the study of Wagner *et al.* (1989) in Morocco. They traced 166 children (83 Berber L1, and 83 Arab L1) from year one to year five, administering annual tests of reading in Arabic, the language in which the children were being taught to read. Although there were differences in favour of the Arab L1 children in year one, these differences had almost disappeared by year five, and Wagner *et al.* contest the view that "learning to read in one's "mother tongue" or first language enhances a child's achievement relative to that of children obliged to learn to read in a second language" (*ibid.* 32), claiming that minority children need not be taught to read in L1 "in order to achieve literacy norms of the majority language group". However, it is clear that the Berber L1 children were in daily contact with Arab L1 children and were learning Arabic outside the school as well as inside. Indeed it is likely that the "second language", Arabic, had become their psycholinguistically dominant language by year five. In most educational contexts it is assumed that a child's "first language" is the most widely used (and often the sole) language of the community and school, and the language which is best known by the child. The case of the Berber children described by Wagner would appear to be an instance of misleading use of the term "first language" although such "language-dominance shift" is typical of minority or marginalized groups, or individuals (see above 3.3.1.2). Thus, contrary to what Wagner (1998: 181) asserts, Berber speakers reading in Arabic in Morocco have much more in common with minority language speakers reading in English in the USA, than they have with "multilingual societies ... located in Africa", in that both Berbers and minority groups in the USA are encompassed within a dominant majority language group (Arabic or English), whereas this is not the case for African children reading in English.

Further claimed counter-evidence to the view that successful reading must be conducted in L1 is provided by the Canadian immersion programmes (where English pupils were educated through the medium of French), from the late 1960s onwards (see Cummins and Swain, 1986). These immersion programmes (which vary with respect to when, and to what extent, the French medium is introduced) have been subject to a considerable amount of evaluation. The prototypical Canadian immersion programme is that of "early immersion" where French is used from the outset. Longitudinal evaluation from kindergarten to grade 8 suggests that, for the first 3 grades, the French immersion groups (i.e. English groups taught through French) lag significantly behind the control groups (i.e. English groups taught in English) in English reading skills (Cummins and Swain, 1986: 60-61), but that the immersion groups catch up and indeed overtake their English comparison groups thereafter ("English language arts" are introduced, however, to immersion classes in grade 3). It is, however, difficult to generalize from the Canadian immersion situation to situations in other countries, given the rather special background factors which operated, namely:

- parents deliberately opted for the immersion schools for their children
- parents could withdraw their children if the latter experienced problems
- parents, who were largely middle-class, provided informal L1 support at home.

A further point to note concerning the French immersion programmes in Canada is that they are successful primarily in that English students do not appear to suffer in English academic skills by comparison to their English peers who are in "traditional" schools, and in that their French proficiency is much higher than that of those English peers. Their productive capacity (speaking and writing) in French, on the other hand, lags behind that of their French peers, although their receptive capacities (reading and listening) are similar. The general conclusion concerning reading in immersion contexts from Cummins and Swain (1986: 41) is that "it is preferable initially to teach literacy-related skills directly in only one language, whether it be the first or second language. Once literacy related skills are well established in one language, they will transfer readily and rapidly to the other language (provided it is mastered), even possibly without explicit instruction". The proviso on the mastery of language is crucial, both for the Moroccan and Canadian cases.

3.3.4 Explanations for contradictory findings

To account for the contradictions in the effects of a home-school language switch (whereby some children seem to suffer academically, while others do not), various explanations have been put forward. Cummins and Swain (1986) propose, as already mentioned, a linguistic interdependence hypothesis whereby "content learned in one language is interdependent across languages, given, of course sufficient proficiency (threshold levels) in both languages" (*ibid:* 35). This hypothesis is supported by research from numerous developed countries, e.g. Spanish-speaking children in San Diego (Cummins and Swain, 1986: 86), immigrant children in Toronto (*ibid.*), and children of temporary Japanese visitors in Toronto (*ibid.*) where first language academic proficiency was established before the switch to English. Such programme evaluation confirms the experimental findings of Carrell (1991), Bernhardt and Kamil (1995) and Lee and Schallert (1997) on the negative effect if the reader's threshold of language competence is lower than that required by the text.

It is of course obvious that the favourable factors surrounding French immersion schools, whereby second language proficiency can be raised to apparently adequate levels, cannot be replicated in most schools in developing countries (c.f. Bamgbose, 1991: 77). In brief, the French immersion school programmes, and similar programmes where similar conditions obtain, result in what has been termed "additive" bilingualism (Lambert's original term, cited in Cummins and Swain, 1986: 18); in such cases competence in the language of instruction is achieved, but at no cost to academic competence in the first language.

On the other hand, in the case of developing countries, and indeed of many minority groups in developed countries, the result of a home-school language switch is often "subtractive" bilingualism, where students "may be characterized by a less than native-like competence in both languages" (*ibid.*) especially with respect to academic competence. Serpell (1989: 102) specifically points out the inapplicability of the Canadian immersion model to Zambia for similar reasons. The findings from Morocco and Canada are entirely consistent with the view that second language reading is in large part a function of second language proficiency. In fact, all the evidence is consistent with the view that learner proficiency in the language of instruction, is an important factor – although not the only important factor – in educational achievement generally, and reading in particular.

A further explanation for the differing academic achievements associated with home-school language switches is adduced by Bratt-Paulston (1992). She considers different minority groups in American and European, and attributes failure in education to the low socio-economic status of the students, which she sees as a causative variable, yielding negative self-perceptions, rather than instruction in a second language *per se*. In short, her view is that "education cannot compensate for society". On the other hand, in low-income countries, the findings of Heyneman and Loxley (1983: 1162) are that, "the predominant influence on student learning is the quality of the schools and teachers" and not social status, which suggests that Bratt-Paulston's explanation may only be valid for minority groups in developed countries.

3.4 Research objectives

3.4.1 General aims

The research project which is to be described here aimed to investigate Zambian and Malawian children's reading ability, both in English and in local languages, in the context of contrasting language policies in their countries' primary education systems. The investigation was carried out at year 5 of formal schooling, since it is at this year that Malawian pupils switch to English as a medium of instruction, having spent the previous 4 years with ChiChewa as the medium. Accordingly it is at the beginning of year 5 that one would expect to find the greatest differences between the pupils in the two countries.

It was considered essential to test reading proficiency in the local languages also, not only as a necessary part of the enquiry into the effects of the different policies, but also in an attempt to disentangle proficiency in reading from proficiency in English. Simply investigating reading in English could not be regarded as yielding illuminating data on the child's reading proficiency *per se*, since it is clearly possible that some children may have low proficiency in English, but can nevertheless read adequately in their own language. By way of comparison, parents and teachers in a British school would be unlikely to accept the result of a reading test in French as a valid indication of their children's *reading* proficiency.

Cross-cutting the general concern with reading levels, however, there is increasing attention in both countries to issues of gender and also of the rural/urban divide. On the gender issue, in Malawi the proportion of males who are literate was reported to be 71.9%, and that of females 41.8%; in Zambia 85.6% of males are said to be literate, and 71.3% of females[6]. The MOE, Zambia (1992: 81), claims that boys outperform girls in public examinations, and attributes this to traditional attitudes that education is more

---

[6] World Factbook, 1999. See section 2.2.1 for doubts about the definitions of literacy used in that source; however, the relative proportions are still suggestive.

important for boys than for girls. Gadsden (1992: 107) likewise says "the failure of girls to utilize the meagre education facilities available to them surely lies in the economic organization of Zambian societies", where girls are involved in cultivation from an early age. This view is supported by research in neighbouring Mozambique (Åkesson, 1992: 52) which, on the basis of interviews with parents, reported that the attitude was particularly prevalent among poor subsistence farmers, who constitute the largest single group in the country.

As far as the urban/rural dichotomy is concerned, informal observation suggests that there is much greater use of English in urban environments in both Malawi and Zambia. There are in both countries many urban-based commercial companies and international agencies where English is the sole working language or at least an important language of communication within the organization. Furthermore it is in urban areas that we find the major offices of civil administration, and public utilities, where English is the official "working language". There are also far more opportunities in towns for casual reading of publicly displayed texts such as signs, advertisements, campaign posters; these are always in English in Zambia, although in Malawi they may also occur in ChiChewa, ChiYao and Chitumbuka. In rural areas, on the other hand, particularly off-road areas, there are relatively few opportunities to practice English.

3.4.2 Research hypotheses

Given that the general question addressed in this study is "What is the effect of the differing language policies in Malawi and Zambia on the reading abilities of the children in the relevant languages?", then a number of hypotheses emerge in the context of the preceding discussion. It was initially decided to test the following 10 null hypotheses:

Hypothesis A: there will be no significant difference in English reading test scores between year 5 pupils in Zambia and year 5 pupils in Malawi.

Hypothesis B1: there will be no significant difference in local language reading test scores year between year 5 children in Malawi and year 5 children in Zambia.

Hypothesis B2: there will be no significant difference in local language reading test scores between year 5 boys in Malawi and year 5 girls in Malawi.

Hypothesis B3: there will be no significant difference in local language reading test scores between year 5 boys in Zambia and year 5 girls in

Zambia.

Hypothesis B4: there will be no significant difference in local language reading test scores between at year 5 children in urban schools in Malawi and year 5 children in rural schools in Malawi

Hypothesis B5: there will be no significant difference in local language reading test scores between year 5 children in urban schools in Zambia and year 5 children in rural schools in Zambia

Hypothesis C1: there will be no significant difference in English reading test scores between year 5 boys in Malawi and year 5 girls in Malawi.

Hypothesis C2: there will be no significant difference in English reading test scores between year 5 boys in Zambia and year 5 girls in Zambia.

Hypothesis C3: there will be no significant difference in English reading test scores between at year 5 children in urban schools in Malawi and year 5 children in rural schools in Malawi

Hypothesis C4: there will be no significant difference in English reading test scores between year 5 children in urban schools in Zambia and year 5 children in rural schools in Zambia

In addition to these 10 hypotheses, one further hypothesis was added while field-work was being carried out. While under normal circumstances hypotheses are set up before embarking on data collection, it seems admissible to adopt a flexible and prudently reactive approach in the field. In this case it had been initially considered undesirable to administer the Nyanja (i.e. Zambian) version of the reading test in Malawi, but rather the near identical ChiChewa. However, the fact that Malawian children in the first 4 schools tested were scoring highly on their ChiChewa tests led to the view that Malawian pupils would be able to cope with the Nyanja version of the test. In the last two Malawian schools tested, therefore, the Zambian test was administered in addition to the English and ChiChewa tests. Although, as has been said, the ChiChewa and Nyanja versions were almost the same, the opportunity to assess Malawian pupils' reading using an identical test to the Zambian pupils' would allow for unequivocal conclusions to be drawn. The following hypothesis (B6) was therefore put forward and tested in the last two schools in Malawi.

Hypothesis B6: there will be no significant difference in Nyanja reading test scores between year 5 children in Malawi and year 5 children in Zambia.

These 11 hypotheses are amenable to answers through conventional group tests of reading.

However, a simple quantitative approach through group testing, although instructive, must be illuminated by a consideration of the general circumstances of formal education, and also by some insight into the reading strategies of the learners. Data was therefore collected from a sample of testees in each school, through informal discussions of texts in English and the local language. These individual reading sessions were intended to explore the difficulties in reading reported by high and low scorers, and the extent to which they differed.

These research instruments, namely the tests, and reading discussions are intended to be complementary, although it is of course acknowledged that they do not provide an exhaustive picture of practices related to reading, far less of literacy practices generally (which was not, of course, their aim). To have restricted the research to case studies of individuals would possibly have provided insightful data on those individuals. However, the main aim in this present research was to obtain a broad, general picture of reading ability in English and local languages, an aim for which group tests were the best data collecting approach.

4. The Reading Tests

4.1 The schools

To investigate students' reading abilities, two urban schools and four rural schools were selected, in both Malawi and Zambia. These twelve schools were not chosen at random, since the choice was affected by those ever present constraints of applied linguistics research, time and money. Random sampling procedures were not practical, as the time available for visiting schools was only two weeks in each country, which meant that there could be no visits to schools that were too far from each other or difficult of access. By way of example, it takes 3 days on foot, from the point of nearest vehicle access to get to Liteta primary school in the Luano Valley (Lungwangwa, 1989: 64).

The research is therefore a survey of schools selected under the constraints of practicality, rather than a randomly selected sample. Kamil, Langer and Shanahan (1991: 53) term generalizations deriving from such samples as "logical", rather than "statistical" saying that "Logical generalizations are drawn when the researcher has no direct evidence of the sample's ability to represent the population. Instead the researcher attempts to use logic or intuition in supporting the generalisability of the evidence collected from the sample. The decision to attempt a logical generalization is usually made on the basis of cost." Although their use of "logical" does not seem entirely justifiable, the distinction concerns the manner in which the selection is made: expediency tempered with experience guides the process. Furthermore, I had carried out a number of previous visits to both Malawi and Zambia, visiting over a hundred schools in both countries, and to that had extent did indeed have direct personal evidence that the sample of schools in this research was representative.

A further consideration in the selection of schools was that of African language use. Since tests of reading in African languages (ChiChewa in Malawi; Nyanja in Zambia), were to be administered, then the testing had to be carried out in areas where that language was known to be the dominant language, and additionally, in the case of Zambia, where Nyanja was the language officially prescribed to be taught (recall that seven Zambian languages are officially taught as subjects). The schools were in all cases selected by the Ministries of Education in Zambia and Malawi, following a written request, plus follow-up discussion. The Ministry subsequently contacted the District Education Officers, who informed the relevant schools. However, difficulties in communication meant that in all but two cases (one urban school in each country) the schools had not been fore-warned of the visits.

In Malawi three schools were selected in the Zomba area (two in Zomba rural district, one in Zomba urban district) and three in the Lilongwe area (two rural, one urban). In Zambia all schools were in the Lusaka urban or rural districts. The areas in the two countries are comparable in that they contain large towns (in Malawi, Zomba is the old colonial capital of Ma-lawi, and still houses the parliament, while Lilongwe is the present capital; in Zambia, Lusaka is the capital). However, because of time pressure, little ethnographic investigation was possible of the local communities which constituted the catchments for the schools. The local community is important in both countries in that it may provide a framework, sup-portive or otherwise, which affects teachers' well-being and motivation, especially in rural villages, where, for example, it is the community (in conjunction with civil authorities or, in the case of "unalienated land" with traditional chiefs) which provides housing for teachers – a crucial element in teachers' lives.

4.1.1 Selected schools in Malawi

School 1 - A boy's school in rural Zomba, some 20 kilometres south of the town on a metalled road. The school is brick-built, but classrooms have no doors, or desks; the windows are latticed breeze blocks. The buildings were, however, clean and well-maintained, and the teachers, most of whom were trained, appeared knowledgeable and committed. Because of short-age of classrooms, three classes were taking place outside in the playground during the visit.

School 2 - A girls' school in rural Zomba, some 30 kilometres from Zomba, and 14 kilometres off the metalled road. The school is a Catholic mission school; ten of the twelve teachers were nuns and two were laymen. The school buildings appeared neglected, and although teachers' accommoda-tion was said to be adequate, the teachers appeared dispirited. In a year 5 social science lesson which I visited with the head teacher, the class teacher was not present (reportedly in the staff room). At his request, one of the students was copying out sections from the teacher's book on to the black-board (this transcription, which contained many errors and omissions, included copying *verbatim* instructions intended for the teacher such as *Ask the pupils to ...*). The rest of the class were in turn copying this from the blackboard into their exercise books.

School 3 - An old school, located in a central area of the town of Zomba. The buildings are showing signs of age, but are well maintained: they stand, island-like, their bases almost a metre above the level of the surrounding earth playground, that has been eroded by decades of daily sweeping, plus tropical rainstorms. Classes were large, with over 100 registered in many. The teachers, the majority of whom were women, were trained and appeared committed to their work. The students included the children of civil servants and people running small businesses, as well as those of casual manual workers.

School 4 - A rural school some 40 kilometres from Lilongwe and about 25 kilometres off the metalled road. Most parents are poor subsistence farmers. Students are frequently absent to sell produce at market, or to help in the fields. The school was in a dilapidated condition, with many classes taking place outside. The teachers complained that their housing was inadequate: some had to rent in a larger village nearby, while others had old mud-brick houses provided free on the school site. It was clear from the huge cracks that ran from the ground to the roofs of these houses, that they were in an extremely poor state of repair. The teachers were demoralised, and also complained that the students were "rude".

School 5 - A rural on-road school some 15 kilometres south of Lilongwe. The buildings have brick walls, with both floors and benches made of smeared mud-brick (which the girls re-smear every Friday afternoon). There are no doors or windows. The students are for the most part children of subsistence farmers and labourers who, according to the teachers, are themselves very poor, and unable to read or write. The head teacher was absent when we arrived, reportedly seeing to his crops. Most of the teachers were young, and had been recently appointed. Their morale did not seem very high: three said that they would like to leave to work in Lilongwe, and all complained of inadequate housing.

School 6 - A large urban school in Lilongwe. Most of the parents are civil servants, household workers, or manual workers. The school buildings are in reasonable condition, the school having been built in the mid-1970s. The head teacher seemed particularly efficient and energetic; teachers observed in 2 lessons seemed capable and well-motivated, and the general atmosphere was purposeful. Again, the majority of teachers were women.

4.1.2 Selected schools in Zambia

School 7 - An urban school in an old established neighbourhood of Lusaka. The classrooms were in good condition and of an unusual design, with light coming through clear plastic corrugated sheets in the roofs, and ventilation via latticed breeze block "windows" set into the walls. The students are from economically very poor backgrounds. The teachers seemed committed to their work and to the upkeep of the school (two were repairing a door when we arrived); they are all trained. The school probably receives more attention from donor agencies than the average school, due to its location on a main road. However, it has no perimeter wall, and the head teacher reported the buildings were subject to almost nightly attack by thieves, who were normally (although not always) deterred by the nightwatchmen.

School 8 - A rural school in a village some 10 kilometres from Lusaka. The parents are for the most part subsistence farmers, manual labourers and hawkers. The school buildings were in an extremely dilapidated condition, and the school had suffered from considerable theft, with desks, roof sheeting and doors taken from many classrooms. All but two of the nine teachers, including the head teacher, were absent when we visited, and reported to be attending a funeral.[1]

School 9 - A rural school some 20 kilometres from Lusaka, and 5 off the metalled road. Students are almost all children of peasant farmers, living in a single village under a chief, who appeared to be active in support of the school, and had organised the building of houses for the teachers. The school had had many changes of teachers in recent years, but those present seemed happy to be there, possibly because of the degree of community support and security which obtained. The school building is in good condition, and teachers present, who were mostly trained and male, seemed to be reasonably well motivated.

---

[1] It should perhaps be mentioned that this is the "classic" reason provided to excuse absence, although there is no doubt that it may be genuine, given the incidence of HIV/AIDS related deaths. So frequent had absence because of funerals become in the early 90s that the government of Zambia had ordered civil servants (teachers are counted as such) that they could only attend funerals at the weekends – an order frequently ignored, as here.

School 10 - A rural school some 15 kilometres outside Lusaka. The school was in poor material condition, with roof sheeting missing from two school blocks, and no desks in any of the classrooms. There is a large commercial farm nearby, and many fathers work on this farm, with most of the remaining parents working on their own fields, as manual labourers, or as hawkers. Many of the children were said to work seasonally on the commercial farm, a practice which contributed to absenteeism.

School 11 - An urban school with a relatively privileged catchment, including children of civil servants. A minority of students seemed from reasonably well-off backgrounds (judging by their clothes, footwear, and school bags), and were clearly accustomed to speaking in English. However, there were also many children whose parents were the cleaners, gardeners, and security guards. The staff, who were overwhelmingly female, were all trained and seemed committed. The school buildings were in good condition, with rooms for all classes, and desks for most children.

School 12 - A rural school close to a metalled road some 15 kilometres from Lusaka. Although the school is regarded as rural, there is a cement factory nearby, which covers the school in a fine dust during the dry season. Some parents work in this factory; others are labourers or peasant farmers. The teachers are mostly trained, and seemed reasonably well motivated. The majority were living in accommodation provided by the school.

4.2 The students

The tests were administered to intact classes, except for two classes in Malawi where the numbers present were over 80 (school 1, where numbers were 82, and school 3, where they were 86). In these a sample of 50 students was randomly selected so as to allow sufficient space in the classrooms for students to take the test comfortably. In cases where there was more than one class at year 5 in the school, the class that was in the school at the time was selected (classes are not streamed in either country). In total 517 students were tested, 290 in Malawi and 227 in Zambia, with the testee structure being as indicated in Tables 4.1 and 4.2 below.

As indicated in Table 4.1, Schools 1 and 2 in Malawi were all boys and all girls, respectively. While it would clearly have been preferable for all schools to be mixed, it did not become apparent until we had actually arrived at School 1 that it was a single sex school, by which time it was too late to locate a different school.

School	1	2	3(U)	4	5	6(U)	Total
Girls	0	32	25	23	21	28	129
Boys	50	0	25	32	26	28	161
Total	50	32	50	55	47	56	290

Note: U = urban

Table 4.1 Data structure for reading tests (English and ChiChewa), Malawi

School	7(U)	8	9	10	11(U)	12	Total
Girls	17	11	12	14	27	19	100
Boys	22	28	19	20	28	10	127
Total	39	39	31	34	55	29	227

Note: U = urban

Table 4.2 Data structure for reading tests (English and Nyanja), Zambia

The tests were administered in the dry season, when agricultural demands on children's labour are relatively low, and when rains and floods do not affect attendance. Many children routinely stay at home in heavy rain; given the number of classrooms held in the open, this is a reasonable precaution. Flooding can also affect access to school, especially in rural areas. Lungwangwa (1989: 63) speaks of a school on the Mulungushi river in Zambia which is "heavily infested with crocodiles and is usually flooded in the months of January and February" and observes that "The combination of floods and crocodiles has worked to discourage parents from sending their children to school."

Personal data collected on each child included their name, date of birth, sex and home language. Many children, mainly in the rural areas, did not know their month of birth, in which case the mid-point of the claimed year was used. There was a small number who did not know how old they were, in which case they were attributed the age of friends who claimed that they were "the same age". Thus calculated, the mean age of the testees in Zambia was 12 years and 3 months, and in Malawi 13 years and 7 months. That the mean age of year 5 students in Malawi is higher than those in Zambia, despite the fact that Malawi children officially start school aged 6 as opposed to 7 in Zambia, is explained by two factors: first many students in Malawi actually start school later than 6, and secondly more Malawian students may repeat years than Zambians.

Without exception, the testees in all 12 schools claimed to speak ChiChewa (for Malawi) or Nyanja (for Zambia). This was supported by the teachers and by observation outside the class. However ChiChewa or Nyanja was not the home language for all the children. Of the Malawian testees 18% claimed to speak a language other than ChiChewa at home, while 46% of the Zambians spoke a language other than Nyanja at home. The languages spoken were in all cases other Malawian or Zambian languages of the Bantu language family.

Information on the child's principal carers was not sought directly from all the students, since piloting had suggested that written responses to the question would not yield sufficiently precise data, and would be far too time-consuming. For example, a question asking for the job of the principal carer often elicited a response such as "X's Farm", without specifying either the size of the farm, or whether the carer worked on the farm as a casual labourer, a driver, or a clerk, occupations which imply very different socio-economic circumstances. Additionally many students answer "Nothing" or "No work" if their carer is a subsistence farmer, since there is a tendency for Malawians and Zambians to consider only waged or salaried occupations as "work" (c.f. Åkesson, 1992: 29 for a similar attitude in Mozambique). In addition, requiring students to read questions and write responses, makes assumptions which it is precisely part of the purpose of the inquiry to investigate, namely the competence of the students in reading and writing.

General information on students' background was provided by teachers. In addition, there was discussion with 6 students from each class on their family background following the tests (see Chapter 5). Information from the teachers and students indicated that the carers – both male and female – of the majority of the rural children were subsistence farmers, and/or casual labourers, while those of urban children had a range of occupations including security guards, drivers, cleaners, market traders and a variety of clerical occupations.

It is certain that the testees from both countries are representative, in that most come from backgrounds that are economically poor, as the following quotations from interviews indicate. The first is from a 13 year old Zambian girl, who had been absent 14 times that term. The student has just told the interviewer that she cannot read in either English or Nyanja. (Italics indicate that the original Nyanja has been translated into English. I = interviewer; S = student). The interview continues:

I: *How often do you come to school?*
S: *Ah ... when I don't have a pen, I don't come to school.*
I: *If you don't have a pen, you don't come?*
S: *Yes. So like - since we opened, I have only been twice, because*

> *I didn't have a pen.*
>
> I: *You usually miss school. Doesn't your mother scold you when you miss school?*
> S: *But because I did not have the books .....*
> I: *I see, even if you miss class, they don't scold you if you don't have books.*
> S: *That's right.*

The following example is from a 12 year old Zambian boy, again translated from Nyanja:

> I: *(...) you are sometimes absent?*
> S: *Yes.*
> I: *When do you miss school?*
> S: *Like when I don't have an exercise book.*
> I: *When you don't have books?*
> S: *Yes, or when I wash my uniform.*
> I: *Oh, when you miss school, does your mother tell you off?*
> S: *Yes, she does.*
> I: *And when she tells you off, what do you do?*
> S: *Nothing.*

While some children do not dare to come to school without books, shoes, or uniform (no longer compulsory according to the Ministry officials in both countries, but often insisted on by teachers), some may face problems at home if their parents disapprove of absence:

> I: *(...) How often do you come to school?*
> S: *Very often.*
> I: *Do you ever miss school?*
> S: *Once in a while.*
> I: *Like when?*
> S: *Like when I have a pain in my leg.*
> I: *When you miss school doesn't your mother scold you?*
> S: *She does.*
> I: *What about at home?*
> S: *My father beats me.*

Anecdotal evidence and observation suggests that, in both countries, corporal punishment by parents and teachers is not infrequent. Many people in both countries believe that beating children encourages them to learn, although no teachers professed that attitude.

It should also be pointed out that the concept of the nuclear family, where children's life styles are heavily influenced by their parents, does not accord with the reality for many African families, especially in rural areas. There is, for example, a much higher degree of communal living, with children brought up in extended family mode. Further, the role of the mother's brother is traditionally important in much of Zambia and Malawi. He is often the one to take decisions (either positive or negative) relating to his nieces' or nephews' education. Thus a rich and supportive uncle could make a significant positive difference to a child's circumstance, by buying note books or footwear, for example, whereas an exploitative uncle might prevent a child from going to school in order to obtain their services as a domestic or agricultural worker. However, the traditional extended family has been affected by the HIV/AIDS epidemic, with over one and a half million maternal and double AIDS orphans below the age of 15 projected for Malawi in 2010 (Kadzamira et al, 2001: 102).

4.3 The reading tests

4.3.1 Test construction

As there were no standard reading tests in any language available for Malawi or Zambia, resource constraints meant that this research was in the unsatisfactory, but common, situation of having to construct a test and use it for measuring purposes without going through the process of test validation. In such circumstances, the best one can do is to construct tests that have *prima facie* claims to be valid in terms of a construct of reading, of socio-cultural appropriacy and in this case, in terms of the content of the English syllabuses, and then carry out a pilot.

The testing of reading is always difficult because the requirement for an observable response means that all reading tests interfere with the reading process to some extent. A number of formats for the assessment of reading were trialled (text plus comprehension questions, text plus multiple choice questions, 'classical' cloze, and 'modified' cloze). Results suggested that a form of modified cloze test was the most user-friendly format for this population of learners, in particular in that it allowed weak students to register a score. It was accordingly decided to employ it for tests in English, ChiChewa and Nyanja.

In the modification employed here the correct option, plus incorrect options, are provided in scrambled order in a box above each paragraph.

This modification addresses three points of criticism of classical cloze: (i) in this modification the testee is not required to *produce* language to fill a gap, but only to *process* written language (the text and the options); (ii) this modification has the advantage of being objectively markable, provided of course that only one of the options is appropriate for each gap; (iii) this modification also has the potential, depending on the words deleted, to test an overall understanding of the texts (see Alderson, 2000: 210), thus addressing the criticism that cloze focuses on the sentence level. A final important advantage is that this is a format that children in Malawi and Zambia are familiar with (see Appendix 4) from their English textbooks.

The language for the English tests was taken from the English language course books *English in Malawi* and *New Zambia Primary Course, English Language*. In both countries these were the courses that the students at year 5 would have used. The English syllabus of the two countries is sufficiently similar for language common to both courses to be used in the test: the year of introduction of the various English lexical items according to the English course books appears in Appendix 5. Both countries for the most part take standard British English as their model, although there are in both sets of course books some borrowing of African language lexical items (e.g. *nsima*: maize meal), and some cases of lexical items which have different meanings in Malawian and Zambian English from those of standard British English (e.g. *relish* used to refer to meat or vegetables accompanying *nsima*).

Four passages were prepared, the last two being divided into two sections. Each passage or section contains 4 or 6 gaps. The box above the section contains 50% more options than there are gaps, so that the last item cannot be completed by simple elimination; thus there are 6 options provided for sections with 4 gaps, and 9 options provided for sections with 6 gaps. Testees were told that options could only be used once.

All language in the tests (both the text and the options) occur in the Zambian and Malawian English course books at year 5 or below, with most coming from years 1 to 3. In terms of grammar, all structural items and syntactic structures which feature in the test have been introduced by year 4 in both countries, with the exception of the so-called "second conditional" (of which there is one example towards the end of the test), which in both countries appears in year 5.

In terms of socio-cultural appropriacy the passages contain topics and episodes with which students were, according to their teachers, likely to be familiar and which also closely resemble texts in their text books. The titles and numbers of items for the English passages were as follows:

1. 'Ruth and her brother': 4 items;
2. 'Simon's Accident': 6 items;
3. 'Kalulu goes fishing': 2 sections of 4 and 6 items;
4. 'Trees': 2 sections of 4 and 6 items.

As text types, the four passages may be rather weakly characterised as descriptive (1), narrative (2) and (3) and expository (4). The overarching category, however, is manifestly the rather bland 'English language teaching text'. However, there is ample justification for this, since such text types are among the few written text types which can safely be assumed to be within the experience of all the children tested, particularly those attending rural schools. The children of subsistence farmers in Malawi and Zambia rarely see cereal packets, sweet papers, or tin labels, far less newspapers or other "authentic texts" of the consumer society, for the simple reason that most rural villages do not have shops. For children in such communities, the notion of being "socialized into reading" (Wallace, 1988:1) or "joining the literacy club" as Smith (1988) puts it, is not an option. In fact, in rural Zambia, Hoppers (1981) suggests that primary school leavers who do not go on to secondary school, tend to loose their literacy skills in English, and are in effect "socialised out of reading". A test of reading based on "authentic texts", would not therefore have been appropriate. It is, however, likely that many Malawian and Zambian children hear religious texts (both Christian and Muslim) being read, and may see such texts themselves. In view of these considerations, it was concluded that using texts similar to school texts was the only fair option, while the choice also provided direct information as to student's probable ability to cope with their school textbooks.

A copy of passage 1 appears in Appendix 6, while the first section of passage 3 appears below. Deletions were normally made every sixth word, although that was extended on a few occasions to avoid more than one free structural element (grammatical word) per section[2], the reason being that they were judged to be difficult for children at this level. This was a subjective decision, supported by teachers and observation; Nyanja/ChiChewa does not normally mark definiteness or non-definiteness through an article system and many schoolchildren have difficulty with the appropriate production of articles, although this might not be a major obstacle to comprehension. Likewise there are said to be only three "preposition

[2] Modification with respect to being selective about deletions is sometimes referred to as 'rational cloze'. Alderson (2000: 208) refers to such tests as 'gap-filling tests', and deplores the use of 'cloze' to refer to any but nth word random deletion tests.

equivalents" in ChiChewa/Nyanja, which again may lead to difficulties in production, but not in comprehension. There are in all six gaps (20% of the total), which require to be filled with the following free structural elements: *is, not, but, near, the, when.*

While this "motivated" selection of gaps undermines the justification for nth word deletion in classical cloze, namely that a wide selection of long texts will randomly tap lexis and structure in proportion to their occurrence in natural written language, the gaps in these texts were motivated with a view to making the test easier than it would otherwise have been. The penultimate version of the English test was piloted during a preliminary visit to both countries. Minor changes were made as a result of this piloting. In addition local judgements were sought as to the "ease" or otherwise of the test. In each school the class teacher examined a copy of the test while it was being administered, and gave their opinion on what the "average" student in that class would score. Their pooled views were:

	Malawi	Zambia
Urban teachers	21.33	21.83
Rural teachers	17.50	16.00

Table 4.3 Pooled teacher estimates for English test scores

4.3.2 Rationale for modified cloze tests

The rationale for the construction of these tests is that competence in the relevant language, together with the ability to map the orthographic words onto the mental representation of language, are necessary but not sufficient conditions to enable reading. Bernhardt, for example, claims that 'knowledge of words and how words can be related to each other is a necessary yet insufficient prerequisite for understanding' (1991a: 95). It is evidence for precisely such "low level" capacities that this modified cloze test format attempts to capture.

As low level reading skills are said to be confined to intrasentential processing, it might be argued that the fact that each passage is a coherent whole is irrelevant, and that single sentences could have been used. However, even if overt intersentential cohesive devices (i.e. connectives, and lexical and syntactic reference) are absent, the readers' "meaning making" process will normally take account of incoming information across clause boundaries. This "meaning making" is the process whereby the reader interacts with the text to achieve coherence; it includes scanning the lexical and syntactic elements in the text, and matching the "incoming data" from the page to the evolving text-level discourse, in the context of an appropriate activated schema. Textual coherence is thus generated by the reader. This necessary interaction of the reader's background knowledge with the linguistic elements in the text may be exemplified by examining the following extract from the test:

Kalulu goes fishing

eating	but	bicycle	cooked	hand	fish

One morning Kalulu went fishing in the river.
He caught a lot of _____, then made   11
a fire, and _____ the fish. While   12
he was _____ the fish, Leopard   13
saw him, _____ Kalulu didn't see Leopard.   14

One relevant piece of background knowledge is that Kalulu is a hare, and a well-known trickster, the hero of many folk tales in Malawi and Zambia. The word *kalulu* (hare or rabbit) is the same in ChiChewa and Nyanja (and a number of other languages in the region) and the character is certainly well known to the testees from home or from previous school stories.

Assuming the case of an adequate reader, with the appropriate background knowledge, then the first sentence will activate the 'fishing in a river' schema. Catching a fish is an expected (or at least, devoutly hoped for) occurrence in such a schema. Next 'making a fire' leads to the possibility of cooking the fish, and in turn, eating it. In completing this test, the appropriate lexical choices 'fish', 'cooked' and 'eating' are facilitated by the reader attending to the local clause, but in the context of the relevant background knowledge. Thus, background knowledge and incoming data from the text are mutually supportive, and contribute to the evolving message which the reader is constructing. As long as the incoming data is congruent with background knowledge and the evolving message, then the reader proceeds 'in harmony' with the text. If an incoming element cannot be accommodated, then the reader has 'problems'. Obviously such modified cloze tests operate at what has traditionally been termed "low level", and they "can be assumed to draw strongly on the test taker's lexical knowledge" (Read, 1997: 309). However, as we saw in Chapter 2, lexical competence is an important factor in reading comprehension, and may therefore justifiably feature in a test of reading.

4.3.3 African language tests

The same format was employed to test the students' reading performance in African languages as in English. Two 30 item tests were produced, one in ChiChewa (for Malawi) and one in Nyanja (for Zambia). Since previous research (Williams, 1993a and 1993b) had suggested that Malawian children had higher proficiency in reading their local language than did Zambian children, the texts for both African language tests were modified versions of texts from the Zambian school textbook *Werenga Cinyanja*. The Malawian version of the texts was appropriately modified by ChiChewa specialists working in the Malawi Institute of Education. This modification resulted in a small number of minor differences between the two versions. For the purposes of comparison, the practice section of both tests is provided, with instances of differences being underlined:

Extract from the ChiChewa (Malawi) Test

Atate <u>ake</u> a Mumbi

nyemba	amawathandiza	pafupi
<u>amadzuka</u>	onse	njinga

Atate <u>ake</u> a Mumbi ndi mlimi. Ali ndi dimba lalikuklu.

Liri _____ ndi mudzi wawo. Matsiku onse	1
_____ m'mawa ndi <u>kupita</u> kudimba kwao.	2
Amalima _____, matimati ndi <u>chimanga chambiri</u>.	3
Mumbi _____ kudimba.	4

Extract from the Nyanja (Zambia) Test

Atate <u>ace</u> a Mumbi

nyemba	amawathandiza	pafupi
<u>amauka</u>	onse	njinga

Atate <u>ace</u> a Mumbi ndi mlimi. Ali ndi dimba lalikuklu.

Liri _____ ndi mudzi wawo. Matsiku onse	1
_____ m'mawa ndi <u>kuyenda</u> kudimba kwao.	2
Amalima _____, matimati ndi <u>cimanga cambiri</u>.	3
Mumbi _____ kudimba.	4

Translation:
[In box: beans; helps; near; he-wakes-up; all; bicycle]
Mumbi's father is a farmer. He has a large field. It's (near) his village. Every day (he-wakes-up) in the morning and goes to his field.

*He grows (beans), tomatoes, and a lot of maize. Mumbi (helps) him
in the field.*

Both test extracts have the same total of words (36 including the title and
correct options, plus 2 incorrect options) and only 6 words differ in the
two versions. Of the differences 4 are in terms of c/ch/k spelling variants,
(*ake/ace: 'of' (two occurrences); chimanga/cimanga 'maize'; chambiri/
cambiri: 'a lot of'*). A further difference occurs in the verb forms *amadzuka/
amauka: 'he wakes up'*. In the spoken form this occurs with and without
elision of the voiced alveolar affricate represented by the letters *dz*. However, the unelided form has been standardised in written Malawian
ChiChewa, and the elided form in written Zambian Nyanja. The final difference is a lexical choice *(kupita/kuyenda)* where again both items occur
in both languages, where the former was considered to be more 'normal'
in Malawian ChiChewa. Otherwise, the same gaps are inserted in both,
and on the basis of close similarity the texts may be regarded as "linguistically equivalent". The pooled views of the teachers from the schools as
to the scores that average students would score, were:

	Malawi	Zambia
Urban teachers	25.50	23.33
Rural teachers	23.67	14.00

Table 4.4 Pooled teacher estimates for African language test scores

The titles of the four sections in the Malawian and Zambian versions of
the tests were as follows (Malawian version first):

— Atate ace a Mumbi / Atate ake a Mumbi (Mumbi's father): 4 items
— Mabvuto ndi njinga yache / Mabvuto ndi njinga yake (Mabvuto and
   his bicycle): 6 items
— Magule / Magule (Dancing): 2 sections of 4 and 6 items
— Maphinziro ena amakono / Maphunziro ena amakono (Farming to-
   day): 2 sections of 4 items and 6 items.

The total number of orthographic words for each test (including gaps)
was: English, 294; Nyanja, 249; ChiChewa, 250. The English passages
contain some 20% more orthographic words than the local language texts
but not necessarily 20% more information. This is due to the fact that in
Nyanja/ChiChewa many grammatical elements are prefixed or suffixed
to the related lexical item in the orthographic form, while definiteness and

non-definiteness are not normally marked by articles. Thus the single ChiChewa/Nyanja orthographic word *kunyumba* translates into three English orthographic words *in the house*. The so-called "conjunctive" nature of Nyanja orthography (see Kashoki, 1990: 69 ff.) whereby "the Bantu locative prefixes as manifested in Zambian languages [are] spelt conjunctively with the noun to which they are closely structurally related" (Kashoki, 1990: 70) has been a matter for some controversy. From the perspective of recognition of written words, however, one might surmise that the strategy of identifying initial letters in orthographic words, and then making an informed guess from context, is not as readily applicable in cases where grammatical elements (e.g. locative or singular/plural morphemes such as *ku-* and *ma-*) occur systematically at the beginning of orthographic words, as they do in written ChiChewa/Nyanja[3].

4.4 Test administration

The tests were administered over a 2 week period in each country, Zambia first, followed by Malawi. In each school visit, the English tests were administered first, and the African language tests second, to the same students, after an interval varying from 15 to 30 minutes. Immediately before the administration of both English and African language tests, the students were taken through a "warm up" phase where the research team members introduced themselves, and interacted with the class, often using blackboard drawings. The purpose of the visit was then explained, and students were told in local languages that they were not obliged to take part. This was followed by a practice session, with local languages being used by the assistants, and finally the test administrations proper. No students dropped out, and there seemed to be no doubt that they understood what the test task required of them. Most appeared to enjoy doing the tests, with many asking if we could return to give them some more. Up to 35 minutes were allowed for completion of each test, with some students completing within half that time, and the weaker students taking by far the most time.

---

[3] However, examination of audio recordings of Malawian children reading aloud in ChiChewa, suggests that many recognise the "conjunctive" prefixes fairly readily, then "attack" the remainder of the orthographic word employing much the same "psycholinguistic guessing" strategy as English unpractised readers.

5. Results of the English Reading Tests

5.1 General description

Readers who are left cold by statistical information may at this point wish to skip to Section 5.2 of this chapter. The data presented in the chapter consist of answers to the modified cloze tests, each of which had a maximum score of 30 points. The statistical tables were generated using the SAS programmes (SAS, 1985). For the purpose of hypothesis testing the conventional statistical significance level of 0.05 is employed.

The English test results are first briefly reviewed in general statistical terms; next they are discussed on a country-by-country basis in terms of the factors addressed by the hypotheses; finally the inter-country comparisons are investigated. Bar charts and box plots are employed in addition to tables, since they offer an effective visual presentation of information. These were generated using the SPSS 6.1 programme, or Excel 5.0a programme. The statistical significance for the main effects which feature in the hypotheses are noted in the discussion that accompanies each section.

Tests of significance were produced using the General Linear Model (GLM) procedure in SAS. The analysis takes account of the fact that the data has a hierarchical structure with two levels, pupils within schools. Some variables (namely sex and home language) apply to individual pupils, while others (location and country) apply to schools. If the hierarchical structure is not taken into account, in particular the fact that there are only two urban schools in each country, and only four rural schools (with obvious potential for sampling error if just one school is atypical), then misleadingly high significance levels will be generated with respect to location, particularly as the number of pupils is relatively large. In order to present the reporting of results as an "unfolding narrative", relevant details regarding statistical significance from the General Linear Model (GLM) are provided on a section-by-section basis, with the *post hoc* Bonferroni procedure employed in cases where the GLM yielded significant differences in main effects. The complete tables for the statistical significance of all main effects are provided at the end of the chapter.

Test reliability for the English reading test is high: the alpha figure calculated for the combined results for both countries, is over 0.9 and the "alpha if item deleted" figures are also over 0.9 for all 30 items. This indicates that all items are in line with the overall results. This is confirmed by the point biserial correlation, which measures the extent to which "single items are related to, or 'fit' with, other items" (Hatch and Lazaraton, 1991: 448). The point biserial correlation was calculated separately for

Malawi and Zambia, and is positive for results on all items in both countries (i.e. there were no "aberrant" items), with 26 out of 30 items in the range 0.32 to 0.61 for Malawi, and all items within the range 0.46 to 0.78 for Zambia (see Appendix 7). This high reliability is confirmed by the KR-21 results of 0.84 for Malawi and 0.95 for Zambia.

The facility value of items overall ranges from a high of 0.785 (item 1) to a low of 0.178 (item 28). The following histogram gives a visual presentation of the facility values. More detailed information appears in Appendix 8.

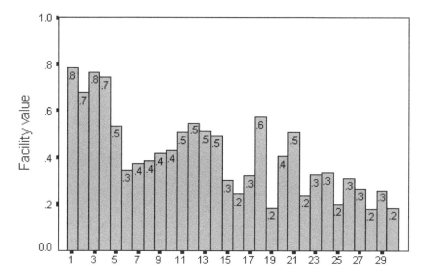

Figure 5.1 Facility values of items in English test, Malawi and Zambia.

While there was no aim of grading all the items in terms of anticipated facility values, it was intended that the first 4 items should be relatively easy, and that the last 8 items relatively difficult. Figure 5.1 shows that by and large this was the case. The items which involved free structural elements (grammatical words) were items 2, 10, 14, 15, and 22. The facility value for these ranged from 0.238 (item 22) up to 0.677 (item 2), with a mean facility value of 0.357. The remaining gaps to be filled by lexical words had facility values which ranged from 0.178 (item 28) up to 0.785 (item 1), with a mean of 0.425. As anticipated, the items requiring grammatical words for completion had proved slightly more difficult overall than those requiring lexical items.

The overall scores for both Malawi and Zambia combined in the English reading tests are as follows:

N	Mean	Sd	Max	Median	Min
517	12.35	7.83	30	11	0

Table 5.1 Summary statistics for English test results, Malawi and Zambia (Maximum possible 30)

Figure 5.2 provides a visual account of the distribution of scores (i.e. the number of testees achieving each score).

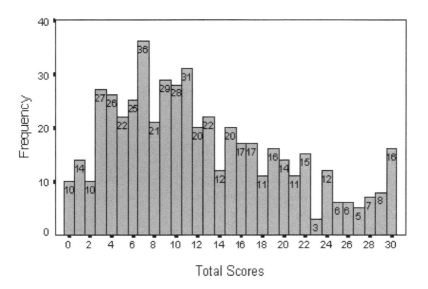

Figure 5.2 Histogram of total scores in English test, Malawi and Zambia

The full range of scores appears, with 10 pupils scoring 0, and 16 scoring the maximum of 30. The shape of the curve is obviously not that of the regular "bell-shaped" curve, although 95% of the scores fall within ± 2 standard deviations of the mean score[1]. Most obviously, the scores

---

[1] In language testing if 95% of the population fall within ± 2 standard deviations of the mean then this accepted "as being sufficiently close to that of a normal distribution (Green and Weir, 1998: 34). However, satisfying this criterion alone does not ensure normal distribution.

generally are skewed towards the bottom end of the range, and there is also the 16 pupil "peak" at the very top of the range. One should not, however, make too much here of whether the results are normally distributed: it could be argued that, since the test content is based on the content of the previous four years' English course books in the two countries, then what we are dealing with is an achievement test (where the main focus of interest should be on a criterion score, or threshold level), rather than a language proficiency test, where a distribution approaching the normal may be expected. In fact if all testees had scored close to the maximum (and assuming the test was valid in content and construct terms), one might simply conclude that the learning outcomes were highly satisfactory. Nonetheless, because of individual differences (in factors such as attendance, motivation, etc.), it is not unusual for the results of achievement tests to display near-normal distribution. However, as we shall see, the distribution of scores within each of the two countries follows a different pattern.

5.2 English reading tests results – Malawi

5.2.1 National level

The mean score of nearly 13 out of 30 is not high, given that the test material was drawn overwhelmingly from material from year 4 and below, i.e. supposedly below the level of these year 5 pupils. However, as we shall see, this mean score conceals considerable differences between schools, sexes, and the rural/urban divide, as well as between individual pupils within schools.

N	Mean	Sd	Max	Median	Min
290	12.84	6.22	30	12	1

Reliability (KR-21): 0.84

Table 5.2 Summary statistics for English test results, Malawi

The histogram (Figure 5.3) reveals that there is a small number of high scoring testees, only 14 students out of the 290 scored above 25, and a far larger number of low scoring testees.

It is apparent that, assuming the test is valid, in the sense of being reasonably in line with the expectations of the curriculum (bearing in mind that English is now for these year 5 children the medium of instruction for all subjects except ChiChewa), then the majority of these children must be experiencing considerable difficulty in coping with the curriculum demands.

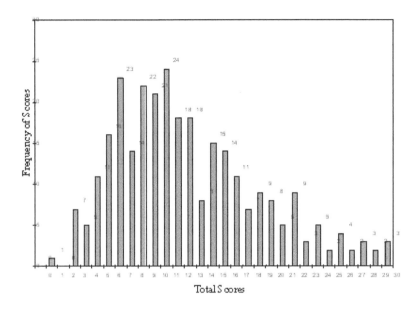

Figure 5.3 Frequency of total scores in English test, Malawi

5.2.2 Differences between schools

There are considerable differences between schools, with the highest scoring school (school 6) having a mean approximately twice as large as that of the lowest scoring school (school 5), although it should be noted that all schools display a very roughly similar range of scores, the minimum being 1 to 5, the maximum 24 to 30.

School	N	Mean	Sd	Max	Median	Min
1	50	15.18	4.93	27	14.5	5
2	32	11.69	4.87	26	10.5	3
3 (U)	50	13.66	5.96	29	13.0	4
4	55	10.42	4.69	28	9.0	3
5	47	8.47	3.71	24	8.0	3
6 (U)	56	16.75	7.72	30	16.5	1

Note: U = urban

Table 5.3 Summary statistics for English test results by school, Malawi

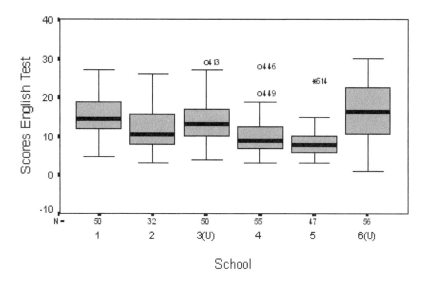

Figure 5.4 Box plots of English test results by school, Malawi

The above box plot[2] possibly allows the overall picture to be more readily apprehended. Testees from School 5 are confirmed as the lowest scoring, with the box plot highlighting the fact that the maximum score of 24 is exceptional (an "extreme value") in that school. While in general one might expect urban schools to do better in English tests than rural schools, it is obvious that there are considerable differences in results between rural schools themselves. The socio-economic status of the school catchments appeared to be very similar, as did the attendance rates of students. It would therefore appear possible that the different rural school results are due to a teacher effect. As subjectively assessed during the visit, such differences between schools were possibly to do with teacher commitment.

---

[2] The box indicates the middle 50% of testees (from the 25th to the 75th percentile), while the line across it indicates the median, with the number of pupils in the lower section of the box being equal to the number in upper section. Thus if the lower section is narrower than the upper, as in school 2, it indicates simply that there is a "bunching" of lower scores. Likewise "flat" boxes simply indicate "bunching" around the median, not the number of testees in the box. Maximum and minimum scores are indicated by the "whiskers", apart from (i) "outlier" scores (those more than 1.5 box lengths from the box) which are indicated by circles, and (ii) "extreme" scores (those more than 3 box lengths away from the box), indicated by asterisks. The numbers are those assigned to the testees by the SPSS programme (See Kinnear and Gray, 1994: 64).

The teachers in school 4 seemed demoralised, while many of those in school 5 expressed discontent about having been posted to a rural school; in school 2, the class 5 teacher was in the staffroom, while his pupils copied from the Teachers' Guide. It may also be noted in passing that schools 4 and 5 were in the worst material condition, although this does not necessarily reflect teacher commitment.

5.2.3 Sex differences

Sex	N	Mean	Sd	Max	Median	Min
Boys	161	13.72	6.40	30	13	3
Girls	129	11.75	5.83	30	11	1

Table 5.4 Summary statistics for English test results by sex, Malawi

The corresponding box plot is:

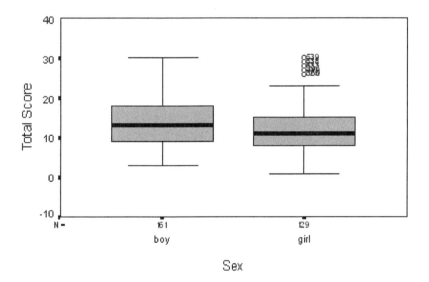

Figure 5.5 Box plots of English test results by sex, Malawi

The difference between the sexes in the English test is statistically signifi-cant (Pr>F: 0.0308), with boys scoring on average some 2 points higher than girls. The box plot (Figure 5.5) indicates that there are relatively fewer high scoring girls than boys, although a cluster of 5 girls are "outliers". There are a number of possible explanations for the girls' relatively weaker performance. First girls' attendance is generally less regular than that of boys, since girls more often miss school to look after younger siblings or sick family members. Girls also have a heavier load of domestic chores, such as cleaning, or carrying wood and water, than do boys, which makes them more tired and less able to concentrate during school. Although females are disadvantaged in Malawian life and society in general, my subjective impression from classroom observations is that girls do not appear to be discriminated against directly in the classroom (e.g. in terms of seating arrangements, access to books, or teacher attention). It may well be, therefore, that it is the disadvantage suffered by girls outside school that negatively affects their achievement inside school. As the histogram below indicates, boys perform relatively better than girls in all mixed schools, and also in the single sex schools (School 1, all boys and School 2, all girls).

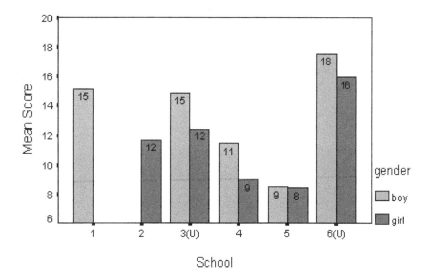

Figure 5.6 Mean scores in English, schools by sex, Malawi.

The mean difference is small in rural school 5 (the boys' mean is in fact 8.50 and the girls' 8.43; the histogram label rounds up/down to the nearest whole), while the girls' median score is actually slightly higher than the boys'. (Such "untypical" findings are, however, a feature of *post hoc* data "trawling", where unexpected results will emerge if the "trawl" is persistent.) Although there is no hypothesis on the effect of single sex schools, it may be observed (Table 5.5), that the one single sex girls' school (school 2, a rural school) has a much higher mean score than that of the girls in the other two rural schools.

Testees, girls in:	N	Mean	Sd	Max	Min
School 2 (rural single sex)	32	11.69	4.87	26	3
Schools 4 & 5 (rural mixed sex)	44	8.73	3.14	16	3
Schools 3 & 6 (urban mixed sex)	53	14.30	6.86	30	1

Table 5.5 Mean scores, English test of girls in single sex and mixed sex schools, by location, Malawi

A similar picture emerges in the single sex boys' school (school 1):

Testees, boys in:	N	Mean	Sd	Max	Min
School 1 (rural single sex)	50	15.18	4.93	27	5
Schools 4 & 5 (rural mixed sex)	58	10.12	5.03	28	3
Schools 3 & 6 (urban mixed sex)	53	16.28	7.23	30	4

Table 5.6 Mean scores, English test, of boys in single sex and mixed sex schools, by location, Malawi

As in the case of the girls, the mean score of the boys in single sex schools is between that of rural boys and urban boys in mixed sex schools. There is a suggestion here that being in a single sex school in Malawi may be of advantage to both boys and girls. However, since there was no hypothesis on the effect of single sex schools, and since the number of such schools in the data is minimal, the above suggestion is speculation.

5.2.4 Location (urban/rural) differences

Loc	N	Mean	SD	Max	Median	Min
Rural	184	11.43	5.18	28	11	3
Urban	106	15.29	7.08	30	15	1

Table 5.7 Summary statistics for English test results by location, Malawi

While the urban mean is higher than the rural, the location variable fails to reach statistical significance (Pr>F: 0.1518). Since there are only two urban schools there is clearly scope for sampling error, and a larger sample of schools (not pupils) would be needed to examine the differences between rural and urban schools.

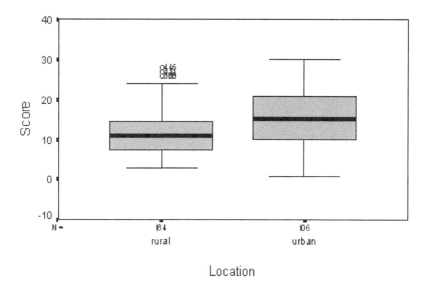

Figure 5.7 Box plots of English test scores by location, Malawi

The box plot shows fewer high scoring rural pupils than urban pupils, with the urban mean at roughly the same point as the rural 75th percentile.

Figure 5.8 shows that urban testees tend to predominate in the high scores, while rural testees do so at the lower end.

In terms of the generalisability of our overall results, it should be noted that the rural proportion of the total population in Malawi is estimated at

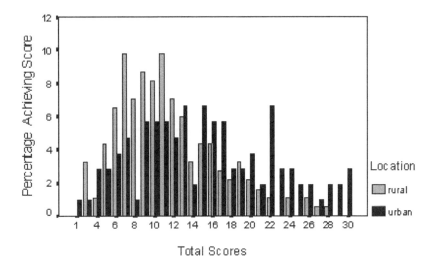

Figure 5.8 Distribution of English scores by location, Malawi
(expressed as percentages[3])

about 90%, whereas in this research the rural proportion is only something over 63%. Taking this into account, and assuming our schools are
representative, then the "true" overall mean score for Malawi would have
been slightly lower than 12.84 (see 5.4).

5.2.5 Location and sex effects combined

Location	Sex	N	Mean	S.D.	Max	Median	Min
Rural	Boys	108	12.46	5.57	28	12	3
Rural	Girls	76	9.97	4.20	26	10	3
Urban	Boys	53	16.28	7.23	30	16	4
Urban	Girls	53	14.30	6.86	30	13	1

Table 5.8 Mean scores by location and sex, English test, Malawi

---

[3] The results in Figures 5.8 and 5.14 are expressed in percentages (urban total =
100%), rural total = 100%) since there are many more rural testees than urban.
These figures (generated by SPSS) do not show scores for which the frequency is
zero.

Combining the effects of location and sex for Malawian testees reveals, as would be expected, considerable differences with urban boys scoring most highly, followed by urban girls, rural boys and rural girls. The difference between the first group and the last is some 6 points. The pattern is clearly revealed in the box plots (Figure 5.9).

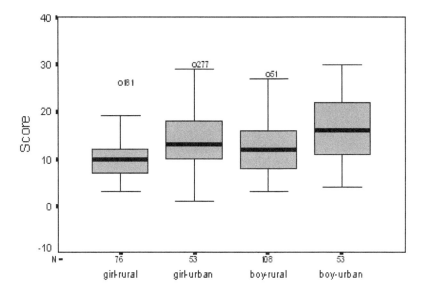

Figure 5.9 Box plots of English scores by location and sex, Malawi

In short, it would seem that urban boys are considerably more advantaged than rural girls in Malawi. However, since urban girls score more highly than rural boys, it seems that advantage is also conferred through being urban.

5.3 English reading test results – Zambia

5.3.1 National level

N	Mean	Sd	Max	Med	Min
227	11.72	9.48	30	8	0

Reliability (KR-21): 0.95

Table 5.9 Summary statistics for English test results, Zambia

As in Malawi, the mean score of 11.72 out of 30 is not high, given that the test material was drawn from material from year 4 and below, i.e. supposedly below the level of these year 5 pupils. However, this mean score conceals even greater differences than was the case in Malawi, between schools, sexes, and the rural/urban divide, as well as between individual pupils within schools; these differences are examined below.

A striking feature of Figure 5.10 is the unexpected distribution of scores: instead of tending towards a bell-shaped normal curve (as was the case with the Malawi scores), the curve here is rather U-shaped, with a relatively large number of low scores, and considerable numbers of high scores. The number of pupils scoring 21 to 30 is 51 (18.8% of the total) while the number scoring 0 to 9 is 121 (44.8% of the total), resulting in a high standard deviation of 9.48.

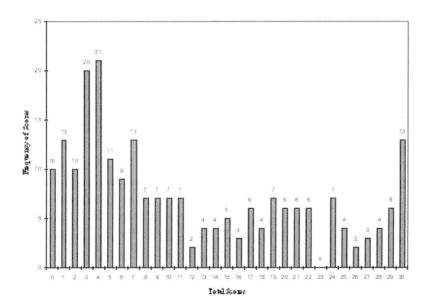

Figure 5.10 Frequency of total scores of English Test, Zambia

The very high test KR-21 reliability of 0.95 suggests that the items are not behaving in a random fashion, but that there are consistent differences between the more and less proficient pupils. The reasons behind this unusual distribution will be investigated in the following sections.

5.3.2 Differences between schools

School	N	Mean	Sd	Max	Median	Min
7 (U)	39	11.85	9.76	30	8.0	0
8	39	5.79	5.40	26	4.0	0
9	31	9.23	7.74	29	7.0	0
10	34	9.41	9.04	30	6.5	0
11 (U)	55	19.51	9.15	30	21.0	0
12	29	10.10	7.08	24	8.0	0

Note: U = urban

Table 5.10 Summary statistics for English test results by school, Zambia

The inter-school mean differences are large and statistically highly significant (Pr>F: 0.0008). The mean in the highest scoring school is almost 4 times more than that in the lowest, although, as in the case of Malawi, a roughly similar range of scores appears in the six schools (a minimum of 0 up to a maximum of 24 to 30). Notice that all schools have testees with the minimum scores of 0, while 3 schools also have testees who achieved the maximum score of 30. This extremely large intra-class range suggests that appropriate teaching for pupils of different proficiencies is needed. However, classroom evidence is that a "lockstep" teaching approach, with the teacher dominating the pace and activities, is the norm.

Figure 5.11 confirms that school 8 has the lowest general performance with high scores being exceptional: the scores are clustered around the chance score of 4. The other rural schools (9, 10, 12) have results much in line with each other, and the results in school 8 would seem to give cause for concern. It may be that the high degree of teacher absenteeism noted on the day of the visit for test administration was not unusual.

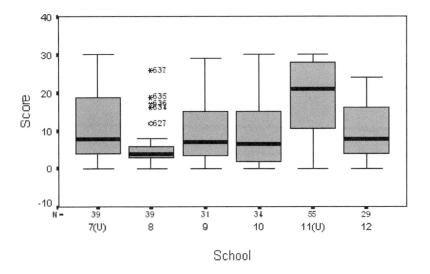

Figure 5.11 Box plots of English scores by school, Zambia

5.3.3 Sex differences

Sch	N	Mean	Sd	Max	Med	Min
Boys	127	11.13	9.51	30	7	0
Girls	100	12.46	9.43	30	10	0

Table 5.11 Summary statistics for English test results by sex, Zambia

The girls overall have a marginally higher mean than the boys, but this is not statistically significant (Pr>F: 0.8019). Hypothesis C2 (that at year 5 there will be no significant difference between the scores of boys and girls in Zambia on reading tests in English) is therefore supported.

That many results are concentrated in a narrow band of low scores, particularly in the case of the boys, is indicated by the position of the median lines in the box plot of Figure 5.12.

While there is a common assumption that in Zambia boys outperform girls in school-based assessments, and the general findings of Zambian public examinations, held at the end of year 7, support this (MOE [Zambia], 1992: 9.11), the present research provides no evidence for that view. A similar result (i.e. a slight but non-significant superiority for girls) is

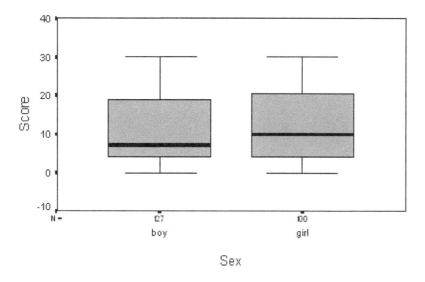

Figure 5.12 Box plots of English scores by sex, Zambia

reported in Williams (1993b) for grades 3, 4 and 6 in five Zambian schools on similar reading tests. These results taken together suggest there may be a real, but small, difference in favour of girls in reading in English at year 5, although it should be repeated that there is no evidence for such a claim in this present study.

Possible reasons as to the lack of superiority on the part of boys in Zambia in these tests, although they are reportedly (see above) superior in Zambian public examinations, may be that *subsequent* to year 5, some Zambian families put pressure on their academically successful girls to drop out of school, while keeping their academically successful boys at school. This would be in keeping with the view that education is more likely to be economically rewarded in later life for a boy. It is also possible, of course, that the Zambian public examinations referred to above favour boys, or that boys receive more intensive "coaching" in year 7.

5.3.4 Location (urban/rural) differences

Loc	N	Mean	Sd	Max	Med	Min
R	133	8.46	7.49	30	6.0	0
U	94	16.33	10.10	30	17.5	0

Table 5.12 Summary statistics for English test results by location, Zambia

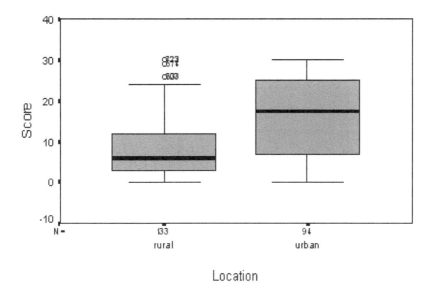

Figure 5.13 Box plots of English test scores by location, Zambia

The GLM output for this variable is as follows:

Source	DF	Type III SS	Mean Square	F Value	Pr > F
Location	1	2538.781	2538.781	7.44	0.0526

There is a large difference in favour of urban schools, which just fails to reach statistical significance. However, the result is nonetheless extremely close . Additionally, when the data sets from Malawi and Zambia are combined, then the difference in favour of urban schools does achieve significance (see section 5.5 below).

One comment that may be made at the outset is that the differences between rural and urban pupils are an important factor in the distribution of English test scores, which as mentioned above, does not display a normal bell-shaped curve, such as one would expect from one population, but rather a U-shaped curve. Examination of Figure 5.14, reveals that a strong contributory reason is that rural students predominate in the lower scores, while urban students dominate the higher scores.

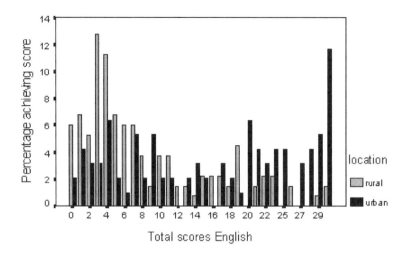

Figure 5.14 Distribution of English scores by location, Zambia (as percentages)

Rather than suggesting the outline of a single population with the expected normal distribution of scoring pattern (peaking around the mean) these results suggest a more complex picture in terms of English reading ability: rural children are overall achieving low scores, while urban distribution suggests possibly two sub-populations, one similar to the rural, the other a high scoring one. Again, as is the case in Malawi, the likely explanation for this difference is that there is more English available in urban settings than in rural ones. There, is also, as in Malawi, the possibility that rural children are absent more than urban children, or that teachers are more effective. However, the rural/urban difference does raise concerns as to the divisive effect of the current language policy.

5.3.5 Location and sex effects combined

Location	Sex	N	Mean	S.D.	Max	Median	Min
Rural	Boys	77	8.73	7.92	30	5.0	0
Rural	Girls	56	8.09	6.92	26	6.0	0
Urban	Boys	50	14.84	10.61	30	14.5	0
Urban	Girls	44	18.02	9.31	30	20.0	1

Table 5.13 Summary statistics for English test results by location and sex, Zambia

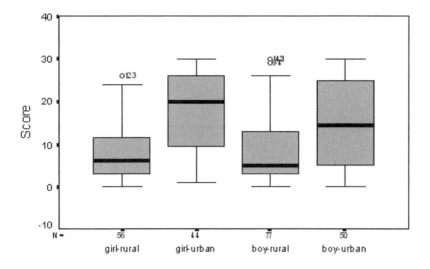

Figure 5.15 Box plots, English test results by location and sex, Zambia

Combining the effects of location and sex reveals, as would be expected, considerable differences with urban girls scoring most highly, followed by urban boys, rural boys and rural girls. The difference between the first group and the last is some 10 points. However, although urban girls score more highly than urban boys, the situation in rural schools does not correspond: here rural girls have a slightly lower mean score than rural boys (although they have a higher median score than boys – 6 as opposed to 5).

Investigating at the school level shows that girls have outperformed boys in both of the urban schools (schools 7 and 11), whereas the opposite is the case in 3 of the 4 rural schools (the exception being school 9), as shown in Figure 5.16.

It seems possible that in Zambia, rural schools and communities have a more "traditional" attitude to girls (possibly comparable to the Malawian attitude) than urban schools. It should also be pointed out that while negative attitudes towards girls' education may well be more prevalent in rural areas, rural boys in Zambia do not fare particularly well either. We might finally note that the proportion of Zambian urban schools in the research is some 33% (2 out of 6) while the proportion of urban dwellers throughout Zambia is some 43%, suggesting that the "real" mean for this test in Zambia as a whole might possibly be higher (see 5.4 below).

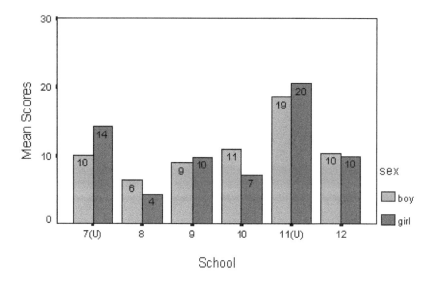

Figure 5.16 Histogram, mean English scores by sex and school, Zambia

Country	N	Mean	Sd	Max	Med	Min
Malawi	290	12.84	6.22	30	12	1
Zambia	227	11.72	9.48	30	8	0

Table 5.14 Summary statistics for Malawi and Zambia, English test results

5.4   General comparison of the English test results in Malawi and Zambia

Table 5.13 shows that Malawi has a slightly higher mean score than Zambia, but the GLM output (Pr>F: 0.3337) indicates this is far from statistically significant. The hypothesis that there will be no difference in reading ability between children in Zambia and children in Malawi at year 5 in primary schools is therefore supported. The evidence is, contrary to what one might expect, that year 5 Zambian children who have officially had their first four years of education through the medium of English are not superior to Malawian children who have had Chichewa as a medium of instruction for those years.

The number of rural to urban subjects in this research is not proportional to the estimated distribution of rural to urban population in Malawi and Zambia, and this can affect the overall cross-country comparability. However, even if the actual proportions are taken into account and the results recalculated, then the Malawi overall mean for the English tests is 11.73, while the Zambia overall mean 11.60. In short, we still find that the overall mean for Malawi is slightly higher than that for Zambia.

The higher standard deviation in Zambia indicates a generally wider spread of scores, while the fact that the median is considerably lower than the mean indicates the Zambian results are skewed towards the lower scores, as confirmed by Figure 5.17.

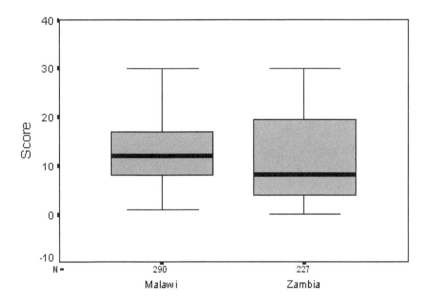

Figure 5.17 Box plots of English test scores, Malawi and Zambia

The Malawi population displays relatively less variation than the Zambian population, not only of the populations as a whole, but also of the individual schools, as juxtaposing the school box plots graphically demonstrates. The Malawian boxes are more compact, indicating that scores are bunched together.

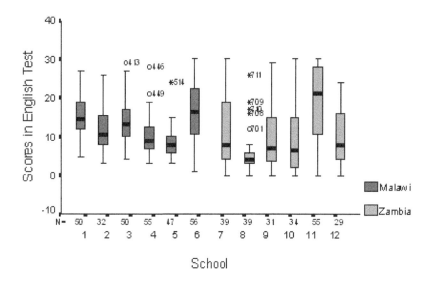

Figure 5.18 Box plots of English test results by school, Malawi and Zambia

5.5 Testing of the hypotheses for English – summary

Overall means: These are very slightly in favour of Malawi, but not at a statistically significant level. Hypothesis A "that there will be no difference in reading ability between children in Zambia and children in Malawi at year 5 in primary schools" is therefore supported.

Sex (boys/girls): In Malawi, the difference between the sexes in the English test is statistically significant with boys scoring some 2 points higher than girls. Hypothesis C1 "that at year 5 there will be no significant difference between the scores of boys and girls in Malawi on reading tests in English" is thus not supported. In Zambia, on the other hand, there is no statistically significant sex difference although girls have in general a higher mean than boys. Hypothesis C2 "that at year 5 there will be no significant difference between the scores of boys and girls in Zambia on reading tests in English" is supported.

Location (urban/rural): In Malawi, while urban pupils have a mean score more than 3 points higher than rural pupils, this is not statistically significant. In Zambia, there are much larger mean differences (over 7 points) in favour of urban schools, but these just fail to attain statistical significance. Hypotheses C3 and C4 that for Malawi and Zambia respectively, there will, at year 5, "be no significant difference between the scores of pupils in urban schools and rural schools in reading tests in English" are therefore supported.

It is however, worthy of note that when the data sets from the two countries are combined, the location effect is significant, and had there been a hypothesis worded "for Malawi and Zambia combined, there will, at year 5 be no significant difference between the scores of pupils in urban schools and rural schools in reading tests in English" then it would not have been supported. It seems likely that a location effect is present in both countries, but that the small number of schools (not pupils) in the study prevents this being detected.

As far as the reasons for the general superiority of urban over rural pupils in the English tests are concerned, we may speculate that it is because there is far less English in the rural environment; in fact it is likely that the vast majority of rural children are only exposed to English while at school. Interpersonal communication outside school is entirely in African languages (mainly ChiChewa or Nyanja for these children), newspapers are very unusual, television is non-existent (rural communities usually have no electricity), and battery-powered radios extremely rare. While urban areas are also very poor, there is more exposure to English through public advertisements, posters, newspapers, and to some extent radio.

The edited results of the significance tests with details of the main effects specified in the hypotheses, are produced in Tables 5.14 to 5.16.

Source	DF	Type III SS	Mean Square	F Value	Pr > F
Location	1	931.982	931.982	3.12	0.518
School	4	1192.985	298.246	9.76	0.0001
Sex	1	144.035	144.035	4.71	0.0308
Home Lang.	1	0.594	0.594	0.02	0.8892
Model	7	2570.994	367.285	12.02	0.0001
Error	282	8617.024	30.557		

Table 5.15 Malawi, significance tests for English test scores

Source	DF	Type III SS	Mean Square	F Value	Pr > F
Location	1	2538.781	2538.781	7.44	0.0526
School	4	1365.724	341.431	4.96	0.0008
Sex	1	4.342	4.342	0.06	0.8019
Home Lang.	1	68.663	68.663	1.00	0.3189
Model	7	5232.354	747.479	10.87	0.0001
Error	219	15065.602	68.793		

Table 5.16 Zambia, significance tests for English test scores

Source	DF	Type III SS	Mean Square	F Value	Pr > F
Location	1	3318.407	3318.407	8.81	0.0157
Country	1	392.814	392.814	1.04	0.3337
School	9	3388.753	376.528	7.95	0.0001
Sex	1	43.115	43.115	0.91	0.3406
Home Lang.	1	26.447	26.447	0.56	0.4554
Model	13	7813.360	601.028	12.68	0.0001
Error	503	23834.272	47.384		

Table 5.17 Malawi and Zambia combined, significance tests for English test scores

6. Results of the African Language Reading Tests

6.1 General

This chapter reports on the African language test results, opening with brief general consideration, then examining the results for each country in turn. There is also a comparison of the African language tests for Malawi and Zambia across the two countries, and finally we look at the English and African language test results relatively, across the two countries.

6.2 Results of African language reading tests, Zambia

6.2.1 National level

N	Mean	Sd	Max	Median	Min
227	4.40	3.70	22	3	0

Reliability Index (KR-21): 0.75

Table 6.1 Summary statistics for Nyanja test results, Zambia (Maximum possible 30)

The mean score in the Nyanja test is considerably lower than that which the same people scored for English (no claim of course is made that the texts are of "equivalent difficulty" for the population). The mean score is in fact only marginally above the chance score of 4 and suggests that the vast majority of the Zambian testees could not cope with this test. Test reliability was high at 0.75 (KR-21). The bar chart in Figure 6.1 reveals, as one would expect, a marked preponderance of very low scores.

Although the results will be considered in terms of school, sex and location, it is apparent from Figure 6.1 that little differentiation is likely. We shall therefore proceed through these factors in a fairly cursory manner, before discussing the possible causes for this overall very weak performance. All of the items have proved difficult for the testees, although no item has a zero facility value, the lowest facility value being 0.02 on item 27 (see Appendix 5 for details of facility values).

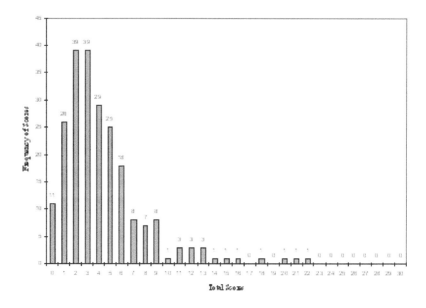

Figure 6.1 Histogram of frequency of scores for the Nyanja reading test, Zambia.

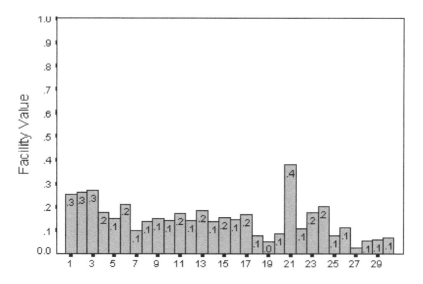

Figure 6.2 Facility values of items in Nyanja test, Zambia

6.2.2 School differences

Three schools have means below the chance score of 4, and the median scores are at or below chance in five of the six schools. The box plots in

School	N	Mean	Sd	Max	Median	Min
7(U)	39	5.31	3.40	22	5	1
8	39	4.41	2.64	14	4	2
9	31	3.77	4.36	21	2	0
10	34	3.12	2.35	9	2	0
11(U)	55	5.49	4.65	20	4	0
12	29	3.24	3.09	13	2	0

Table 6.2 Summary statistics for Nyanja test results by school, Zambia

Figure 6.3 indicate that the handful of higher scores are exceptional, being "outliers" or "extreme values".

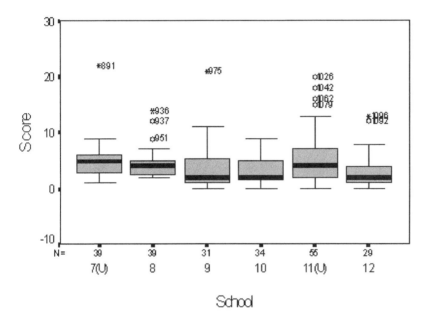

Figure 6.3 Box plots of Nyanja test results by school, Zambia

However, it is interesting to note that the high scores are not confined to one school – three schools have a maximum score of 20 or over, while only one school has a maximum of below 10. This suggests that compe-tence in reading Nyanja in Zambia may not be a school or teacher effect,

but due to personal reasons[1]. Unfortunately, since these Nyanja test papers
were marked after the school visits, there was no opportunity of investigating further the pupils concerned. These results show that inter-school
differences for Nyanja are much smaller than those in English, and also
indicate that the scores are generally low in all schools. The school variable overall (Pr>F: 0.5963) fails to achieve statistical significance. Although
in the event the test proved "too difficult" for these Zambian pupils, it
should be born in mind that the texts were taken from Zambian Nyanja
course books at or below grade 5, and when the identical Nyanja test was
administered to 74 pupils in Malawi the mean score was 18.66.

6.2.3 Sex differences

Sex	N	Mean	Sd	Max	Med	Min
B	127	4.46	3.50	21	4	0
G	100	4.31	3.96	22	3	0

Table 6.3 Summary statistics for Nyanja test results by sex, Zambia

Both sexes have a very similar set of low scores – a pattern confirmed by
the box plots:

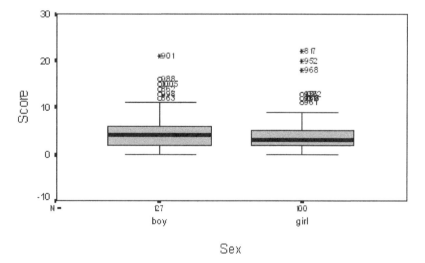

Figure 6.4 Box plot of Nyanja results by sex, Zambia

[1] One urban boy in an earlier test series obtained near perfect scores (58 and 60

There is no statistically significant difference by sex, (Pr>F: 0.7905. However, given the weak performance of both boys and girls, this near equality is hardly to be attributed to gender sensitive education policies.

6.2.4 Location (urban/rural) differences

Loc	N	Mean	SD	Max	Med	Min
R	133	3.68	3.17	21	3	0
U	94	5.41	4.16	22	4	0

Table 6.4 Summary statistics for test score in Nyanja by location, Zambia

The urban/rural difference is small in the case of Nyanja, and again both means are extremely close to the chance score of 4. It is, however, of interest that the urban mean is nonetheless higher than the rural mean (which is below chance). In fact the GLM yields the rather strange finding that the difference between the urban and rural means is statistically significant (Pr>F: 0.0135). Clearly the fact that the scores are so low has not only contributed to this significance finding, but also means that little importance can be attributed to it[2]. Statistics are a useful servant, but they cannot redeem an unsatisfactory test outcome. While this finding is statistically significant, it is not meaningful (in the sense of "important in the real world"), and sometimes we need to distinguish between the two.

One possible explanation for the slightly higher urban mean is that the urban children may have had a stronger tendency than rural children to write something in all the gaps and thus give themselves a better statistical chance of getting items correct. Given the very low scores, no exploration of this possibility has been carried out; in marking the tests, both incorrect answers and gaps left unfilled were counted as incorrect answers.

6.2.5 Sex and location differences combined

As in the English test results, rural girls have the lowest mean, and urban girls the highest, but the differences are of a much smaller order.

---

out of 60) in the English and Nyanja tests respectively (see Williams, 1993b). Conversation with him some months later suggested he was something of a "loner" whose mother bought him books in Nyanja.

[2] The test of statistical significance is not "aware" of the chance score, which is a function of the modified cloze format employed.

Location	Sex	N	Mean	S.D.	Max	Median	Min
Rural	Boys	77	4.00	3.52	21	3	0
Rural	Girls	56	3.23	2.57	13	2.5	0
Urban	Boys	50	5.18	3.40	16	4	0
Urban	Girls	44	5.68	4.91	22	4	1

Table 6.5 Summary statistics for Nyanja results by location and sex, Zambia

The "flat" box plots confirm the overwhelmingly low scores, with a few exceptions in each group.

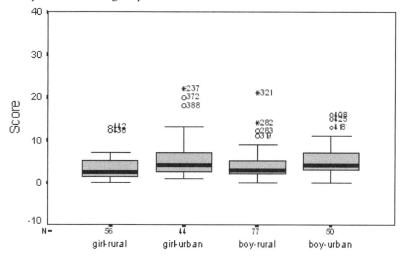

Figure 6.5 Box plots of Nyanja test scores by sex and location, Zambia

As before, the results overall are again too close to chance for the differences to merit detailed discussion of the effect of these factors.

6.2.6 Testees from non-Nyanja homes

Although the test was administered in Nyanja speaking areas, only just over half of the pupils (122 out of a total of 227) claimed the language as their home language. When the results were analysed for home language effect, there was a very small and non-significant difference in favour of those from non-Nyanja speaking homes (e.g. SiLozi, or IciBemba), over those who had Nyanja as their home language (the means were 4.50 as opposed to 4.30). It may be worth noting that urban school 11, which has by far the highest mean in English, and also the highest mean in Nyanja, has more than twice as many testees from non-Nyanja speaking homes than it has from Nyanja speaking homes (38 as opposed to 17), and that the former had a Nyanja mean of 6.37, whereas the latter had a mean of only 3.53. However, possible explanations for this unexpected finding (similar to that in Malawi), will not be pursued – other than to repeat that the languages involved are very similar to each other.

This lack of difference is in contrast to the findings of research carried out over 20 years ago (reported in Serpell, 1987: 172) which discovered considerable superiority in Nyanja comprehension in favour of children from Nyanja-speaking homes. A speculative explanation for these different findings is that at the time of Serpell's investigation, there was relatively little integration between various language groups in Lusaka, whereas this had increased by the time the present study was carried out, nearly two decades later. This speculation gains some support from Siachitema (1991: 478), who, in a survey which happened to be in the same Lusaka urban district as school 7 in this present research, found that there was a language shift to Nyanja in this district of the capital.

6.2.7 Comparison of English and Nyanja test results

At the school level Figure 6.6 confirms that the two urban schools have the highest means in both English and Nyanja, but the Nyanja scores in general are of course very close to chance.

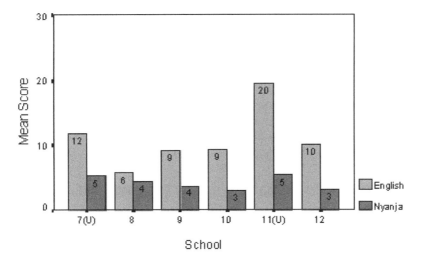

Figure 6.6 Mean scores in Nyanja and English by school, Zambia

The correlations between test scores in English and in Nyanja by school are positive but very low, and the overall correlation coefficient between the English and Nyanja test at 0.38 ($P < 0.0001$) is again low, as confirmed by the scatterplot in Figure 6.7 which shows that increasing scores in English show very little corresponding increase in Nyanja, where scores are distributed in a rather "flat" manner.

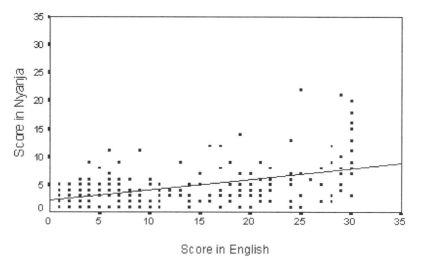

Figure 6.7 Scatterplot of English and Nyanja scores

However, the scatterplot shows that above a cut-off score of 15 in Nyanja, then English scores are high – in other words, one might claim that if testees achieve above a threshold score in Nyanja, which is not the language of instruction, then they are likely to score reasonably in the language which is that of instruction. More data with more Nyanja scores above the threshold of 15 would be needed to test such a claim.

There is, incidentally, no evidence in any of the above analyses to support the view that competence in one language is gained at the expense of competence in another. (Indeed, we may note that school 11, with the third highest English-Nyanja correlation, has the highest mean in English, as well as the highest mean in Nyanja.)

6.3 Results of African language reading tests, Malawi

6.3.1 National level

The mean score in the Chichewa test is high at 19.88 out of 30 (approximately 66%), and is obviously higher than the mean score in the English

N	Mean	Sd	Max	Med	Min
290	19.88	5.44	30	20.5	4

Reliability Index (KR-21): 0.80

Table 6.6 Summary statistics for Chichewa test results, Malawi

test, but no claim is made that the tests are of "equivalent difficulty". See 6.2.7 below for further discussion of this issue. Test reliability was also high at 0.80 (KR-21).

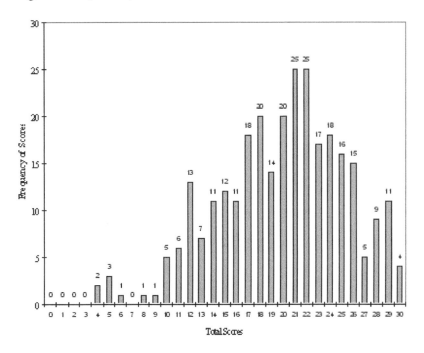

Figure 6.8 Histogram of frequency of total scores in ChiChewa, Malawi.

The histogram confirms the overall high scores; the pattern of scoring also suggests the outline of a fairly normal distribution, albeit skewed towards the high end of the range. There also a handful of very low scorers, which, as in the case of the Zambian high scorers, it was not possible to investigate individually. Facility values for the test items are high, as one would expect (see Figure 6.9).

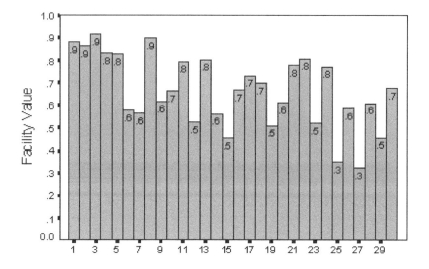

Figure 6.9 Facility values, ChiChewa test, Malawi

The items correspond to those in the Zambian Nyanja test, although as previously mentioned, there are a few minor differences. The impression from these facility values is that the African language test overall has proved rather easy for these Malawian pupils, in contrast to their Zambian peers.

6.3.2 School differences

Table 6.7 reveals clearly that inter-school differences for Chichewa are smaller than those in English.

School	N	Mean	Sd	Max	Median	Min
1	50	21.80	4.80	29	22	11
2	32	19.75	5.39	30	21	4
3 (U)	50	19.84	5.20	29	20	6
4	55	18.45	4.78	30	18	10
5	47	17.85	5.19	27	18	5
6 (U)	56	21.38	6.20	30	23	4

Table 6.7 Summary statistics for Chichewa test results by school, Malawi

The box plots (Figure 6.10) confirm this visually:

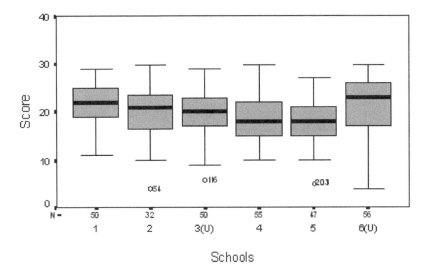

Figure 6.10 Box plot of Chichewa test results by school, Malawi

The differences are relatively smaller in ChiChewa than English, but school remains a statistically significant factor (Pr>F 0.0038) according to the GLM output. However, there are significant differences in only three pairs of comparisons, as Table 6.8 shows. The reasons for the smaller degree of differentiation are almost certainly that all pupils in all schools have access to ChiChewa; indeed, even if pupils are absent, they will still have access to ChiChewa in the community.

Mean	School	5	4	2	3	6	1
17.85	5						
18.45	4						
19.75	2						
19.84	3						
21.38	6	*					
21.80	1	*	*				

Note: * Indicates significant differences (p<0.05)

Table 6.8 Significant differences by school means, ChiChewa,
Malawi (Bonferroni)

However, bearing in mind that the test was a test of *reading* in ChiChewa, not simply of *proficiency* in ChiChewa, the results would appear to indicate that not only do pupils know ChiChewa, but that for the most part they are able to read in the language as well, a skill that they are unlikely to have acquired outside school.

6.3.3 Sex differences

Sex	N	Mean	Sd	Max	Median	Min
Boys	161	20.35	5.45	30	21	6
Girls	129	19.29	5.39	30	20	4

Table 6.9 Summary statistics for Chichewa test results by sex, Malawi

Although boys have slightly higher mean and median scores than girls in the Chichewa test, this is not statistically significant (Pr > F: 0.3271). This contrasts with the results in English, where boys were superior to a statistically significant degree. The box plots in Figure 6.11 confirm the relative lack of difference between the sexes in ChiChewa.

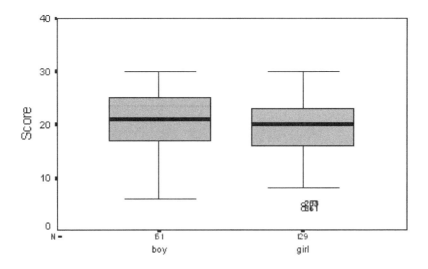

Figure 6.11 Box plots of Chichewa scores by sex, Malawi

It may be speculated that both sexes "know" Chichewa, whereas English results are more dependant on "being taught" and therefore variables such as teacher attention and accessibility of books, as well as access to English outside school, may play a more decisive role. Figure 6.12 confirms that there are no striking sex differences, but reveals a slight tendency for a higher proportion of boys than girls to score above 25, and for a higher proportion of girls than boys to obtain scores of 10 or below, with no great differences in between.

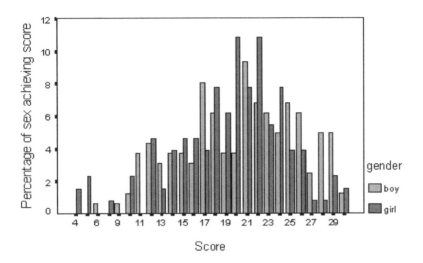

Figure 6.12 Distribution of ChiChewa scores
(as percentages for each sex), Malawi

6.3.4 Location (rural/urban) differences

There is no statistically significant urban/rural difference. While this was also true for the English test, it is evident that for Chichewa the differences are not as marked.

Loc	N	Mean	SD	Max	Median	Min
Rural	184	19.43	5.20	30	20.0	4
Urban	106	20.65	5.77	30	21.5	4

Table 6.10 Summary statistics for test score in Chichewa by location, Malawi

Needless to observe, such differences are not statistically significant. Figure 6.13 confirms this near identity of score distribution:

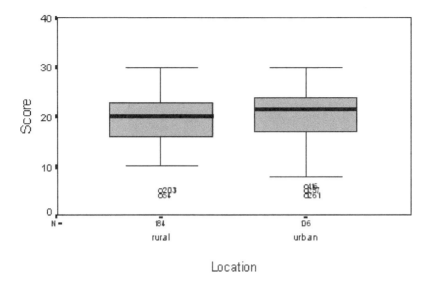

Figure 6.13 Box plot of Chichewa test scores by location, Malawi

Again, one might suggest that this similarity is due to the fact that both rural and urban children "already know" Chichewa, and that urban/rural variables in the teaching situation accordingly have less effect.

6.3.5 Sex and location differences combined

As in the English test results, rural girls have the lowest mean, and urban boys the highest, but the differences are much smaller in the Chichewa results, and not statistically significant.

Location	Sex	N	Mean	S.D.	Max	Median	Min
Rural	Boys	108	20.19	5.16	30	21	10
Rural	Girls	76	18.36	5.11	30	19.5	4
Urban	Boys	53	20.68	6.04	30	22	6
Urban	Girls	53	20.62	5.54	30	21	4

Table 6.11 Summary statistics of test scores in Chichewa
by sex and location, Malawi

An "interesting" statistic, again suggesting the relative lack of rural disadvantage, is that rural boys have the highest minimum score of 10.

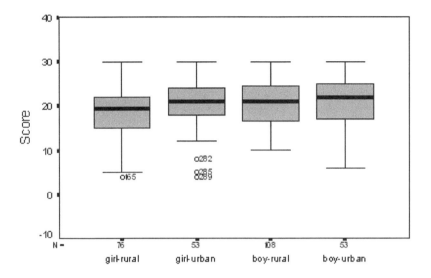

Figure 6.14 Box plot of test scores in Chichewa by sex and location for Malawi

6.3.6 Testees from non-Chichewa homes

The test was administered in Chichewa speaking areas with the majority of pupils claiming the language as their home language (237 against 53 who said that ChiChewa was not their home language). When the results were analysed for home language effect, it was found, against expectations, that those from non-Chichewa speaking homes had a very slight but not statistically significant advantage over those who claimed to speak ChiChewa at home (a mean of 20.40 as opposed to 19.77). Of the 53 pupils from non-ChiChewa speaking homes, 29 (54.7%) came from the two urban schools.

There is no immediate explanation for this lack of difference (which is similar to that for Nyanja in Zambia). In the Chichewa speaking areas investigated, the minority of children from non-Chichewa speaking homes do, of course, acquire the language from the peer group interaction, and use it in the playground. ChiChewa is therefore the "local" language of these children, if not their "home" language. We should also bear in mind the considerable similarity to ChiChewa of the languages involved here (principally ChiTumbuka, ChiLomwe, and ChiYao). The possibility that the non-ChiChewa "migrant" families have greater ambition for their children is possible, but cannot be checked, as the ChiChewa families may also be "migrants" especially in the case of the urban schools.

6.3.7 Comparison of English and Chichewa results

At the school level the relative performances of schools in the two language tests are roughly similar, although the rank order is not the same for the two languages. The histogram of mean scores by school (rounded to the nearest whole on the bar labels) confirms this:

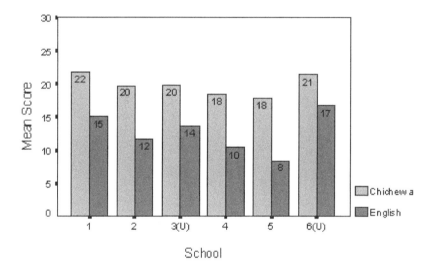

Figure 6.15 Mean scores by school in ChiChewa and English, Malawi.

Clearly the pupils have achieved higher scores in Chichewa than in English. While no claim can be made that these tests are of "equivalent difficulty", the scores indicate that the pupils overall found the Chichewa test easier, a fact that may reasonably be attributed to their greater proficiency in the language. It might of course be simply maintained that the ChiChewa test was "easier" in an absolute sense, a theoretically untestable proposition. One can only establish equivalence of two tests of different languages if "balanced bilinguals" achieve the same score in them. Unfortunately one can only establish whether people are "balanced bilinguals" through tests.

The correlation in terms of pupils' results in English and ChiChewa by school is moderately positive (from 0.4 to 0.6), but not high. The overall correlation (Spearman Coefficient) between the English and Chichewa test was 0.57 (see Table 6.12). These correlations suggest that the two tests ranked the pupils in roughly the same order. It would seem that proficiency in one of the languages is not gained at the expense of proficiency in the other, for if that were the case pupils would be good at one and poor at the other (giving a negative correlation).

Sch.	Corr.	Sig.	N
1	0.50701	0.0002	50
2	0.40555	0.0213	32
3	0.45476	0.0009	50
4	0.61487	0.0001	55
5	0.49935	0.0004	47
6	0.43943	0.0007	56
All	0.57416	0.0001	290

Table 6.12 Spearman correlation coefficients between test score in English and in Chichewa, by school

The concept of equivalent difficulty of tests in two different languages raises considerable problems, since "difficulty" depends on the competence of the population under investigation. In a British secondary school, for example, a given English test could not be claimed, in an absolute sense, to be easier than a French test simply because the pupils had scored higher on the former. The crucial question is "easier for whom?" In these tests, out of a total of 290 testees, 26 achieved higher scores in English than in Chichewa, of whom 18 came from the two urban schools, while 10 pupils achieved the same score in both tests, of whom 7 came from the two urban schools (see Table 6.13).

There are also smaller differences with respect to sex, location (urban/ rural) and school effects in the ChiChewa tests than in the English test. This is reflected in the lower standard deviation of the Chichewa score compared to the English score (5.44 as opposed to 6.22) and is more striking when compared to the mean scores (Chichewa 19.89, English 12.84), where the standard deviation in Chichewa is about 25% of the mean, and in English about 50%. The scatterplot and the regression line confirm the moderately positive relationship between the scores in the two tests. However, the points do not cluster very closely around the regression line, and one could hardly predict the score in one test from the score in another.

School	Frequency	Percent
1	5	13.9
2	3	8.3
3 (U)	9	25.0
4	1	2.8
5	2	5.6
6 (U)	16	44.4
Total	36	100.0

Table 6.13 Frequency of pupils with English scores greater than, or equal to, ChiChewa scores, by school, Malawi

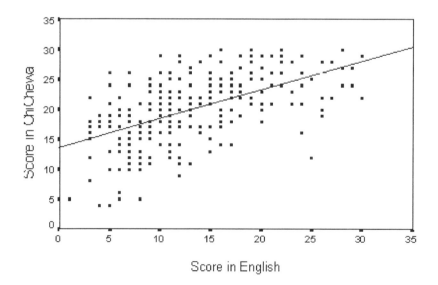

Figure 6.16 Scatterplot of scores in English and in ChiChewa, Malawi

## 6.4	African language reading – Malawi and Zambia compared

The results by country for the African language tests are summarised in Table 6.14:

Country	N	Mean	Sd	Max	Med	Min
Zambia	227	4.40	3.70	22	3	0
Malawi	290	19.88	5.44	30	20.5	4

Table 6.14 Summary statistics for African language test results, Zambia and Malawi

The considerable differences are rather dramatically displayed in the box plots (Figure 6.17):

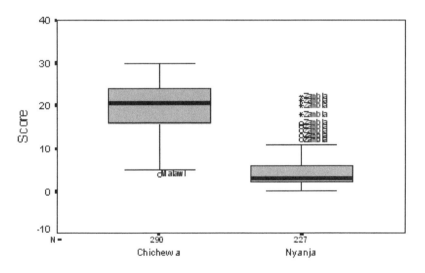

Figure 6.17 Box plot of African language reading test results, Malawi and Zambia

The most striking feature of these results is of course the vastly superior performance of the Malawian children (Pr > F: 0.0001). As already mentioned, the overall mean for Zambia at 4.4 is only just above the chance level of 4. Hypothesis B1 (that there will be no significant difference in African language reading test scores between year 5 pupils in Zambia and year 5 pupils in Malawi) is clearly rejected. If it is accepted that the Chichewa and Nyanja tests are "the same tests", then the evidence is that Malawian children read better in Chichewa than Zambian children read in Nyanja.

The African language results suggest that there is relatively little difference associated with the variables of sex and location, although probably for different reasons: in Zambia the results, although statistically significant for location, are very low (close to chance), and accordingly not meaningful. The lack of difference stems essentially from a very low level of reading proficiency in Nyanja. In Malawi, on the other hand, scores are much higher, and would suggest that most of the pupils, whether male or female, rural or urban, are competent readers at this level in ChiChewa. It is clear that tests of ChiChewa in Malawi discriminate less against girls and against rural pupils than do tests of English, and the probable reasons have already been alluded to, namely that ChiChewa is equally available to both rural and urban pupils, as well as male and female pupils.

There are, however, comments to be made on the observation that ChiChewa is equally available to boys and girls in rural and urban environments: in the first place, it is overwhelmingly spoken rather than written ChiChewa that is available; exposure to written ChiChewa is largely experienced through school. However, the relatively shallow orthography of ChiChewa, combined with the syllabic method of teaching initial reading (see Appendix 3), plus, of course, the fact that the children already know the language, may well mean that "basic reading" in the sense of being able to recognise written words, is fairly readily achieved[3], and may not be significantly affected by the girls' tendency to be absent more than boys. We may speculate that once the skill of reading has been acquired, then language competence becomes crucial, and any favourable treatment which boys may receive, in families or in schools, is insufficient to give them a large advantage. It would further appear that even if boys attend school more than girls, and thereby gain more exposure to written Chi-Chewa, and possibly more practice in reading, this is insufficient to make them significantly more fluent, in the sense of having more rapid automatic recognition of words than girls. However, no investigation of relative reading speeds was carried out, and this suggestion must therefore remain at the level of speculation.

---

[3] An untrained Zambian teacher in a community school (i.e. not a government school), claimed her pupils learned to read Nyanja using the syllabic method within 9 weeks.

6.5   Cross country comparison of English and African language results

As we have seen, English mean scores are fairly similar in both countries, while there are considerable differences between African language scores. One obvious conclusion to be drawn is that testees have generally performed better on the test in the language that is used for instruction for the first 4 years, than they have on the language that is not so used. The paired t-test confirms that the differences are, as expected, significant:

Malawi	Paired t-Test: one-tailed		Zambia	Paired t-Test: one-tailed	
	Chichewa	*English*		*Chichewa*	*English*
Mean	19.88	12.84	Mean	19.88	12.84
Variance	29.59	38.71	Variance	29.59	38.71
df	289		df	289	
t	21.53		t	21.53	
P one-tail	0.0000		P one-tail	0.0000	

Table 6.15 t-Test of differences by language of instruction,
Malawi and Zambia

However, these differences in favour of the language of instruction (English for Zambia, ChiChewa for Malawi) are relative: while English test results are roughly the same in both countries, the African language test results are very different, and to a statistically significant extent. (Recalculation of the national African language means on the basis of the "real" proportion of the urban to rural population in each country makes little difference: for Malawi the recalculated mean is 19.53 and for Zambia 4.37.)

It would seem that not using the language used by the children has resulted in a classic case of "subtractive bilingualism" in Zambia, with relatively little evidence of reading achievement in Nyanja (although this observation will need to be qualified) on the one hand, and low levels of English on the other. In Malawi, however, although one might hesitate to claim the results are in line with "additive" bilingualism (since scores in English are not high), it seems that most pupils can cope as well in English as can Zambians, and much better in the African language.

While the scatterplots (Figures 6.7 and 6.16) show that score in one language test is not predictive of score in another, there is some weak evidence, especially in the case of Zambia, that a score above a certain threshold (15 in the case of Zambia) in the language *which is not* the medium of instruction (i.e. Nyanja in Zambia) is predictive of a high score in the language *which is* the medium of instruction. In brief, it seems that if students can read reasonably in a language where they have had relatively little practice in reading, then it is highly likely that they will be able to read very well in a language in which they have had more reading practice.

6.6 Malawian performance on the Nyanja (Zambian) test

It will be recalled that it had been decided in the field to administer the Zambian (Nyanja) test to the Malawian testees, in addition to their own ChiChewa test. The test was administered to 74 children in two schools (all 47 in school 5 and a sample of 27 in school 6). The Nyanja test was done after the ChiChewa test, with a break of some 20 minutes. Because of the break, plus the fact that the children did not know that they were going to do the Nyanja test, it is unlikely that memory played a part in the result, although of course it cannot be discounted. The results for those 74 children in the ChiChewa and Nyanja tests (plus Zambian Nyanja results for comparison) were:

Country	Language	N	Mean	SD	Max	Median	Min
Malawi	Chichewa	74	19.78	5.65	30	20	5
Malawi	Nyanja	74	18.66	5.49	30	19	8
Zambia	Nyanja	227	4.40	3.70	22	3	0

Reliability index for Malawi Nyanja test (KR-21): 0.79

Table 6.16 Statistical summary of results of Nyanja reading test for Malawian pupils

These results confirm that the two tests (Chichewa and Nyanja) are of comparable difficulty for the Malawian students, and that these students are superior to the Zambian students in African language reading ability, to a highly statistically significant extent (Pr > F: 0.0001). Hypothesis B6 (that there will be no significant difference in Nyanja test scores between year 5 pupils in Malawi and year 5 pupils in Zambia), is clearly rejected.

6.7 Testing of hypotheses for African Language results – summary

6.7.1 Cross-country comparisons (Malawi and Zambia)

Overall means: The large difference in African language means (19.88 for ChiChewa in Malawi as against 4.40 for Nyanja in Zambia) is highly statistically significant. Hypothesis B1, that there would be no significant difference in African language reading test scores year between year 5 children in Malawi and year 5 children in Zambia is rejected. Accepting this result of course, means accepting that the minor differences (see section 4.3.4) between the two African language (ChiChewa and Nyanja) tests, have not yielded two "different" tests.

Source	DF	Type III SS	Mean Square	F Value	Pr > F
Country	1	27304.771	27304.771	484.16	0.0001
Location	1	240.845	240.845	4.27	0.06
School	9	507.564	56.396	2.62	0.00
Sex	1	19.037	19.037	0.89	0.3470
Homelang	1	3.111	3.111	0.14	0.7037
Model	13	1365.266	2412.713	112.29	0.0001
Error	503	10807.322	21.485		

Table 6.17 Malawi and Zambia, significance tests for African language results

When we compare the difference between the two schools in Malawi who did the same Zambian Nyanja test, and the Nyanja scores in the six Zambian schools, it is likewise large and statistically significant. As we have just noted, Hypothesis B6, that there would be no significant difference in Nyanja reading test scores between year 5 children in Malawi and year 5 children in Zambia is also rejected.

6.7.2 Within-country African language comparisons

6.7.2.1 Malawi
Sex (boys/girls) Here, the difference is very small and statistically non-significant, and Hypothesis B2, that there would be no significant difference in African language reading test scores between year 5 boys in Malawi and year 5 girls in Malawi, is supported.

Location (rural/urban) Again there is only a small and statistically non-significant difference between urban and rural scores, and Hypothesis B4, that there would be no significant difference in African language reading test scores at year 5, between children in urban schools in Malawi and children in rural schools in Malawi, is supported.

Source	DF	Type III SS	Mean Square	F Value	Pr > F
Location	1	81.986	81.986	0.74	0.4388
School	4	444.475	111.119	3.96	0.0038
Sex	1	27.020	27.020	0.96	0.3271
Home Lang.	1	1.628	1.628	0.06	0.8098
Model	7	644.749	92.107	3.29	0.0023
Error	282	7906.026	28.036		

Table 6.18 Malawi, significance tests for Chichewa results

6.7.2.2 Zambia
The Nyanja scores in Zambia were overall low and close to chance, and therefore, apart from the observation that the Zambian year 5 pupils seem to be weak at reading standard Nyanja, little weight can be attached to the results in terms of comparisons.

Sex (boys/girls) There was no significant difference in Nyanja reading test scores between year 5 boys in Zambia and year 5 girls in Zambia (Hypothesis B3).

Location (rural/urban) In terms of statistical significance, there was no support for Hypothesis B5, namely that there would be no significant difference in African language reading test scores between year 5 children in urban schools in Zambia, and year 5 children in rural schools in Zambia (see Table 6.19). In fact, the urban students have outscored the rural students to a statistically significant extent. However, as mentioned in 6.2.4 above, the mean scores were in both cases very low, being close to the chance score of 4.

Source	DF	Type III SS	Mean Square	F Value	Pr > F
Location	1	162.949	162.949	17.76	0.0135
School	4	36.699	9.175	0.69	0.5963
Sex	1	0.934	0.934	0.07	0.7905
Home Lang.	1	0.901	0.901	0.07	0.7942
Model	7	206.267	29.467	2.23	0.0328
Error	219	2892.051	13.206		

Table 6.19 Significance tests for Nyanja reading test results, Zambia

The fact that urban children in Zambia have marginally higher scores than rural children is therefore a "statistically significant but meaningless" result, although it may indicate that the urban children were in general more "test-wise".

7.   Individual Reading Sessions

7.1 The participants – assistants and students

To help carry out the individual reading sessions, three research assistants had been appointed for each country. All six either had been, or were at the time of the research, primary school teachers. Some three months before the main data collection they had received two days of initial orientation for the research. Unfortunately two of the trained assistants in Malawi, and one of the trained assistants in Zambia had to withdraw shortly before the data collection exercise. Of these three, one had received promotion to another post, one had been awarded a scholarship overseas, and in the third case a husband unexpectedly refused to let his wife travel with strangers. (He recanted, but the Primary Education Adviser refused to accept the change of heart.) These last-minute losses – amounting to half the research assistants – were replaced, but the replacements received very brief preparation. Such eventualities are not, of course, peculiar to Africa: the skills and qualities which make for good research assistants are much sought after. The assistants who eventually carried out the sessions were two men and one woman in Malawi, two women and one man in Zambia.

Students were selected for the individual sessions according to their English reading test scores (high, mid, or low), and where possible one girl and one boy at each level was chosen, making 6 students from each school, and thirty-six from each country, a grand total of seventy two. The original intention was to report on high, mid, and low scoring students separately. However, in Zambia eight of the twelve low scoring students proved to be non-readers in any language, and were therefore not appropriate for the second part of the individual sessions, namely the investigation of reading strategies. Eight mid-scoring Zambian students were therefore recategorised as low scorers for the purpose of the reading investigation (while for the interview the group is as originally selected).

The range of scores over the high and low scoring groups for all schools was:

> Malawi: High scoring range: 13 - 30; Low scoring range: 3 - 9
> Zambia: High-scoring range: 19 - 30; Low scoring range for interviews 0 - 8, and for reading sessions 1 - 17

The students were aged from 12 to 14, and it was felt they were mature enough to be able in principle to provide accurate information. No statistical analysis of significance has been carried out, since the numbers concerned are small, although there is no reason to believe that the students selected were unrepresentative.

7.2 The reading sessions

The individual reading sessions took place shortly after the tests. To reduce the stress on the individuals selected, each of them was asked to choose two friends to accompany them for the whole session. The sessions were preceded by short discussions about their family background, and biscuits and soft drinks were provided in a further attempt to put the students at ease, and as a small reward. Questions were also put to the friends, but only answers from the "target student" have been included in the quantitative reports.

The aims of the individual reading sessions were:

- to identify the difficulties in reading the text reported by high and low scorers
- to examine the extent to which high and low scorers differed in terms of difficulties encountered
- to gain insight into the strategies they employed to overcome their difficulties.

The sessions also provide an opportunity to validate the results of the reading tests.

7.3 Techniques in the investigation of reading strategies

Investigating the strategies that readers use to make sense of texts is problematic because the attempt disrupts (even more than do tests of reading), the very process that it is intended to illuminate. Researchers have nonetheless adopted a "nothing ventured, nothing gained" approach, and addressed the problem through a variety of techniques, both indirect and direct. In the former, they attempt to infer process from product, for example by scrutinizing answers to comprehension questions and inferring how readers may have arrived them; in direct techniques, on the other hand, researchers ask readers to report their thoughts directly.

Indirect techniques include reading aloud, recalling text content, or answering comprehension questions. Depending on the nature of the task associated with the text, various reader strategies may then be inferred. Thus reading aloud tasks may give insights into word recognition strategies (e.g. Goodman, 1967); recall tasks may reveal strategies of activating and using background knowledge (e.g. Steffensen and Joag Dev, 1984); comprehension questions may provide clues to a variety of strategies, from guessing word meaning by utilizing similarity of form, to utilizing background knowledge. Early opinions (e.g. Simons, 1971) that product-centred research produced little knowledge of process are misleading reactions to the product-oriented orthodoxy of that period. A popular dictum of the 1980s "You can no more infer process from product than you can infer a pig from a pork sausage" is likewise misleading, as any molecular biologist can confirm.

Direct investigation techniques involve "think aloud" procedures, where an individual reads a text, and thinks aloud or "verbalises" their thoughts, these verbalizations being then recorded and analysed. A number of procedural options are available in second language "think aloud" investigations (for example, readers may think aloud either during or after the reading; they may verbalise in their first language, or in the language of the text; the text may be marked to prompt the reader, and of course the degree of investigator intervention may vary). Direct techniques were not employed in the research with Malawian and Zambian students partly because they may not be reliable, but mainly because neither research assistants nor students were familiar with the techniques, and it would have taken more time than was available to adequately present them. In particular there is a strong risk that the students would have been confused, since their classroom experience leads them to very strong expectations that questions (whether from teachers or researchers) have right and wrong answers.

The individual sessions in this research were therefore carried out through indirect means, with which learners were broadly familiar. It should be stressed that the reading investigation was informal, and carried out by local researchers relatively inexperienced in this type of work. The questions did not have fixed wordings (or even a fixed language), they varied slightly from student to student, and the responses of the researchers to the students' answers – or lack of answers – were matters of on-the-spot subjective judgement. The time taken for the reading sessions varied from a couple of minutes (in cases where the student was clearly a non-reader) up to 20 minutes.

7.4 Individual reading of English

7.4.1 The English reading text

The English text had been specially constructed so that the topic (waiting at a bus stop) would be familiar, together with most, but not all, of the language. Five words judged unlikely to be familiar were deliberately introduced, namely: *elapsed, trundling, vermilion, snapdragons, grenadine.*

The exact meaning of these words is not crucial to an understanding of the text as a whole, and the main features of their meanings are recoverable from context. The purpose of including words which it was predicted would be unknown, was to ensure that there would be some words which students did not know, so that their strategies in dealing with these words could be investigated. The purpose of the questions (which could be asked and answered in either English or ChiChewa/Nyanja) was:

* to assess the extent to which the students had understood the text
* to investigate the difficulties that students identified in reading
* to investigate the students' inferential ability in reading
* to investigate the students' ability to attribute meaning to unknown words from context.

The text of the passage (for which the font was courier 10 cpi) was as follows:

Jane and Mary

Jane was at the bus stop. She was waiting for her sister Mary. The bus was late. After ten minutes had elapsed, the old bus came trundling along the road and stopped at the bus stop.

When Mary got off the bus, Jane was surprised. Her sister was not wearing a blue dress but a vermilion one. And she was carrying a big bunch of flowers –there were roses, daisies and yellow snapdragons.

Jane ran up to her sister. "Mary, how are you?" she said. "Where did you get that new dress, and why are you carrying those flowers?"

"Hello, Jane," said Mary. "Oh, I'm so thirsty. Let's go and have a grenadine. Then I'll tell you everything."

Sample of Suggested Questions and Prompts (asked in English or ChiChewa/Nyanja)

1)   What's this passage about?
(1a)   Where was Jane?
(1b)   What was she doing?
(1c)   Who is Mary?

2)   Is there anything you don't understand?

3a)   Was the bus late?
3b)   Why do you think it was late?

4a)   Was Jane surprised?
4b)   Why was Jane surprised?

5)   What is "vermilion"?
5a)   What was Mary wearing?

6)   What is a "snapdragon"?
6a)   What was Mary carrying?

7.4.2 Findings for the English reading sessions

Since this data is essentially "talk" it does not lend itself in all instances to quantifiable analysis. Many of the findings will be reported by quoting from the conversations between the students and the researchers (with translations where necessary), since these extracts largely speak for themselves. However, there has been some quantification of answers to comprehension questions. In assessing the acceptability of these answers, all that were deemed to indicate comprehension of the text were counted as acceptable irrespective of pronunciation or deviancy from standard grammar.

(i) Understanding the gist of the text

All of the high scoring group in both Zambia and Malawi, and most of the low scoring group (11 in Zambia, 6 in Malawi) were able to give adequate answers to the question *What's the passage about?* Acceptable responses included *It's for (sic) Jane and Mary* or *Jane was waiting for her sister.* Unacceptable responses included rereading the text, or giving responses judged to be plainly inaccurate, such as *Buying a dress.*

(ii) Direct reference questions

Direct reference questions may by definition be answered by quotation of the appropriate section of the text. The direct reference questions most commonly asked were *Where was Jane?* and *What was she doing?* These questions were generally correctly answered, although it may be that students are simply reading aloud the sentences from the text in sequence, and assuming that the questions follow that sequence. This strategy is revealed if the third sentence of the text is read out in answer to the third question as in the following sequence, which is one of many examples:

MAB27[1]
I: Where was Jane?

---

[1] In all extracts, I = interviewer; S = student; SF = student's friend. Items in the code preceding the extracts signify: 1st letter: M, Malawi; Z, Zambia; 2nd letter: school A=1, B=2 etc. 3rd letter: B=boy; G=girl; the number identifies the individual.

S: Jane was at the bus stop. *(first sentence of text)*
I: What was she doing?
S: She was waiting for her sister. *(second sentence of text)*
I: Did Mary get off the bus?
S: The bus was late. *(third sentence of text)*

Of course, in cases of inappropriate responses to questions put in English we cannot be sure if the student cannot understand the question or cannot understand the text. If the question is put in the local language, however, either the text is causing problems, or the student has acquired (possibly from classroom experience) the habit of answering questions by repeating sentences in sequence, as in the following example (it will be recalled that italics in the transcripts indicate a translation from ChiChewa or Nyanja):

MDG15
I: Where was Jane?
S: At the bus stop.
I: *What was she doing?*[2]
S: She waiting for her sister Mary. (*sic*)
I: *Did Mary get off the bus?*
S: The bus was late.

However, students generally provided acceptable answers to direct reference questions, and there does not seem to be any striking differentiation between the high and low scorers for such questions:

	Acceptable	Unacceptable	Total
High scorers	17 (81%)	4 (19%)	21 (100%)
Low scorers	18 (86%)	3 (16%)	21 (100%)

Table 7.1 Responses to Direct Reference Questions, Malawi

	Acceptable	Unacceptable	Total
High scorers	34 (97%)	1 (3%)	35 (100%)
Low scorers	12 (75%)	4 (25%)	16 (100%)

Table 7.2 Responses to Direct Reference Questions, Zambia

---

[2] As mentioned, italics in transcripts of talk indicate translation from the African language.

The relatively high scores achieved in this category by students who in other respects had great difficulties suggest that direct reference questions are unreliable indicators of comprehension. They should therefore be used with caution in the classroom and in tests, particularly where, as here, some could be answered acceptably by simply reading sentences in sequence from the text. The ease with which otherwise poor comprehenders achieve correct answers in this type of question is presumably the reason why they are employed in class "safe-talk" (see Chapter Two).

(iii) Inference questions

The questions asked in this case were of two types:

(i)   text based, where the answer may be inferred from another section of the text (e.g. *Why was Jane surprised?* where the answer provided in the text is: *Her sister was not wearing a blue dress.*)

(ii) based on the student's knowledge of the world (e.g. *Why do you think Mary was carrying a bunch of flowers?*), where the answer is not in the text, and therefore has to come from the student's head. Such suppositional or pragmatic inferences cannot be judged "right" or "wrong", but simply more or less reasonable in the light of world knowledge.

(a) Text based inference

There are a number of examples of appropriate text-based inferences are provided below (recall that italics indicate translation from ChiChewa/Nyanja):

ZEG21
I: Was Jane surprised?
S: Yes, she was.
I: Why do you think she was surprised?
S: Her sister was not wearing a blue dress.

MEG06
I: *Was Jane surprised?*
S: *Yes.*
I: Why was she surprised?
S: *At the dress Mary was wearing.*

MDG17
I: Now, was Jane surprised?
S: Jane was surprised when Mary got off the bus.
I: Why was Jane surprised?
S: (Pause) Because her sister was not wearing a blue dress.

Inappropriate inferences from the text include:

MDG15
I: Was Jane surprised?
S: Yes, she was.
I: Why was Jane surprised?
S: At the bus coming late.

ZCB04
I: Was Jane surprised?
S: Yes.
I: Why was she surprised?
S: Because she saw her sister.
I: Because she saw her sister doing what?
S: Coming.
I: Do you know the meaning of "surprised"?
S: Yes.
I: What does it mean? Can you say it in Nyanja?
S: *Surprised.*
I: *Good. Why was Jane surprised?*
S: *Because she saw her sister coming.*

The results of text-based inference questions for each country are as follows:

	Unacceptable	Acceptable	Total
High scorers	3	8	11
Low scorers	5	1	6

Table 7.3 Results of text-based inference questions, Malawi

	Unacceptable	Acceptable	Total
High scorers	2	2	4
Low scorers	2	1	3

Table 7.4 Results of text-based inference questions, Zambia

As expected, there is a tendency for high scorers to produce a greater number of acceptable responses. However, even high scorers have a degree of difficulty with inference questions.

(b) Inference from world knowledge

Here we see the effect of cultural knowledge "filling in the gaps" in the text. Reasonable answers derived from inferencing based on knowledge of the world, include the following:

ZEB08:
I: [...] did you understand the passage?
S: Yes.
I: What is it all about?
S: I thought Jane was going to a funeral.
I: What makes you think she was going to a funeral? Maybe you
     can have some ideas.
S: Because she was carrying roses, flowers.

For many Zambians funerals would be particularly associated with carry-ing flowers. In the following instances we may surmise that the students are drawing on their personal experience of why buses are late:

MAB41
I: Was the bus late?
S: Yes, the bus was late.
I: Why do you think it was late?
S: Because the driver drive the bus slowly.

ZEG21:
I: Was the bus late?
S: Yes, it was.
I: Why do you think the bus was late?
S: Because it was old.

ZDB12
I: Was the bus late?
S: Yes.
I: Why do you think the bus was late? *Why do you think the bus
     was late? What could make the bus late?*
S: *If not many people come.*

In the last example it should be appreciated that buses in Zambia and Ma-lawi often have approximate departure times from the bus station, but usually do not leave until they are almost full. The bus departure is there-fore delayed – sometimes up to a day - if there are too few passengers.

   Students may provide answers based on world knowledge even in cases where the question is intended to be a direct reference question, as in:

ZFB6
I: What was Mary carrying?
S: She was carrying a handbag and a watch.

Instead of reading aloud the expected answer "She was carrying a bunch of flowers", this student evokes the schema of a relatively well-off Malawian woman. An unusual example of an inference which almost certainly results from a linguistic error (interpreting "flower" as its homophone "flour"), combined with knowledge of the world is the following:

MBG14
I: *What was Mary carrying?*
S: *Flour.*
I: *No.*
S: Mary was carrying a big bag of flour.
I: A ...?
S: Mary was ... Mary was take bag of flour (sic).

Since the student uses the ChiChewa word for maize flour (*ufa*) in her response to first question, there seems little doubt as to her interpretation. It is in fact more likely that someone on a bus in Malawi would be carrying a bag of maize flour, rather than a bunch of flowers. Such responses provide compelling evidence that the student is attempting to construct meaning from the text, and are a positive indication.

7.4.3 Difficulties in the English text reported by students

In answer to the general question of whether they had understood the text, approximately half of the students, from both high and low scoring groups responded in the affirmative, e.g.

ZEB08
I: Did you understand the passage?
S: Yes.

Examples of negative responses include:

ZCG05
I: *Did you understand what you've read? What this passage is about?*
S: *No.*

I: *You didn't understand anything?*
S: *No.*

It is likely that those low scorers who claimed to have understood, have been conditioned by a very common routine in both countries, whereby the teacher asks the class "Do you understand?" to which the answer is always a choral "Yes" (the routine is much deplored by education advisers and teacher trainers, but nonetheless very persistent). One student, however, who read aloud haltingly and with many miscues, revised his answer under mild pressure:

ZDB13
I: *Did you understand what you read?*
S: *Did I understand?*
I: *Yes.*
S: *Yes, I did.*
I: *Sorry?*
S: *Ah, I didn't understand very much.*

However, when the interviewers asked a more specific question along the lines of "Is there anything which you don't understand?" rather than "Did you understand this passage?" then the majority of students report problems. With one exception in each country, all the difficulties identified by students were individual words. The single exception in Malawi, where difficulty did not arise from a vocabulary item, was the following:

MEG12
I: *Is there anything you don't understand in this story?*
S: *Yes.*
I: *What is it? ... What is it that you don't understand?*
S: *Where Jane was coming from.*
I: *Jane was coming from home.*

Here it is the interviewer who makes the inference! The following example from Zambia is rather more obscure, but the student does not seem to have a vocabulary problem:

ZFG17
I: Is there anything you didn't understand?
S: That Jane gave – Mary – Jane gave or greeted Mary that "Hello Jane". (sic)
I: OK – good, Jane. Now-

> S: That her sister had put on a blue dress.
> I: I can't understand because you are looking down.
> S: That her sister was putting on a blue dress.
> I: Her sister was not wearing a blue dress.

On listening to the recording, the research assistant suspected that the child was asking why Mary had simply said "Hello" rather than the more elaborate greeting normal (even when people are speaking English) in Zambia. In the second part of this extract the student is perhaps trying to ask why Mary was wearing a blue dress (although she wasn't). Such confusing moments occur from time to time in interviewing.

Apart from those examples, all other identified sources of difficulty were vocabulary items. In both countries more high scorers than low scorers (a total of 16 as opposed to 12) identify unknown words as difficulties. Possibly good readers have more confidence in admitting ignorance; possibly low scorers are not aware of what they do not know, or do not wish to admit ignorance, or have a model of response to text which does not focus on meaning. However, subsequent questioning revealed that in fact the low scorers had considerable difficulties with vocabulary.

The words most commonly reported as unknown were, as expected, one or more of the 5 words deliberately included which were prejudged to be unfamiliar (*elapsed, trundling, vermilion, snapdragon, grenadine*). In Zambia they accounted for 56 of the 66 tokens identified by students as unknown. Other words which some students did not know included: *daisies, bunch, surprised, sister, everything, thirsty.*

7.4.4 Strategies for assigning meaning in English

The main strategies that the students seem to have used for assigning meaning to unknown words may be categorised as:

(i) guessing based on the appearance of the word
(ii) use of world knowledge
(iii)using context

(i) Guessing based on the appearance of words
Guessing meanings of unknown words on the basis of their similarity to known words is the prime strategy, even if the guess appears quite inappropriate to the context. Guesses based on appearance include: *vermilion:* guessed as *chameleon, nylon* and *million; daisies:* guessed as *many days* and *days; snapdragon* guessed as *photograph* (from "snap"); *thirsty* (which

it was not predicted would be unknown) was guessed as *Thursday* (twice) and *first* (three times). Examples of such guessing include:

ZFG17
I: What other word in here was difficult for you?
S: Dai- ..dai-..
I: Daisies – so what could daisies be?
S: They can be many days.
I: Not really.

MFB19
I: Thirsty. *What is it in Chichewa?*
S: Thirsty?
I: Mm.
S: *On Wednesday,* thirsty *is Wednesday*[3].
I: *Not* Thursday, *thirsty.*
S: Thirsty.
SF: First.
I: Again?
SF: First thing.

MEB11
I: What is thirsty in Chichewa?
S: To be first.
I: Not first, but thirsty.
S: I've forgotten.

MBG20
I: *What is* vermilion?
S: *It's a million.*
I: *Not* million, *but* vermilion.
S: *I only know million.*

By a process of extension "vermilion" is also more plausibly glossed as "expensive" by four students, e.g.:

---

[3] This identification of *thirsty* as *first* is probably a function of ChiChewa phonology, which causes many ChiChewa speakers to pronounce these two words identically. English /q/ in *thirsty* is realised as [f] and the CV (consonant-vowel) phonotactic structure of ChiChewa has generated an epenthetic vowel, in this case [I], following the word final consonant in *first*. (The phenomenon of epenthesis is widely observed in the English of speakers of CV languages e.g. Japanese; see Brasington [1978] cited in Woods *et al* [1986: 142-143] for very similar examples from Rennellese, also a CV language).

MAB43
I: This word is vermilion. Now read the sentence -
S: Her sister was not wearing a blue dress but a vermilion one.
I: Now, what does the word mean?
S: *Maybe it means she bought a dress costing one million.*

"Money" is likewise for one student a plausible extension of meaning for "vermilion":

MBG14
I: What is vermilion?
S: Money.
I: No.
S: She will find you once.
I: No.
S: Was not properly dressed.
SF: "You are not properly dressed, go and get dressed again."

None of the research assistants could offer an explanation for this student's subsequent attempts; some direct questioning by the interviewer on these unexpected answers might have been illuminating. Occasionally students seem to focus on part of an unknown word only, as in the following:

MEG10
I: *That sentence is* And she was carrying a big bunch of flowers. There were roses, daisies, and yellow snapdragons. *What do you think Mary carried as she got off the bus?*
S: She carried a bag.
I: *OK. She was carrying flowers. What are* snap-dragons *then?*
S: *She was carrying her sister's photograph.*

It seems likely that snap is associated with "photograph", as photographs are widely referred to as "snaps" in Malawi and Zambia (a usage which tends now to be restricted to the older generation in the UK).

(ii) Attributing meaning from context
In this investigation, use of context to attribute meaning to unknown words is usually prompted by the interviewer, and does not appear to be a strategy that students spontaneously have recourse to. It may be that students

see an admission of ignorance as the appropriate response to a question about a word which they do not know, and possibly regard attempts to guess through context as constituting a dishonest pretence to know a word which in reality one "doesn't know". Certainly classroom observation suggests that students are not encouraged to guess meanings of words. (Classroom observations have also yielded occasional instances of teachers saying "You are lying!" in response to an incorrect answer from a student: whether incorrect answers are being judged as immoral, or whether the response is synonymous with "You are wrong!" is not clear.)

In all instances the relevant context for the words which it was anticipated would be unknown is the local context (i.e. the sentence where the word occurs or an immediately adjoining sentence), rather than global context (i.e. from the whole text). This is in line with the findings of Haynes (1993) that second language learners tend to use local context rather than global. Context, whether local or global is, of course, unlikely to yield the exact meaning of an unknown word, but rather a partial meaning. Thus in the present text students might guess that "vermilion" is a colour, but not exactly what sort of colour. Clearly there is an element of subjectivity in assessing the acceptability of these guesses; anything that indicated that a crucial semantic feature had been identified was accepted (e.g. "slowly" or "moving" were accepted for "trundling", and any colour was accepted for "vermilion"). The following are examples of acceptable prompted guessing:

ZAG06 (this student has just identified "snapdragons" as unknown):
I: OK – now could you read from where we ended "vermilion one"? After that, read the sentence.
S: And she was carrying a big bunch of flowers - there were roses...
I: Daisies.
S: Daisies and yellow snapdragons.
I: So, what does snapdragon mean from what you've read? (Pause) Again you can tell from the sentence. You can tell what snapdragon could be. In reading this sentence, just to understand the sentence. Read again.
S: And she was carrying a big bunch of flowers – there were roses ...
I: Daisies.
S: Daisies and yellow snapdragons.
I: So, what does snapdragon mean now?
S: Flowers.
I: Yes, they are a type of flower. Now you've got it. Thanks. What other word didn't you understand?
S: Daisies.

I: What could they be?

S: Flowers.

MBG11

I: What is vermilion? (Pause) What was Mary wearing?

S: Mary is wearing...

SF: Mary was wearing blue dress.

I: Yes. What did Jane think Mary would be wearing?

S: How are you?

I: No.

S: Hello Jane.

I: No. Mary was wearing a blue dress and Jane thought ... It's a ... Mary was not wearing a blue dress - *was not wearing a blue dress, but Jane thought Mary would be wearing a blue dress, but Mary was wearing* a vermilion dress. *What is* vermilion?

S: *A red one.*

MCG24

I: What is a snapdragon?

S: *I don't know.*

I: *What was Mary carrying? (Pause)*

S: A big bunch of flowers.

R: What is a rose?

S: Rose – *I think they are flowers.*

I: Then what is a snapdragon?

S: *I don't know.*

I: *You read from* "And she was carrying – (Pause, student reads silently)

S: *So they are flowers too.*

On some occasions, the interviewer devises a situational context outside the text in an attempt to help the student with the unknown word. This strategy may be thwarted by the students reacting unpredictably, as in this example:

MBG20

S: (identifies as a word she doesn't know) Surprised.

I: You mean this one? Read the sentence again.

S: When Mary got off the bus, Jane was surprised.

I: *What's the meaning? Mmm?*

S: *She was shouting.*

I: *Shouting? If you see four policemen coming in here, how would you feel?*

S: *I would be frightened.*
I: Frightened - before you are frightened, what might happen first?
S: I will tell my friend.
I: Telling a friend. Right. How would you feel if you saw your father come into school?
S: Happy.
I: Happy? Oh, what about seeing your mother coming in a pair of short trousers?
S: It would be a disgrace.
I: All right. Thanks very much.

The moral of this exchange is that local researchers do not necessarily share the same values and schemata as the students.

There is a tendency for high scorers to produce a higher frequency of acceptable answers when prompted, than low scorers. Of the words that were identified as unknown, high scorers were able to arrive at a higher proportion of acceptable answers, as the following tables indicate:

	Number of prompted occasions	Number of acceptable responses	Percentage of acceptable responses
High scorers	47	26	57.8%
Low scorers	38	9	23.7%

Table 7.5 Acceptable responses by Malawian students to prompts for unknown words

	Number of prompted occasions	Number of acceptable responses	Percentage of acceptable responses
High scorers	43	38	88 %
Low scorers	31	16	52%

Table 7.6 Acceptable responses by Zambian students to prompts for unknown words

One might speculate that high scorers are probably able to use the context more appropriately because they understand it better, and because they may have more confidence than low scorers. Again one should not read too much into the quantitative detail of the above tables, not only because the numbers are small, but also because the research assistants varied considerably in sophistication when prompting students to use context.

There are some cases where students draw on world knowledge to help them guess the meaning of a word, although of course this is identifiable only when the answers are inappropriate e.g.:

MAB27
I: What was Mary carrying? (Pause)
S: She was carrying a big bunch of flowers.
I: Yes. What is a rose?
S: There were rose, daisies, and yellow snapdragons.
I: Then what is a rose?
S: Rose is a name of a person.
I: No, in this case it's a flower.

7.4.5 The English reading sessions as validation for the test results

Although they were not conducted with great rigour, the individual reading sessions provided a measure of informal validation for the test results. The performance in the individual English reading sessions of the high scoring groups in both countries was clearly superior to that of the low scoring groups. In Zambia, of the 12 students in the original low scoring group, 7 had scores at or below the chance score of 4, and 1 had scored 5: these 8 all proved to be non-readers in the individual reading sessions.

In cases where processing of meaning is necessary (namely the text-based inference questions and attributing meaning to unknown words from context, which is also a type of text based inference), high test scorers have consistently produced a higher proportion of acceptable responses than low test scorers. (The exception to this expected tendency is the case of direct reference questions, which, as we saw, did not necessarily require the processing of meaning.) It would seem that high scorers in this study, as in the study by Jimenez *et al.* (1996), tend to monitor their comprehension, resulting in a greater readiness to report problems, although low scorers actually encounter more problems. A possible explanation for this is that the low scorers conceive of reading as simply "reading aloud" or transcoding, and if they feel they have encountered no problems in this respect, then they report no problems (c.f. Wallace, 1992: 4).

7.5 African language individual reading sessions

7.5.1 The African language reading text

The reading passage was based upon a text in the Zambian Nyanja Primary book entitled *Werenga Cinyanja* [*Read Nyanja*], MOE, Zambia: 1988-92). It occurs near the end of the year 5 course book and had therefore not been covered by the Zambian schoolchildren at the time of the research. It deals with preparations for building a school, a common occurrence in both urban and rural areas, and was therefore considered to be part of the background knowledge of students at year 5. Exactly the same passage was used for both Malawian and Zambian students, as the Malawian teachers consulted had said the lexis and orthography would be acceptable for a Malawian version.[4] The text reads as follows:

Sukulu limangidwa

Mfumu Mitulo atacoka pamudzi paja nyakwawa Kameta ndi anthu ake pamodzi ndi ena ocokera m'midzi yozungulira, anagundika nayo nchito youmba ncherwa zomangira sukulu.

Azimai ndiwo amabweretsa madzi ndi udzu wophimba pancherwa, pamene anyamata anali kuthamanga ndi zikombole. Azibambo ndiwo anali m'nkhando kumaponda dothi. Panthawiyi amuna ena anali kudala nkhuni zodzatenthera ncherwa.

Ncherwa zitakonzedwa, nyakwawa Kameta anauza Bambo Jamu omwe amadziwa kamangidwe ka nyumba za ncherwa kuti akayambeko kukumba maziko a sukulu.

Translation
Building the School
After Chief Mitulo had left the village, headman Kameta and his people, together with others from the nearby villages, started on the job of making bricks to build a school.

The women brought water and grass to cover the bricks, while the boys carried the brick-moulds. Some of the men were in the pit treading the clay and water. Meanwhile other men were busy cutting wood to bake the bricks.

When the bricks were ready, headman Kameta asked Mr Jamu, who knew how to build with bricks, to start digging the foundation for the school.

---

[4] However, as the episode concerning alternative ChiChewa/Nyanja spellings of the word for "brick" indicates, this view was not entirely born out.

Sample of suggested questions (asked in ChiChewa/Nyanja)

1. *What is this passage about?* (general gist question)
2. *Who was the village Headman?* (direct reference question)
3. *What did the women do?* (direct reference question)
4. *Who cut the wood?* (direct reference question)
5. *Why did the women cover the bricks?* (inference from world knowledge)
6. *Why did Kameta ask Mr Jamu to start digging the foundation?* (inference from text)

In addition a "probing" question such as *Is there anything you don't understand?* was generally asked in the course of the session. The words in the text which the researchers felt might cause difficulty, since they were judged to be infrequent were: "*anagundika*" (started, set about), "*zikombole*" (brick moulds), and "*nkhando*" (pit).

7.5.2 Individual African language reading session – Malawi

Of the 12 students in the high and low groups, two chose to read the Chichewa text silently, while the others read aloud. All these students were able to read aloud fairly fluently with occasional "slips" which were judged to be performance errors, rather than due to lack of competence. However, 4 of the low scoring group read slowly and did not appear to have rapid recognition of the written words; at times they were clearly "sounding out" words prior to identifying them, in the manner of beginner readers. The remaining 8 students however, appeared to read aloud fluently with rapid recognition of the orthographic forms.

The ChiChewa comprehension questions (1 to 6 above) were answered with no difficulty in all cases where they were asked. The direct reference questions (2, 3, 4) posed no problems to students. Question 5 (*Why did the women cover the bricks?*) requires an answer based on knowledge of brick making, and students in all cases volunteered acceptable answers, usually along the lines of "*To protect them from the sun.*" The answer to question 7 is provided by inference based directly on the text ("*Because Mr Jamu knew how to build*") or on an extension to that inference ("*Because Mr Jamu was good at digging*"), and again the question was appropriately answered in all cases.

As in the case of the English text, the only difficulties identified in answer to the question *Is there anything you don't understand?* are lexical items, and as in English, there is an inverse correlation between group level and identification of difficulty, with 4 readers from the high scoring group admitting difficulty, and none from the low scoring group. The word level difficulties identified by the students were: *panthawiyi* (meanwhile), *anagundika* (started, set about), *nyakwawa* (headman, adviser), *ncherwa* (bricks). This last word appears to have been identified because of its spelling: although this had not been mentioned by the Malawian research assistants, the standard spelling of the word in Malawian ChiChewa is *njerwa,* the sole spelling which features in *The Student's English-Chichewa Dictionary* (Zambezi Mission, 1986). However, the unexpected Zambian spelling does not seem to have confused these Malawian students, as this exchange makes clear:

MCG12
I: How about the second paragraph?
*SF: There is a difficult word. The word has the same meaning but
      the spelling is different.*
I: What is the word?
SF: Ncherwa.
I: What is ncherwa?
*SF: Njerwa. I know that the word is spelt "njerwa". I find the spelling
      "ncherwa" strange.*
I: Yes. Then what is "njerwa"?
SF: It is moulded soil.
I: Yes

This episode suggests that Malawian students are quite confident with respect to handling printed words where spelling varies from that which they are accustomed to, and indeed may indicate a different pronunciation. (Three other Malawian students had a third pronunciation, which would correspond to *njwera* rather than *njerwa* as the orthographic realization.)

The only point of difficulty that emerged when assistants focused on particular parts of the text was the word *nkhando* (pit): 10 students in these two groups (4 high scorers, 6 low scorers) were not able to assign the correct meaning to the word. Some responses however did contain appropriate elements, e.g. *"In the soil"* and *"People preparing soil"*. Another answer was *"Something fearsome"*. We may speculate that these students were satisfied with the interpretations they themselves had constructed (in the cases where they did so), or that they did not wish to admit to ignorance, although one did say *"I've forgotten"*. The word is not, however, crucial to an understanding of the text as a whole.

Although no attempt at quantification has been made, the clear overall impression from the recorded data, is that Malawian students are fluent and more confident in responding to the Chichewa text, as compared to the English text. There is less hesitation when they read, less quoting directly from the text in response to answers, and a far higher proportion of acceptable answers. Indeed almost every answer is acceptable. As a result, the Chichewa text is dealt with far more quickly than the English text, with the researchers being able to establish fairly quickly that the text had been processed with understanding.

7.5.3 Individual African language reading sessions – Zambia

The African language reading sessions in Zambia were a complete contrast to those in Malawi. The most striking feature was the very large proportion of students who said they were unable to read the Nyanja text, or who tried to read it, and gave up almost immediately. All 12 low scoring students, and 5 out of the 12 high scoring students, either could not or did not want to read the text (the same was true of 6 out of the 8 mid-scoring students who had been re-categorised as low scoring). In all therefore, only 9 out of these 32 students gave evidence of being able to read the Nyanja text. Given these small numbers, especially from the "low scoring" group, no quantitative reports are presented.

The following extracts are examples of the responses of students who were not prepared to read the text (again italics indicate translation from Nyanja):

ZBB7:
I: OK, now I have a passage in Nyanja which I want you to read as well. I don't know whether you want to read it out aloud or you want to read it silently.
S: I don't know how to read Nyanja.
I: You don't know how to read Nyanja?
S: No.
I: You can't try?
S: I can't.
I: You don't want to try?
S: No.
I: OK, thank you very much.

ZDB12
I: OK. Now we are going to try Nyanja. I'm sure you'll be able to do something. *Do you want to read silently or aloud?*
S: *Aloud.*
I: *Read.*
S: *Nyanja is very difficult for me. I only know a few things.*

I: Why? Don't you learn Nyanja?
S: We do.
I: But why? Because you've said that at home you use Nyanja and you've said you learn it in class? You don't like it? So you can't try even a bit?
S: Just a few bits.
I: OK, what are those few bits? What are they?
S: I just don't think I can manage.
I: Oh, OK...

ZAB14
I: (...) Now let's try the Nyanja passage.
S: You mean to read?
I: Yes, give it a try.
S: I don't know Nyanja.
I: Ah - no - give it a little try. Would you like to read to yourself or aloud, so that I can hear? (pause) Will you? You mean you can't try because it's difficult?
S: Yes.

One student, who makes an obvious effort to read the Nyanja, is forced to give up, as are the two friends accompanying him:

ZFB04
I: (...) Now would you like to try reading the Nyanja passage? It's good to try Nyanja because -
S: Oh yes, let's try the Nyanja, because it is difficult for us. (sic)
I: It is difficult for you? What about you Misheck? Is it difficult for you too?
PF1: I don't know how to read Nyanja.
I: So you don't know how to read? What about you Lufeyo?
PF2: I can try a bit.
I: So we can try - can't we? Are you going to share it or what are you going to do? Before we start reading - may I ask who is going to read?
PF2: Let me try.
I: OK, you start from here at the beginning.
PF2: Mfumu ......
I: OK, Rodney help your friend.
S: Mfumu - Ma - ah, I can't.
I: OK, Rodney can't manage. Maybe Lufeyo can try?
PF1: Mu- Mu- Mfumu ali napita pa- pa-
I: I don't think Lufeyo can manage either, because some of what

you've read is not there in this passage. But, you had a try.
Slowly but surely you will learn how to do it, as long as you
study hard at school. You know Nyanja as well as you know
English – even better.

The interviewer's final remark is something of an understatement – these students are perfectly competent in Nyanja, a language they use daily (including this very conversation); their problem is that they cannot read it. Reasons for the high incidence of refusals or failure to read the Nyanja text are discussed below. Turning to the 9 students who did actually read the Nyanja passage, all appear to have understood the gist of the passage. Typical responses include:

ZDB01
(This student read very hesitantly, sounding out most words)
I: What does the passage talk about?
S: It talks about a school.
I: What about it?
S: Building a school.

ZFG17
(The student had read slowly but seemingly with comprehension)
I: So what is the passage about?
S: That he went to the father. (sic)
I: OK, that's there in the passage, but what's the main thing in the
*   passage?*
S: That the school will be built.

A total of 20 direct reference questions were asked, and (with one exception) all were answered appropriately, e.g.:

ZCB04
I: Which chief came from that village?
S: Chief Mitulo.
I: Who brought the water?
S: Women.
I: What about the men? What were they doing?
S: They were trampling the mud.

The single inappropriate answer occurs in the following exchange:

ZEG21
I: What did the women do?

> S: *They brought the water.*
> I: *What else?*
> S: *Cut wood for cooking.*

This answer is clearly an inference from the student's knowledge of the world rather than the text. Knowledge of the world is also the source of another student's inappropriate attempt to give the gist of the final paragraph:

ZAB11
I: In the first paragraph, you can't understand anything?
S: No.
I: Not even anything (*sic*)?
S: I only understood the last paragraph.
I: What was it saying?
S: Money for buying cement for the school.

The Zambian researchers identified the same potentially difficult words as the Malawians, namely: *anagundika* (started on, undertook), *zikombole* (brick moulds) and *nkhando* (pit). Other words which the researchers asked the students about were *nyakwawa* (headman, adviser), *ncherwa* (bricks) and *zodzathenthera* (burning/firing).

Students were asked about these 6 words a total of 23 occasions. On 14 occasions students gave appropriate responses spontaneously, while on 4 occasions they were prompted to the answer, and on 5 occasions the answers were inappropriate. Examples of correct answers from prompting include:

ZCB13
> I: *What about this word "nyakwawa"? What does it mean?*
> S: *"Nyakwawa"?*
> I: *Yes, "nyakwawa", what do you think it could mean?*
> S: *It's too hard for me.*
> I: *"Mfumu Mitulo atacoka pamudzi paja nyakwawa Kameta ndi anthu ake pamodzi ndi ena ocokera m'midzi yozungulira" Now whenever you read "nyakwawa Kameta and his people", what do you think it means?*
> S: *The adviser.*
> I: *Good. That's it.*

ZEG21
> I: *What about "ncherwa", do you know it?*
> S: *Isn't it those fruits?* [probably thinking of "nchele", the strangler fig]

I: *No, I'm talking about "ncherwa" since they are talking about*
     building a school. What do you think they are?
S: *Isn't it that rope for tying?*
I: *What's that?*
S: *The rope that's made from tree bark.*
O: *No, it not that, because "ncherwa" are made from mud.*
S: *They are bricks.*

Examples of inappropriate responses include:

ZFG17
I: *What are "ncherwa"?*
S: *I don't know.*
I: *What do you think "ncherwa" is?*
S: *That you are late* [probably thinking of the verb "-chedwa", to
     be late]
I: *You mean you don't know "ncherwa"? OK.*

ZFG17
I: *What about this one "zodzatenthera"? What does it mean?*
S: *Where is it? What?*
I: *Zodzathenthera.*
S: *That you will stop crying* ["kuphudzya", to stop crying]
I: *What is "kuphudzya"?*
S: *When you are crying - then you stop crying.*

As in the case of English, the above cases seem to indicate a tendency to attribute meaning to unknown words based on their appearance, or similarity to known words, rather than through using context (although the last example does not accord readily with such an explanation). The general impression of the researchers concerning the nine students who read the Nyanja text is that two had only a very general idea of what the text was about, while seven appeared to have reasonable comprehension, although they had difficulties with individual words.

The relationship between a student having Nyanja as a home language and whether or not that student read the Nyanja text was as follows:

Home language	Did read	Didn't read	Totals
Nyanja	3	14	17
Not Nyanja	6	9	15
Totals	9	23	32

Table 7.7 Students who read Nyanja and claimed Nyanja as home language

Unexpectedly, more students from non-Nyanja home language backgrounds read the Nyanja passage as from Nyanja backgrounds (6 out of 15 as opposed to 3 out of 17). Furthermore, the two highest Nyanja test scores among these 32 students (scoring 21 and 20) came from students who were from non-Nyanja speaking backgrounds, while the highest scorer from a Nyanja speaking background scored 13. The research assistants' view was that the spoken Nyanja of those from non-Nyanja speaking homes was indistinguishable from that of their colleagues.

Nyanja is a language that is used by most of these Zambian students at home, by all of them on a daily basis with their friends, and is also, at least officially, the Zambian language taught in their primary schools. Their poor overall performance in reading it is probably due to two reasons. First the variety of Nyanja used for the individual reading, and second, lack of exposure within the school (and outside) to written Nyanja; both possibilities are discussed below.

7.5.4 Comparison of the African language reading sessions and the reading test results

As in the case of the English test, findings of the individual African language reading sessions were examined to see if they provided informal concurrent validation for the results of the African language reading test. In Malawi, both high and low scoring groups seemed to have comprehended the ChiChewa text equally well. However, this is not surprising since high and low scoring groups were based on scores on the English test, not the ChiChewa test. In the latter test, although the low scoring Malawian group has a lower mean in the Chichewa test than the high scoring group, the mean difference between the two groups is relatively small, as Table 7.8 shows:

Group Level	Mean score English	Mean score Chichewa
High scoring	24.25	24.25
Low scoring	6.92	18.17

Table 7.8 Mean scores of high and low scoring groups in English and Chichewa reading tests, Malawi

The mean score for the high scoring group is, surprisingly, exactly the same (24.25) in English as in Chichewa. Higher scores in English than in

Chichewa occur in 5 of the 12 students in high scoring group, while this is not the case for anyone in the low scoring group.

In the view of the research assistants in Malawi, the evidence of the reading investigation is that even the low scoring group could understand the bulk of the Chichewa text. However, there are no scores below 13 on the ChiChewa test for any of those who took part in the individual reading sessions. Even those who scored 13 (3 in all) seem, on the evidence of the transcripts, to have understood the bulk of the text.

In short the reading sessions provide positive validation, for the ChiChewa/Nyanja test results, in the sense that some students do well on both reading sessions and test. Others, however, score only in the mid-range on the test, and yet seem to cope with the text as well as high test scorers. There is of course no one who scores reasonably on the test and is not able to read the text. This suggests that the ChiChewa reading passage was rather easy compared with the test for these Malawian students.

As far as the Zambian groups are concerned, the high scoring group has a mean in the English test which is comparable to that of the Malawian high scoring group's (24.25). In the Nyanja test results, however, their mean is much lower. The low scoring Zambian group, as might be expected, achieves very low scores not only on the English test, but also on the Nyanja test, with a mean lower than the chance score of four in both cases. Indeed, as previously mentioned, eight of the twelve original low scorers could not, as far as could be ascertained, provide evidence that they were able to read in any language, and had to be replaced by students from a mid-scoring group.

Table 7.9 provides the means scores for these groups:

Group Level	Mean score English	Mean score Nyanja
High scoring	25.83	8.17
Low scoring (1)	3.33	2.25
Low scoring (2)	10.17	3.33

Table 7.9 Mean scores of high and low scoring groups in English and Nyanja reading tests, Zambia

Note: Low scoring (1): the original 12 students in the low scoring group
Low scoring (2): the reconstituted group with 8 non-readers substituted by mid-scorers

Again we can see that the Zambian individual reading investigations support the validity of the Nyanja test results. The mean score on the Nyanja tests of all 32 Zambian students who were selected for the individual reading investigation is 4.8, while the mean scores on the same tests of the 9 students who were actually able to read the Nyanja passage is 10.2. This, taken with the extremely low mean score (2.25) of the original low scoring group who included 8 non-readers, suggests that the results in the Nyanja tests are a fair reflection of actual reading competence in Nyanja.

7.5.5 Conclusion on African language reading

The Malawian superiority in ChiChewa reading tests is supported by the findings of the reading investigation, in which all Malawian students were judged to have read the text with understanding, while fewer than a third of Zambian students were prepared even to read the text. There appear to be two reasons for the difference between the Malawian and Zambian groups: the first is to do with the fact that the variety of Nyanja which the Zambian students know (their L1 in most cases) differs from the Nyanja used in the tests; the second, and probably the more substantial reason, is the lack of attention to African languages in Zambian primary schools.

The variety of Nyanja in which many Zambian students are competent is "town Nyanja" (see Kashoki, 1990: 137; Serpell, 1987: 147; de Gaay Fortnum, 1978: 182). This is a non-standard variety characterised by lexical borrowing from English as well as other Zambian languages, together with syntactic deviancies from standard Nyanja. On the other hand, the "standard Nyanja" of the Zambian language course books is a different variety, based on a rural variety from the Eastern province, which is generally regarded as a "purer" or, in the African metaphor, "deeper" variety. De Gaay Fortnum (1978: 182) points out that "A variety has now developed which may be called "Lusaka Town Nyanja" but this is far from standardised. The Nyanja taught in Zambian primary schools, both in the Eastern Province and in Lusaka, is supposed to be Nyanja as it is spoken in Zambia's Eastern Province."

Thus many Zambians are more familiar with the "Town Nyanja" term *mabirikisi* (from the English "bricks", but with Nyanja *ma-* as a plural marker, and influenced by Nyanja consonant-vowel phonological structure) rather than the "school standard Nyanja" *ncherwa*. It is significant that while one Zambian boy in the reading investigation sessions only knew the borrowed form *mabrikisi*, for "bricks" but not the standard *ncherwa*, a Malawian girl could not only read and understood *ncherwa*, but was able to cope with this unfamiliar spelling of the word. Kashoki (1990: 139-140) provides a number of other borrowings from English largely to do with "objects and concepts of the lending culture" (*ibid*: 130). In terms of syntax, de Gaay Fortnum (1978: 186) cites children in Lusaka producing the non-standard noun phrase *nyumba awiri* ("two houses"), rather than assigning *nyumba* ("house") to the *zi*-class of nouns and attracting the appropriate prefix (*zi*-) to -*wiri* ("two") to yield standard Nyanja *nyumba ziwiri* ("two houses"). There were a number of references by the Zambian students to the problem caused by the difference between their language variety and that used in the course books e.g.:

ZDB12
I: *By the way, why do think this Nyanja is difficult for you? Is it*
      different from the one you speak?
S: *Yes.*
I: *How is this Nyanja here?* [indicating text]
S: **This is very deep.**
I: *But if you studied hard, you could understand it, couldn't you?*
S: *Yes.*

The Zambian students are well aware of these differences between "town Nyanja" and "standard Nyanja" and also of the fact that the former is used in speaking and the latter in writing, as the following extracts (with the significant comments in bold) indicate:

ZEG21
S: *I don't know Nyanja so well.* **The way we read it is different**
      from the way we speak.
I: *So, if the Nyanja that you speak is what you were given to read,*
      would you like it?
S: *Yes.*

ZDB19
I: *Do you like Nyanja?*
S: *Writing Nyanja?*
I: *Yes.*
S: *No.*
I: *What about speaking?*
S: *Yes, we like it a lot.*
I: *Why do you like speaking Nyanja, but not writing?*
S: *Because* **when we are told to write, we are given different things,**
      things that are spoken by other people, and not the Nyanja we
      speak.

The fact that these students are faced with an unfamiliar variety of their own language when reading has certainly caused them difficulties, and may possibly have alienated some of them. However, if standard school Nyanja had been taught consistently from year one, and students had achieved literacy in it, then not only would it be more familiar to students by the time they reached year 5, but such teaching could contribute to disseminating the standard form. The prevailing attitude in Zambia is that "town Nyanja" is not appropriate for formal educational purposes. The lack of acceptance of non-standard varieties in the educational domain is widespread in countries other than Zambia, of course, and there is a parallel in the attitude towards standard English in the UK, where school children from non-standard language backgrounds may initially be unfamiliar with standard forms although they acquire them over time (Williams, A., 1989). Of course, Nyanja is not the only language in Zambia with standard and non-standard varieties. Indeed, not one of Zambia's seven official languages is standardised with respect to dialectal variation "as regards pronunciation, grammar or vocabulary" according to Kashoki (1990: 75).

While caution is usually urged on attempts to claim causality from correlation, it is difficult to see any alternative explanation for Malawian students' superiority in the African language reading tests other than the fact that Chichewa is used as the language of instruction for the first four years in Malawian primary schools, while English is used for that purpose in Zambia. This means that Malawian students are accustomed to seeing standard Chichewa in written form. Zambian students on the other hand, rarely see Zambian languages in written form inside their classroom, and even more rarely outside it (in Malawi, on the other hand, one may see posters, comics and sections of newspapers in ChiChewa).

Not only were Zambian languages not used as media of instruction, they were also neglected even as subjects in primary school teaching, despite the fact that provision is officially made for teaching them for 4 thirty minute periods per week. The reason for this neglect is identified in *Focus on Learning* (MOE, 1992: 45):

> Teachers teach what is examined. (...) Curriculum areas that are not examined are not likely to be taught or learned. (...) The present practice is to attach theoretical importance to Zambian Languages and to practical subjects. But the examination results in these areas do not contribute in any way to the overall mark for secondary selection[5].

This neglect of Zambian languages is also born out by what the students say in interviews, as the following extracts reveal:

---

[5] Zambian languages have in recent years counted towards selection (Linehan, 2004: 4).

ZAG13:

I: Don't you do Nyanja?

S: We sometimes do Nyanja, but it was a long time ago. We did it from time to time unless English, we learn English every day. (sic)

ZFB09:

I: Why didn't you want to read Nyanja?

S: We don't know it.

I: But don't you study Nyanja?

S: We study it sometimes, once in a while.

ZEG21:

I: Was it [the Nyanja passage] *difficult for you?*

S: It was.

I: Why?

S: Because we don't know the words.

SF: We don't learn Nyanja. We used to do it in grade 4.

I: OK, but you know how to speak Nyanja?

S: Yes.

I: So why is it difficult for you to read?

SF: I used to like Nyanja when our teacher was a woman – Mrs. [..] and Mrs. [...]. They used to teach us Nyanja a lot.

I: What about the man you have now?

S: He doesn't teach us Nyanja.

I: So because you've stopped doing Nyanja, you've come to dis like it?

S: No, we've just forgotten it.

Precise information on how much teaching of Nyanja these students had experienced in their school careers was not sought, and indeed reliable information would have been difficult to obtain. In this connection it is of interest to note that Verhoeven and Aarts (1998: 130) conclude that "although L1 instruction takes up only a very modest part of the timetable in Dutch schools, Turkish children in the Netherlands appear quite proficient at acquiring literacy in their L1". However, the authors give no indication of actual time spent on Turkish. In addition the respective community literacy practices in, as well as attitudes towards, Turkish and Nyanja are almost certainly different. The prevailing language ideology in Zambia, challenged only by very few, is that English is "strong" and Zambian languages "weak": classroom practices and students' attitudes appear to flow from that ideology.

8. The Language Dilemma in African Schools

8.1 General

The main findings which emerge from the tests, interviews and individual reading investigations that have been described in previous chapters, are:

- In English reading proficiency there is little difference between Malawian and Zambian students at year 5, although the Zambians have officially had English medium teaching for the previous 4 years (i.e. throughout their schooling), while the Malawians have only had English as a subject during the same period.
- As far as local language is concerned, Malawian students appear in general to be very proficient in reading their local language – ChiChewa – whereas the overwhelming majority of Zambian students from Nyanja speaking areas have extremely low proficiency in reading their local language – Nyanja.
- There are considerable urban/rural differences in English reading proficiency in both Malawi and Zambia, with the urban areas outperforming the rural areas. However, the superior urban averages conceal a large urban "tail" of low scores
- In both Malawi and Zambia, many students do not appear to see reading in English as a "meaning making" process, possibly because their level of English is too low. They are highly text and word bound, and do not apply inferencing strategies to textual relations or word meanings when reading English. This approach to reading is encouraged by a teaching style which focuses on reading as reading aloud, and seems to give higher priority to pronunciation rather than to understanding.
- In Malawi the findings suggest that English discriminates against rural students and against girls, with rural girls having by far the lowest average English scores. However, the test results in ChiChewa suggest that ChiChewa does not discriminate against rural students and girls.

It was not, of course, possible to completely control all variables in such a naturally occurring experiment. The independent variables which could not be controlled include class sizes, the book per student ratio, the amount of time devoted to language teaching (both English and national languages) in previous years, and the degree of teacher absences in each country.

Such uncontrolled variables have probably had only a marginal effect on results, and could by no means account for the large differences in local language reading performance. In short, despite this lack of control, and the limited nature of the school samples, personal experience plus the views of experienced local professionals, suggests that the main findings outlined above are an accurate representation of reading proficiency in English and in the local languages in these two countries[1].

8.2 Language in reading in Malawi and Zambia

In Chapter Two it was claimed that two necessary, although not sufficient, capacities which people need in order to be able to read texts in a given language, are: (i) the ability to recognise as words the marks on the page, blackboard etc., and (ii) competence in the language concerned. Although the interactive theory suggests that compensation may come into play (such that language knowledge may compensate for poor word recognition through decoding, or that background knowledge may compensate for language deficiencies) it is clear that inadequate reading will occur when the threshold level of language competence is too low for any sort of compensation to be effective, a common-sense notion supported by the studies of Bernhardt and Kamil (1995), Carrell (1991), and Lee and Schallert (1997), referred to in Chapter Three.

    If we apply the above views to these research findings, it seems that the ability of most Malawian students to read and comprehend success-fully in ChiChewa is in part due to the fact that they have competence in this language. Furthermore, the syllabic method of teaching initial reading has enabled them have an understanding of the letter-sound correspond-ences of written language (aided by the "shallow" orthography of ChiChewa), which means that Malawian children learning to read have insight into the principles of representation of ChiChewa in writing. They are accordingly able to operate in an interactive manner in reading that language, helped by both their language competence and their decoding ability. Thus, although even in ChiChewa reading classes at years 4 and 5, Malawian learners are taught through the repetitive "look and say"

---

[1] Another reason for placing confidence in the results is that the IIEP/SACMEQ surveys at year 6 for both countries, which involved very large numbers of schools and students, and a sophisticated sampling procedure, produced almost identical results to research reported in Williams 1993a and 1993b (see Chapter Three for details). I have no doubt that the schools selected for the research reported in this book are as representative as those selected for the 1993 research.

method, what is important is not only that they have insight into the system of representation, but crucially they are in a position to understand what they are "looking at and saying". In brief it seems likely that the syllable-based methodology plus language competence play a positive role in the Malawian success in teaching reading in the local language, a success achieved in the face of school conditions that are among the most materially impoverished in the world. Their proficiency represents a considerable achievement, and the methods by which it has been achieved should not be lightly put aside. One of the main dangers to the high quality of reading in local languages in Malawi is interference from Western "experts" who have prejudices against the teacher-centred classroom, or phonic approaches to initial literacy. The research reported here suggests that the teacher-centred classroom in Malawi is successful to the extent that most students learn to read, despite classes which have a hundred or more students, and despite a severe shortage of books. This is not an achievement to be set aside at the behest of international "experts" or "early years specialists" on flying visits to the country – especially in cases where literacy levels and second language learning are not exemplary in the "expert's" own country, despite its manifest material advantages.

However, although Malawian students are adept at phonological decoding in ChiChewa, there is little evidence in the reading sessions that they employ this strategy very often in English; possibly they are influenced by the predominance of the "look and say" approach in the teaching of reading in English, possibly inhibited by the irregular spelling of so many English words. Moreover, even if they did employ such phonological decoding, it would not assist greatly in their construction of meaning, since, given their limited vocabulary in English, they would not be able to match the result of their phonological decoding to items in their mental lexicon – in brief they would not recognise the words because they don't know many words.

Turning to the Zambian learners reading in Nyanja, it seems that not only do they have problems arising from being speakers of a different (non-standard) variety of Nyanja, but that the teaching of reading in standard Nyanja is neglected. The Zambian learners have not been provided with an explicit word attack strategy in their own language (which either the phonic or syllabic approach might have given), and they do not seem to have induced such a word attack strategy from the "look and say" approach, almost certainly because they have had very little exposure to it in their local language. Unsurprisingly, they have not induced such a strategy from their English reading either – again the "look and say" approach would hardly encourage such an inductive process. The "whole word" approach to reading has accordingly left the majority with no strategies to cope with words which they have never before seen in print, in either English or Nyanja. However, as in the case of the Malawian students, the very limited English vocabulary of many Zambian students means that even if they had acquired phonic attack strategies for words in English, it would serve relatively little purpose.

The fact that some Zambian children in the individual reading sessions had scored reasonably in the English test, and could read the English text well, yet were unable or unwilling to read the Nyanja text, if only at the level of decoding of individual words is rather puzzling. A similar finding is reported by Serpell for adult Zambians who are competent *readers* in English and also competent *speakers* of a Zambian language. Serpell surmises (1989: 101) that this may be due to:

> [A]n inappropriately difficult introduction to the skill of reading [...]
> My hypothesis is that some people are taught reading as an activity
> that is too closely tied to one particular language.

Although in the present research a small number of high scorers in English did achieve reasonably high (15+) scores in Nyanja, one might have expected instances of transfer of reading ability to have taken place from more of those who obtained high scores in English. As intimated previously, the simple view that reading is made up of language competence and reading ability is too simple. Insufficient practice of reading in the language concerned is almost certainly a part of the reason for the weak performance of these Zambian children, although for the moment we can, like Serpell, only hypothesise.

8.3 Lexical competence in English

There is some evidence of a low level of lexical proficiency in English in both Malawian and Zambian students: the evidence of the reading sessions was that a number of words which it was assumed would be known to most students, proved to be unknown to many. They included *surprised, sister, everything,* and *thirsty.* All four words had already featured in previous years in both the Zambian and Malawian English course books.

The total number of English words taught in both countries by the end of year 4 is not large: 840 words for Zambia (MOE, *Writers Guide: Word List* n.d: 1), and approximately 1,300 for Malawi (MOE, *Teacher's Books,* 1965-68*).* The word lists for both countries are a mixture of head words and grammatical items, particularly prepositions. Of course, students the world over do not learn all the words they are exposed to in the foreign language class, so low levels of lexical competence are not entirely unexpected. While the size of individual students' vocabularies is probably as varied as their test scores, it would seem that the "average students" have, at the beginning of year 5 a very small English vocabulary, insufficient to allow them to learn through reading in English as they are now meant to do. A similar situation obtains in South Africa, where Heugh (1999: 303) notes that:

> Macdonald (1990 pp. 137-144) discovered that African language speakers had exposure to about 800 words in English by the end of 4 years of school. However, they needed to have 5000 words of English in order to cope with the content of education in the fifth year of school, the point at which there was an abrupt transition to English. This in itself was problematic.

8.4 Explaining differential reading proficiencies

If consistent repetition over time explains the superiority of the Malawian students in reading the local language, then an obvious question is why do Zambian children – with 4 years extra of English as a medium of instruction – not demonstrate higher proficiency overall in reading English than their Malawian counterparts? The answer probably lies in the dominant pedagogic practice in both countries: as the reports on lessons and the lesson transcripts show, teachers rely very heavily in reading lessons on the "look and say" (whole word and whole sentence) approach, with no attention to the presentation or checking of meaning. This results, as has been pointed out, in "reading-like" behaviour, where students *behave* as if they have automatic recognition – at least while the "look and say" drill is being carried out. The teachers appear to be aiming for a performance which focuses on reading aloud as a product, but which short-circuits the psycholinguistic process of reading.

Experimental work (e.g. Segalowitz *et al.*, 1991: 22) suggests that consistent repetition, such as Malawian students undergo in reading ChiChewa[2], improves speed of automatic recognition in reading. However, automatization of reading skill does not result from repetition alone.

---

[2] No ChiChewa or Nyanja lessons were recorded in this research, but ChiChewa year 4 and 5 lessons which have been observed at other times indicate high levels of repetition.

Segalowitz *et al.* claim that "the issue will be how consistently and frequently a given *meaning* representation is associated with its graphemic representation by the language user" (1991: 22, my italics). Thus, it seems reasonable to suggest that an important reason as to why reading classes in English are relatively unsuccessful in Zambia, whereas reading classes in ChiChewa in Malawi are successful, despite the fact that at years 4 and 5 similar methods are employed, is because in the Zambian case students do not understand what they are repeating, whereas in the Malawian case they do. However, with respect to English reading, as opposed to local language reading, Malawians are in almost the same weak position as Zambians. In short, a major contributory factor to poor reading proficiency in English in the primary schools of both countries is low competence in English.

Language competence, of course, enables readers to deploy "psycho-linguistic guessing" (see Chapter 2) as a strategy to help cope with problems. However, in the case of English, it is not possible for "psycho-linguistic guessing" to be a very productive strategy since many students have low competence in the language. Serpell (1989: 99) cites an unpublished paper by Hvitfeldt (1978) on the behaviour of young Zambian children learning to read which:

> [S]hows very clearly that the mistakes made when guessing a word by those who do not speak English at home are quite different from the guesses made by young English-speaking children using the same books in Zambian schools.

While the discussion in the previous paragraph is somewhat speculative, the moral of the Malawian achievement would appear to be that if resources are scarce, there is a greater likelihood of success in attempting to teach students to read in a known local language, rather than an unknown one. The issue of a known language is crucial – as the test results indicate for Malawian students for whom ChiChewa is not a home language, it is knowing the language, not whether it is a mother tongue, that is important (c.f. Webb, 1999: 357 footnote 7).

An obvious consequence of the heavy reliance on choral repetition is that there is relatively little attention to individual students (apart from the small *élite* known to be competent who supply model readings and answers to comprehension questions). This is possibly a contributory reason to the overestimates by teachers in both countries of the likely test scores of their students. Actual means and teachers' pooled estimates for the English tests were as follows:

	Malawi	Zambia
Urban teachers' pooled estimates	21.33	21.83
Actual urban means	15.29	16.33
Rural teachers' pooled estimates	17.50	16.00
Actual rural means	11.43	8.46

Table 8.1 Pooled teacher estimates and actual scores, English test

Teachers were specifically asked to bear in mind the very weak students, and also estimate what the average student actually "would score", and not "should score". The overestimates suggest that teachers are not familiar with their students' capacities, or that they could not make the connection between those capacities and likely test score. The situation regarding teacher estimates for local language tests is rather different:

	Malawi	Zambia
Urban teachers' pooled estimates	25.50	23.33
Actual urban means	20.65	5.41
Rural teachers' pooled estimates	23.67	14.00
Actual rural means	19.43	3.68

Table 8.2 Pooled teacher estimates and actual scores, local language test

In Malawi we see that the estimates are close to the actual scores. It may be that the teachers have a more accurate judgement of a language that they are more familiar with, and use in "real" communication with the students. However, in the case of Zambia, there are huge discrepancies, and it would seem that teachers have made unwarranted assumptions about their students' competence in reading Nyanja.

8.5 Learning in English across the curriculum

It is difficult to interpret with precision these English test results in terms of the students' comprehension of other school texts. Setting a threshold comprehension score on a reading comprehension test, above which we may assume that students can read with comprehension in other subjects, and below which they cannot, is a hazardous undertaking, and one that would require validation through empirical investigation of reading in other subjects. However, one might reasonably suggest that, since the language in the English reading test was overwhelmingly drawn from year 4 or below of their English course books, then a score of 15 or fewer out of 30 probably suggests that the testees are unable to independently read and understand the material in their year 5 subject course books. In Malawi 203 students out of 290 (70%) were in this position, and in Zambia 150 out of 227 (66.1%). This should not be interpreted as indicating that those scoring above 15 can read English texts in other subjects. This conclusion is roughly in line with previous findings concerning the ability of students in Zambia and Malawi to read across the curriculum. Williams (1993a and1993b) estimated that 74% of Zambian students and 78% of Malawian students at year 6 had "inadequate reading comprehension", while the SACMEQ studies (Nkamba and Kanyika, 1998; Milner et al, 2001) con-cluded that 74.2% of Zambian students and 78.4% of Malawian pupils at year 6 did not reach a minimum "level of mastery" in reading English. The present research suggests that at least two thirds of the students in each country are highly likely to have difficulties in understanding their English school texts in other subjects, and that very few of the remaining third have fluent comprehension.

If students cannot cope with material from their English course books then it follows that they will not be able to understand their content subject course books, for the latter make even greater demands on their English than the former. There must be questions as to the extent to which most year 4 students in Malawi can read with understanding extracts such as the following from their *New Arithmetic* book (MOE, 1980: 75):

(i) When a whole one is divided into 10 equal parts, the parts are called fractions. One tenth is written 1/10 as a vulgar fraction or 0.1 as a decimal.
[...]
(iv) tenths, hundredths, thousandths are usually written as decimal fractions using the **decimal notation** which is based on the **tens number system**. A decimal point (.) is used to separate the whole ones from fractions (or parts) of the whole one.
(v) Also remember how the decimal point is used in money, length, weight (mass) and capacity to separate whole ones from fractions of the whole ones. Money and measures are all based on the **tens number system** or decimal system. You will learn more about this later. (Bold in original.)

As noted in Chapter Two, English appears "unofficially" to have entered into the Malawian arithmetic syllabus. While it is possible that some students have acquired the necessary concepts and associated vocabulary to process the specialised vocabulary in such texts, it would seem highly unlikely that this is the case for the majority, given the low level of achievement on tests tied to their English course books. Similar problems of employing English across the curriculum are reported from South African primary schools (McDonald, 1990, cited in Chick, 1992: 33), where the amount of English up to and including year 2 is said to be inadequate for the sudden transition to English medium at year 3.

It is difficult to see how the majority of students in Zambia and Malawi can learn other subjects successfully through reading in English. The blunt conclusion that, in fact, they do not, is supported by the Zambian Ministry of Education report *Focus on Learning* (MOE, 1992: para. 5.4), which claims that:

> Too early an emphasis on learning through English means that the majority of children form hazy and indistinct concepts in language, mathematics, science and social studies. A number of studies in Zambia have confirmed that children's subsequent learning has been impaired by this policy.

This opinion[3] is confirmed by the previously mentioned research report from Kitwe Teachers' College in Zambia (Chikalanga, 1990: 69; see also section 2.6) which concludes, after testing 583 year 5 children, that:

> [T]here is a large group of very poor readers in most classes and they are unlikely to be able to cope with the English course of the New Zambia Primary Course *nor be able to do much of the work in other subjects*. (my italics).

Apart from weaknesses in the English of students, classroom observation and discussions suggest there are also weaknesses in the English of some teachers. This weakness probably contributes to the excessively text-bound nature of the English reading lessons, and of content lessons. Typically the latter are taught in much the same way as an English reading lesson – the text is read, then questions are asked which simply require the student

---

[3] See Trudell (2005: 240) for similar views from the Cameroons.

to repeat sentences from the text. Such "safetalk" does not serve the cause of conceptual clarification. On the anecdotal level, I have observed lessons in Malawi dealing with the human heart and the structure of flowers, where "auricles" "ventricles" "stamens" and "pistils" were read aloud and copied into students' exercise books, but where there was no reference to "real life" or discussion of the issues: it is certain most students did not have a clear concept of what these words referred to.

For the majority of children in both Malawi and Zambia, all the available evidence suggests there is a clear risk that the policy of using English as a vehicular language may contribute to stunting, rather than promoting, academic and cognitive growth. It is, moreover, obvious from the case of Zambia that the view of Wagner (1998) of "putting second language first" – at least if English is considered the second language – has been a signal failure in that country. Although Wagner's Berber L1 children (see Chapter Three) may have become as proficient in reading Arabic as Arab L1 children, it could hardly be claimed that Nyanja L1 children have become similarly proficient in reading English. Wagner's view that his studies of the Berber speakers in Morocco have relevance to the "complex multilingual societies [...] in Africa" does not (with minor exceptions) apply to sub-Saharan African children reading in English, for the simple reason that most African children have virtually zero exposure to English outside the classroom, and only limited exposure to English inside it. Adequate exposure to a language is a necessary condition for learning it. Wagner (1998: 181), like Schumann (1976), rightly points out the importance of the "motivational structures of language learning". However, the subjects studied by Schumann had not only motivation, but also ample opportunity to interact with English speakers in English, in the same way that Wagner's Berber subjects had motivation and ample opportunity to interact with Arabic speakers in Arabic[4]. For the overwhelming majority of children in Malawi and Zambia, however, especially the rural children who form the majority of the school population, the opportunity to interact with English speakers simply does not exist.

Finally, the argument that instead of learning English *for* content subjects, students could learn English *through* content subjects, does not

---

[4] Wagner's general conclusion, however, that "*only after making a comprehensive and in-depth analysis of each learning and linguistic context should any attempt be made to determine a language and literacy learning policy*" (1998: 182) would in principle prevent inappropriate decisions. But such analyses are virtually never carried out.

seem to offer the prospect of an immediate and general improvement. In principle, it could be occurring in Zambia: this research has added to the mass of evidence indicating decisively that it is not occurring to any significant extent. Learning English through content certainly has theoretical appeal, but would require more careful integration of the content courses with the English courses than seems to be the case currently. Moreover, it would also require more sensitive presentation by teachers, of language and concepts relating to content, than would appear to be possible in current circumstances. It may succeed in particular individual instances, but is unlikely to be effective on a national scale.

8.6   Possibilities for amelioration

The language policies of Malawi and Zambia (and indeed many other African countries), whereby English dominates education in their primary schools, has led to a highly unsatisfactory situation. Obviously, the option of "zero English" in the primary schools is not politically possible for the foreseeable future (see MOE, Zambia, 1996: 39). On the other hand, any realistic plan of "improving English teaching" is unlikely to yield significant immediate amelioration on a national scale, given the magnitude of the problem, and the weakness of much of the human and material infrastructure. Nonetheless, a "two-pronged" approach incorporating parts of these two options might be envisaged: one "prong" would seek to *reduce the dominance of English as a medium,* while the second would seek to *improve the teaching of English as a subject*, especially with respect to reading.

8.6.1 Reducing the dominance of English

As far as Zambia is concerned, the teaching of initial literacy in the child's mother tongue, or at least a local language known to the majority of the children, as is normal practice in most developed countries, must be an option worth investigating. The country's decision in the late 1990s to provide initial literacy in the 7 "officially designated" Zambian languages for the first year is to be applauded, although there are languages with substantial numbers of speakers omitted from this policy (see Table 2.1), and there must also be doubts as to the efficacy of such a short period. Among the positive reasons for promoting initial literacy in a local language are:

- if the example of Malawi is representative, local language literacy seems to be more successfully taught than English literacy.

- local language literacy may provide support for subsequent English literacy: at the very least, it would have the advantage for most children that they would move from the known (their language) to the unknown (reading), rather than confronting two unknowns (the English language and reading) simultaneously. They would thus be familiar with the purpose and conventions of writing (e.g. the approximate sound value of letters, spaces between word boundaries, capitalization and basic punctuation.) Here we may note again that the neglect of African languages did not result in stronger English performance in Zambia.
- to enhance national self-esteem and identity. Even if not all of the local languages could be vehicles for initial literacy, they would nevertheless be more satisfactory for this purpose than English.

A more radical suggestion than simply encouraging initial literacy in a local language in Zambia, would be for local languages to be used as the sole media of instruction throughout primary schooling, in both countries. English would, in view of the political imperative, continue to be taught, but only as a subject. This would allow literacy skills to be established in the local language, and would also help more children to understand what is going on in the classroom. Indeed, if we accept the relevance of the language threshold hypothesis (Cummins and Swain, 1986) for developing countries, it is more likely that the required academic threshold would be achieved in a local language, and that such academic skills and cognitive might then be available to transfer to English[5]. Attempting to teach reading in all the 20 or so Zambian languages identified by Kashoki (1990: 109), would certainly be regarded by government as impractical and expensive[6] – even proposals to use one Zambian language as an alternative medium of instruction to English evoke strong negative reactions:

> The introduction of a language other than English as the official medium of instruction would encounter insoluble implementation problems and would entail enormous costs both in developing and producing materials and in training teachers to use them. (Zambian MOE (1996: 39))

---

[5] See Trudell, 2005: 243 for a similar "two-pronged" programme in the Cameroons.
[6] However, Bunyi (1999: 347) asserts that producing teaching material "even for [...] languages with very small speech communities need not be too expensive".

However, the costs of the present education operation, in terms of the huge bill for teachers' salaries, the supply of books, the opportunity costs for households, all for very little return in the form of learner achievement[7], should also enter into the balance. The current practice whereby English is simply "broadcast" to all students in primary schools is a massive waste of economic resource, as well as debilitating to the morale of the children. In Zambia, the use of English as a medium reduces classroom teaching to a linguistic and behavioural ritual, where what most children learn is how to endure boredom – hardly preparation for an enterprizing life beyond school.

The proposal of using local languages as media throughout primary schooling would bring greater linguistic coherence to many classrooms by extending the local language from speech to writing. Although officially frowned upon, some teacher talk in the local language does occur, particularly in lower years and rural areas, and not only in Zambia and Malawi but throughout Africa – as one primary student in rural South Africa put it, he and his classmates had "no problem learning in English, because the teacher say (*sic*) it in Xhosa".

It might be objected that employing a local language as the medium of instruction would lead to difficulties in secondary schools, which operate entirely through the medium of English. If that is the case, then one solution would be to have a year of intensive English at the beginning of secondary school for those that need it (bearing in mind that all students would have learned English as a subject in primary school). This solution would have the advantage of targeting English only at the minority who have already passed the secondary school entrance examination (usually around 12 to 15 per cent), thus obviating the need for years of incomprehension on the part of many of the primary school students who are currently subjected to English medium[8]. Such flexibility in the system is required to address the differentials in levels of reading achievement, particularly between rural and urban students, which are so great that they

---

[7] In Malawi the view of some parents that English should became a medium in the first four years, rather than a subject, is questioned by educationists: "[S]ince fewer than half of pupils survive in school beyond standard four, the usefulness of learning in English for these children is questionable, and might not be appropriate for the achievement of poverty alleviation." (Kadzamira et al, 2003: 512).
[8] While such a programme may be criticised as representing a transitional bilingual model that ultimately maintains the dominance of English (a) it would not be so for the majority who do not progress to secondary school, and (b) for the present the political imperative excludes more radical steps.

cannot be readily coped with, far less remedied, within the current structure. Similar different policy options for differing sociolinguistic contexts are suggested by Webb (1999: 358-359) for South Africa. There would be practical problems in implementing such a proposal, and there might also be resistance from those objecting that children would learn less at primary school, if they did not learn in English: however, the reality for most students is that they learn very little at present – indeed, the dominance of English means many spend much of their school life in a miasma of incomprehension.

8.6.2 Improving teaching of English reading

As far as classroom approaches are concerned, educationists in countries which use English (or any other "major" language) as a second language medium of instruction, need to be aware that if students are to read effectively in English, then specific attention should be given to a comprehensive English programme where the development of language and skills is integrated. Although perfection in such a programme would be elusive, the following components would nonetheless be widely agreed to be relevant to an effective primary level programme of English as a second language:

(i)   an English language component: this is usually provided by the course book and should attend to meanings and not only to form and pronunciation

(ii)   learning how to read and write in English: ideally this would not be an initial reading programme in English but rather a beginning English reading programme for those who have already learned to read in a local language. There would therefore be no need to re-teach letter formation and the sound values of letters (apart from some modifications).

(iii) intensive reading for practising reading comprehension and improving language proficiency, especially as regards vocabulary expansion: this too is usually provided by the course book in the form of short passages. Typically the language will be slightly above the level of the students, and the gap will "bridged" by the teacher.

(iv)   listening to stories read aloud by the teacher. The purpose of this is to introduce the notion of deriving pleasure from books, and thereby generate a more positive attitude towards reading. The language would normally be at or slightly below the level of the students (there should likewise be story reading in local languages).

(v)   group reading where classes of children read the same books at the same time under the teacher's guidance (possibly with a "Big Book" approach). The purpose of this is to help children develop strategies for individual reading.

(vi) a self-access supplementary reading programme, where students choose their own books and are in charge of their own reading. The purpose of this is to enhance existing reading capacity and encourage interest in reading; the language of most books should be slightly below the level of most students, so that they are truly "self access" (see Day and Bamford, 1998). Such a scheme should only be introduced after careful trialling, into classes which could cope easily with the demands of the texts (Supplementary reading schemes were in fact introduced in the mid-90s in both Malawi and Zambia but most of the books were far too difficult for the majority of children.)

Currently Malawi and Zambia focus on the first three components, often justifying this by claiming that syllabus demands do not allow any other activities. However, in terms of generating a positive attitude towards reading, there are advantages in a planned introduction of the last three components, and particularly the final one, for once students have learned "how to read" they can only develop the skill by reading. It is worth noting however, that there may be resistance from some teachers to reading fiction in the classroom. This is exemplified by a Malawian teacher who, referring to supplementary readers, asked me "*Are these stories true?*" On hearing they were not, he responded "*Then why are we asking the children to learn them?*" This illustrates a view which is not uncommon, and which argues that the place for stories is at home. The solution could well be to provide factual books and "true stories" rather than fiction. Such reactions also indicate that Western attitudes to reading cannot be taken for granted, and that proper piloting of innovations in a range of settings is crucial.

It is also important to realise that people become skilled readers through reading (Nuttall, 1996: 40): simply doing a course of "reading skills exercises" is not sufficient. Students therefore need to be given the opportunity to read. It goes without saying that careful sequencing and integration of the components is important, and there is clearly a significant role for writing.

8.6.3 Comments on the possibilities

Any suggestions for improvements such as those mentioned in the preceding paragraphs should ideally be delivered by a teaching force whose morale is sufficiently high for them to embark on innovative approaches with commitment, whose language competence is adequate, and who have some basic insights into the processes of reading and second language learning. There is a clear danger that simply "unloading" foreign materials and methods onto a teaching force that has neither the willingness nor the pedagogic capacity to implement them will fail. (Further, as King [1986: 118] points out, recipient countries often do not attempt to "assess in great detail what individual donor countries' own education systems are really like".) Before decisions on new approaches are made, careful and critical analysis of the teacher resource potential is needed, as well as investigation into the acceptability of change to families and local communities: denigration of local languages as subjects and as media of instruction is widespread in the very communities that use them, although attitudes do vary considerably (see Baker, 1998). The strongest threat to the implementation of the Zambian Primary Reading Programme (1999-2005; see Chapter 2) whereby initial literacy in year one is being introduced in Zambian languages, was the prospect of parental opposition – despite the fact that English would continue to be the official medium of instruction. A detailed public relations and communication campaign was undertaken through the press, radio and public meetings, together with public pilot trials. The result was that "parents are supportive of the innovations to a surprising degree, taking a new interest in their children's education" (Linehan, 2004: 10).

In addition to such "consciousness raising" exercises, local understanding and ownership of policy initiatives is crucial. This may require rethinking of education by African countries in terms of delivery systems that are more congruent with their own socio-cultural norms, and attuned to their own capacities and needs. In this connection, Serpell (1996) convincingly elucidates the indigenous Chewa perspective on children's development, a perspective which he sees as neglected by "the policy of embedding the curriculum in an exogenous language" (*ibid.* 141) and which has resulted in the counterproductive compartmentalization of school and home in terms of "literate and oral communication, English and Chi-Chewa language, modern and traditional values, high and low prestige occupations, urban and rural existence" (*loc.cit.*). Much the same contradiction between tradition and modernity is documented for Swaziland by Booth (2004). Indeed, such is the hegemony of the Western model that much of present-day African education is arguably a process of "westernization" with the concomitant possibility that those who succeed within it, may well be the most alienated from, or the least sympathetic to, communities in their own countries[9].

---

[9] Thus Kasonde-Ng'andu et al. (2000: 94-95) in the context of cultural practices

Although the simple transfer of foreign approaches to reading has been cautioned against, it is still likely that insights from reading theory in general can be of pedagogic value. For example, the view of reading as the construction of meaning rather than as an exercise in "reading aloud" would appear to be useful, while the value of linguistic competence in the language being read needs to be more widely appreciated in Malawi and Zambia. Reading lessons in Zambia and Malawi could probably benefit from increased teacher familiarity with such issues in both first and second language reading. This would imply, not imposing methods on teachers, but simply developing in teachers a greater awareness of reading principles, and providing them with greater potential to devise their own approaches to problems. If this is to take place, even to a limited extent, then it is important for Malawi and Zambia to possess a larger cadre of their own reading specialists to provide pre-service and in-service training for teachers. Ideally these specialists should be familiar not only with the reading issues in first and second language, but crucially, be familiar with the teaching of reading in the local schools, and an understanding of the application of theory to local conditions. Such a cadre could also raise awareness, in education ministries and schools, of the roles of English and local languages in learning across the curriculum.

This "two pronged" approach is not dissimilar to the successful experiment in the Nigerian Ife-Ife project (see 3.4.2), where Yoruba was the medium of instruction for 6 years of primary school, with English taught as a subject (Bamgbose, 1991: 85-86). It is also similar to a brief academically successful period in the pre-Soweto situation in South Africa (see 1.4), where according to Heugh:

> Ironically, whilst the resistance to "Bantu Education", the role of Afrikaans and the mother tongue, was escalating, the matriculation pass rate of African language speaking students increased dramatically from 43.5% in 1955 to 83.4% in 1976. [...] the increase in the pass rate may very well be partly attributed to the maintenance and development of the home language for eight years of formal education, during which time English and Afrikaans were introduced and taught as subjects. [...] *During the time that the mother tongue was phased in and maintained for 8 years as the primary language of*

---

in Zambia recommend "There is a need to change customs that have outlived their usefulness [...] initiation ceremonies for both boys and girls, the Nyau and the Chimuthali dance in Eastern Province, should be practised during the school holidays. Moreover, the content of the initiation ceremonies should be revised so that the emphasis is on personal cleanliness."

> *learning, the matriculation results steadily improved reaching their*
> *zenith in 1976.* This year is remembered for the rebellion and result-
> ant compromise with regard to language-in-education policy from
> government. It should however, also be noted that it was the end point
> of a period during which the fruits of 8 years of mother tongue in-
> struction could be seen in the matriculation result. (Heugh, 1999:
> 302-303, my italics)[10]

It would seem that the "two-pronged" approach has proved beneficial in
circumstances comparable to those in Malawi and Zambia. Nevertheless,
although present levels of English reading in Malawi and both English
and Zambian language reading in Zambia are far from satisfactory, this is
not to be blamed entirely on official policies or inappropriate pedagogy,
but also on the context for education: dilapidated schools, a shortage of
books, low teacher morale and student absenteeism.

A major reason for student absenteeism is certainly chronic poverty,
since families cannot afford the opportunity costs of sending students to
school regularly, and also because poverty means inadequate diet, which
leads to illness and absence. While a larger role for local languages might,
as has been suggested above, partly address the reading problems as far as
local languages are concerned, its effect on English reading proficiency
would be limited, particularly for students who only attend school spo-
radically. A considerable improvement in the general economic situation
in both countries would probably be needed to make it worthwhile for
poor parents to invest in their children's education by encouraging regular
attendance. In the absence of reasonable attendance, it is unlikely that
proficiency in English reading (as opposed to local language reading) can
register significant improvement.

To conclude, the overall picture is that the aims of the education system in both countries, are not commensurate with what the educational
infrastructures can deliver, nor with what may reasonably be expected of
learners from the majority of Malawian and Zambian communities, where
exposure to English is minimal: there is a mismatch, in that a system of
education which in the main has been imported from the UK, including
the language itself, is not easily accommodated within the "developmen-
tal ecology" of poor African countries such as Malawi and Zambia. The
final chapter considers these issues.

---

[10] While there are more important political decisions than the language of instruction, it would appear that one of the most destructive legacies of apartheid
is the negative attitudes of many communities in South Africa towards their
own languages.

9.   Conclusion

9.1 Language policy and development

One of the paradoxes of education around the world is that poor countries often operate expensive and complex language policies, whereas rich countries usually operate simple and relatively cheap language policies. Thus the policy in Malawi and Zambia involves home-school language switching, with teaching in at least two languages, while countries such as England and France operate what is overwhelmingly a monolingual policy, in a language that is the first language of most learners and teachers.

Although this contrast in present-day language education policies appears superficially as a paradox, it has an historical explanation. In the evolution of most modern European nation-states, there is, crudely speaking, a discernible historical pattern, which involved the emergence of a political unit (by consent or military coercion), accompanied by economic consolidation, a process which was facilitated by, and facilitated, the development and dissemination of a "more or less" standard language,[1] and literacy in that language, although not necessarily mass fluency nor mass literacy in the standard. Coulmas (1992: 214) notes "For a variety of reasons concerning the exchange of goods, people and information, the spread of endoglossic written languages coincided historically with economic advancement." Politics, economics and language are the principal interlocking institutions through which the cultural project which is the nation state (Balibar and Wallerstein, 1991) is enabled.

Within Africa, on the other hand, such "organic" political, economic and linguistic processes, were largely destroyed or curtailed by the colonial scramble for Africa in the nineteenth century. African rulers and communities throughout the continent were made subject to colonial powers, although not necessarily subservient. Bayart (1993: 24) comments that Africans:

> [H]ave been active agents in the *mise en dépendance* of their societies, sometimes opposing it, and at other times joining in it. It would

---

[1] It is of course a dynamic process, where inherent structural conflict between linguistic, ethnic, or religious groups may emerge into violent conflict and secession, as in former Yugoslavia (whose origins, with a boundary artificially encompassing disparate peoples, has parallels with African countries). Conversely the European Union is an emerging political/economic unit, where language issues are still being worked through, although English is by default widely employed as a *lingua franca*.

be naïve to indulge in an anachronistic interpretation of these indigenous strategies in terms of 'nationalism' or 'collaboration' where in fact considerations of local interest came into play, in a world which was indifferent to the national idea.

Boundaries to the colonies were established by the European powers following the General Act of Berlin in 1885. On the one hand these boundaries often encompassed peoples with a history of conflict, while on the other they cut through at least 177 existing ethno-cultural areas "dividing pre-existing economic and social units" (Reader, 1997: 562), which were in large measure replaced by economic and political institutions imported by the colonial powers. The result is a continent is divided into forty-six states, fifteen of which are entirely landlocked (as are Malawi and Zambia), more than the total for the rest of the world. Reader (1997: 567) claims that "no country in Africa is free from problems of access, security and economic instability that are directly attributable to the boundaries they inherited from the colonial era". The pre-eminent colonial powers were Britain and France, countries which had themselves undergone a considerable degree of political, economic and linguistic consolidation[2] by the nineteenth century. These two countries, together with other colonisers such as Portugal, Spain and Belgium (although the colonization of the Congo by the latter is in many respects a special case), introduced their own institutions of government and commerce into their sub-Saharan colonies. These colonial institutions inevitably meant that the process of African language standardization, and the spread of literacy in standard African varieties[3], was short-circuited by the use of the colonial languages, which, of course, extended into formal education. As Spencer, 1985 (cited in Coulmas, 1992:50) puts it, the introduction of colonial languages "froze the opportunity for functional development of almost all the African languages"[4], a point echoed by Mazrui (1996), while Phillipson and Skutnabb-Kangas (1994), point to the same effect with respect to the development of African languages to meet school subject needs.

At independence in the 1960s and 1970s a superficial perspective might have suggested that the economic prospects of African ex-colonies were

---

[2] Although this by no means implies consensus on the part of minorities within those two states; see May (2001), for an incisive historical account.

[3] There were exceptions, notably Amharic in Ethiopia, and to a lesser extent Vai in Liberia.

[4] The phenomenon is not confined to Africa, but an inevitable consequence of dominance of one group over others: Arabic, Bahasa Indonesia, Mandarin Chinese and Spanish have had similar effects in other contexts.

comparable to those of similar countries elsewhere (c.f. Dowden, 1996: 61). Malaysia and Zambia, for example, were in roughly the same economic position in terms of GDP per capita in the 1960s, while South Korea was actually poorer than Chad (Edwards: 1999: 49-50). Thirty years later, however, by the mid-1990s, the two Asian countries had become economic "tigers"[5] while the two African ones were among the world's poorest. With the wisdom of hindsight, it is apparent that many African countries were, relative to Asian countries, in an unenviable starting position – they were saddled with the above-mentioned artificial frontiers (which the OAU had decided, at its formation in 1963, to respect), and they possessed inadequate infrastructural bases. Furthermore, almost throughout the continent, states lacked a sense of national unity, and politicians had to attempt a "state into nation" project.

Although there may have been, at the moment of independence for Malawi and Zambia, no realistic immediate alternative to the use of the ex-colonial language, English, in state institutions, the findings reported in this research suggest that many children in Malawi and Zambia have, over the decades of independence, been the innocent victims of their governments' decisions to perpetuate the dominant role of that language in the educational system. Virtually every other ex-colony in Africa followed similar policies, with largely similar results (see Cleghorn [1992] for the effects of English in education in Kenya). Although the stated aim of the newly-formed governments was to promote unity and modernization within their countries, it is now apparent that using English in education to address these issues has not been an unqualified success for the majority of their populations. Politicians, as well as academic language planners have been victims of the "idealization of the effectiveness of political decisions on social change" (Blommaert, 1999a: 30).

9.1.1 English and unification

National unification was a particular preoccupation for Zambia, in the years following independence. The slogan of the UNIP party of President Kenneth Kaunda was "One Zambia, one nation", and English was clearly perceived as having a role. John Mwanakatwe, Minister of Education in the UNIP government, makes this clear :

> [E]ven the most ardent nationalists of our time have accepted the inevitable fact that English – ironically a foreign language and also the

---

[5] The slump of 1997 in East Asia shook the system, but does not seem to have caused permanent damage (Edwards, 1999: 52). The "Asian tigers" march on.

language of our former colonial master – has definitely a unifying role in Zambia. (Mwanakatwe, 1968: 213)

Further, the primary education system was seen as the instrument that would facilitate this unification through English. In 1976 the MOE's views were expressed in the document *Education for Development: Draft Statement on Educational Reform,* paragraph 47 of which reads:

> [F]or the sake of communication between Zambians whose mother tongues differ and *in order to promote the unity of the nation,* it is necessary for all Zambian children to learn the national language as early as possible, and to use it confidently. (Zambian MOE, 1976; my italics)

The national language referred to is, of course, English, which has been ideologized and promoted as crucial for national *unification* (c.f. Blommaert, 1999a: 31). There does not, however, appear to have been any attempt by Zambian politicians to appropriate English as an ingredient in national *identity*, as FRELIMO did for Portuguese in post-colonial Mozambique (Stroud, 1999). In fact, a degree of doubt about the role of English in the state may be detected in Mwanakatwe's words above, while Kapepwe, Vice President of Zambia, was, one year later in 1969, openly critical:

> [W]e should stop teaching children through English right from the start because it is the surest way of imparting inferiority complex in the children and the society. It is poisonous. It is the surest way of killing African personality and African culture. (cited in Serpell, 1978: 432)

In short, while unification was prime concern in Zambia, there is an absence of public and political debate on language, of the kind that took place in Tanzania and Mozambique, for example, where languages (whether the "indigenous" Swahili or the "appropriated" Portuguese) were promoted as essentialized and homogenized notions in the nation building project. The Zambian political perspective on language is low-key by comparison – it would appear that English is no more than an instrument for unifying Zambia and for accessing the world outside; on the other hand, Zambian languages are not promoted for national authenticity or identity. Given that no language has an absolute majority of first language speakers, the silence may be seen as political discretion.

In Malawi, however, English was not regarded as the sole linguistic means of unification. From 1969, it was the indigenous ChiChewa that

was imposed by President Banda as the medium of instruction in the first
four years of primary education. This was "in the interests of national
unity" (Kayambazinthu, 1999: 49), and President Banda clearly wished to
legitimize this move by appealing to the fact that Chichewa was the language of the majority of Malawians. This is a doubtful "fact" however:
Vail and White (1989: 180) cited in Kayambazinthu (1999: 74) claim that
for the 1966 census:

> President Banda was able to lump together the various dialects of the
> Southern region [...] to produce a national population that was more
> than 50 per cent Chewa. Banda's deep concern for a paper majority
> for the so-called Chewa was demonstrated when he ordered the Uni-
> versity of Malawi to no longer use the services of [...] Prof. Wilfred
> Whitely, after he had observed in a report [...] that the number of
> Chewa speakers was clearly exaggerated in official estimates.

However, it is clear that English was intended to play a communicatively
unifying role at the "upper levels" of state institutions. Thus English was
made compulsory in parliament, and under the regime of President Banda
all MPs were "required to pass a stringent test" in it (Schmied, 1991: 24).
This test was abolished in 1995; however, the Parliament still operates in
English, and Kayambazinthu, a Malawian who runs a UNDP-sponsored
communications skills course for members of the Malawian Parliament,
claims (1999: 73) that it "is doubtful ... that they are able to understand or
follow the bills that they pass in Parliament."

While opting for English may have succeeded in preventing conflict
in the educational arena between competing language groups, and while
its dominance in the same arena is largely welcomed by the public, the
language has created division between, on the one hand, those who have
good access to it, typically members of the reasonably well-off urban
groups, and, on the other hand, those who do not, typically the members
of poor urban and especially rural groups. Djité makes a similar point:

> Reliance and dependency on superimposed international languages
> to achieve development in Africa over the last three decades has proven
> to be a failure. Instead of leading to national unity, this attitude has
> significantly contributed to the socio-economic and political instabil-
> ity of most African countries ... (Djité, 1993: 149)

The English test results reported in this book provide a measure of support for this point: although none of our testees could be counted as
children of the urban élite, the differences between rural and urban Eng-

lish test scores in Zambia suggest that two separate populations are emerging – rural and poor urban on the one hand, and an urban "quasi élite", on the other. In fact, the true disparity with respect to English competence in Malawi and Zambia is certainly under-represented in this study, since it has not included the small but increasing proportion of pupils who attend private fee-paying primary schools in both countries. Referring to this effect of English in Malawi, Kayambazinthu (1998: 52) says that:

> The dominance and limited access to English [...] has created an élite group, [whose] proficiency in English is near-native [...] these élites maintain and regularly use their knowledge of English in their profes- sional environments, where they typically occupy the middle ranks of the political, administrative and academic institutions.

Far from being a source of unity, the use of English in education in both Malawi and Zambia has become a factor in national division, while the distribution of English proficiency in society is an indicator of the extent of this division. As Heugh (1999: 306) puts it: "the role of superimposed international languages has been hugely overestimated in their capacity to serve the interests of the majority on the continent [...] these languages serve only the interests of the élites". Similar suggestions have been made with respect to South Africa (Webb, 1999: 363). "Élite closure" is the term Myers-Scotton (1990) has coined for the process whereby a small dominant establishment in African countries ensures that they and their families have access to high standards of English while inadequate educa- tion systems mean that this is largely denied to the majority.

The issue of "the national language" is of course inextricably tied to the dominance of English. Djité (1993: 149) claims that "real development is not possible in Africa without the integration of national languages" and makes a case for the strengthening of existing indigenous *linguae francae*. However, while one may acknowledge that a characteristic of rich countries is that most of their population share a common language, evidence suggests that such sharing, or even virtual monolingualism, is not in itself a guarantee of unity and development. In Africa there is on the one hand the successful case of Botswana, where Tswana is the first language of the vast majority (al- though the actual proportion is a matter of dispute); on the other hand, there are less felicitous cases. Rwanda where Kinyarwanda is the first language of 95% of inhabitants, saw the massacres of 1994, while Somalia, where Somali is the first language of 98%, according to Bamgbose (1991: 16), has fallen apart into three virtually independent entities, Somaliland, Punt, and Somalia, the latter the scene of chronic armed conflict between rival factions. Again, we need not look as far as Africa to find inter-group friction in monolingual contexts – Northern Ireland has had its "troubles" for over 30 years: these of course have a religious origin, Protestant versus Catholic. There are a variety of lines of cleavage that humans have constructed to divide one group from another, among them religion, ethnicity, location, wealth, any of which may, under certain circumstances, become salient, and mobilised for political ends. Language, however, remains one of the most potent instruments in uniting or dividing groups, because of its role in human communication: most obviously, a language-switch in group discussion results in the abrupt exclusion of those who do not know the language.

9.1.2 English and development

At independence in the 1960s "modernization" was a ubiquitous goal in Africa, and it was thought that English would enhance this goal through facilitating international and commercial contacts. While one may readily criticise the effect that English has had on national unification, the position is less clear with respect to modernization. The term itself, much used in the 1960s and 1970s (c.f. Rubin and Jernudd, 1971; Fishman, 1971), has been largely superseded in public discourse by the term "development". Development, as mentioned in Chapter One, may be conceived of purely in economic terms (growth in GDP), or in human terms (e.g. child mortality, health, education, good governance). Even meeting human needs normally requires some degree of economic input: self-sufficient groups meeting their own human needs, and living in isolation from the outside world have largely disappeared as the remotest areas of the planet have been scoured for mineral or agricultural profit.

Whether one looks at development in terms of the national economic picture or the profile of human needs, neither Zambia nor Malawi has been a success in recent years. Zambia's GDP growth rate[6] was estimated for 2005 as 5.8% (which is due to a recovery in copper prices and a good maize harvest), having stood at minus 2% in 1998. However, to reduce poverty significantly, growth of 6% to 7% is needed. The proportion of the population living below the poverty line of $1 a day stood at a massive 86% in 1993 – the latest currently available figures. In terms of human development, the fertility rate for 2005 was estimated at 5.47 children per woman. Life expectancy at birth was 39.7 years (2005 estimate), and 16.5% of the adult population was affected by HIV/AIDS (2003 estimate).

---

[6] Unless otherwise indicated, information on Zambia and Malawi in this section is from the World Factbook [http://www.odci.gov.cia/publications/factbook/za.html] update 10/01/06.

The picture in Malawi is similarly bleak: the GDP real growth rate estimate for 2005 was 1%, while even this is from a small base, and restricted to a tiny proportion of the population: 55% of the population in 2004 was estimated as being below the $1 a day poverty line. The per capita GDP for 2005 is estimated as $600. The World Bank (1996: 24) estimated that in 1992, 80% of people in rural smallholder households in Malawi (some 90% of the Malawi's total population) had annual incomes less than US$55, while of those 43% "did not have enough income to acquire their most basic needs and 30% had insufficient income to meet their calorie needs." Lack of food was one of two major problems cited by Malawian communities in a study by Khaila et al. (1999), the other problem being lack of health facilities. For 2005 the fertility rate was estimated as 5.98 children per woman, while life expectancy at birth was estimated at 41.43 years. In 1999 HIV prevalence rates of those between 15 and 49 were 16.4% (Kadzamira et al. 2001: 11), while there is widespread agreement among senior education Ministry officers "that the number of AIDS-related deaths among primary staff is increasing very rapidly" (*ibid.* 79). Of Malawi's 1980 university graduates, 25% were dead by 2003: "We can reasonably assume that a very high proportion of these deaths were to HIV/AIDS-related illness" (Allsop, 2005: 93).

9.2 Educational effectiveness and development

Such dismal statistics cannot be laid simply at the door of English dominated education systems. The link between education and development is indirect, and there is no neat space in development theory for language policy to fit into – indeed there is no adequate development theory, if by theory we mean a device with predictive power which specifies the relevant components and the relationships between them. Our state of knowledge is inadequate, as admitted by a UN group briefed in the 1990s to find an answer to 'sustainable human development'. Their conclusion was:

> We simply do not know. Development theories tell us little about how to reconcile economic, social and environmental concerns; markets and states; the local, the national and the global. (Kaul, 1996)

Nonetheless, although there is no adequate theory, we do know that education is a necessary component in the building of human capital i.e. in helping to develop within individuals the skills to contribute to society. Indeed, we have already reviewed in Chapter One evidence which indicates the positive impact of education on economic and human development.

However, research on the quality of formal education in poor countries reveals that much of the potential benefit of education is currently not being realised, even for those who do have access. Oxfam (1999: 12), for example, claims that "it is clear that much of what passes for education in the developing world is of abysmal quality" echoing the sentiment of Williams (1986: 91). The cognitive gains from investment in inadequate education are negligible (Knight and Sabot, 1990), and providing access to such education is of doubtful value.

As far as Malawi and Zambia are concerned, the results of the reading tests and individual reading sessions reported on in this book (with the exception of the local language reading test in Malawi), suggest that the achievements in reading of primary education in these two countries are weak; in this Malawi and Zambia are not unique among African countries (see Watkins, 2000). Indeed, it is very likely that Hobcraft's finding (1993) of the relatively weak effects of maternal education on child survival in Sub-Saharan Africa (see section 1.3), are simply a function of education that is of lower quality, and less effective than that obtaining in the other developing countries which he investigated (in Central and South America, and south east Asia), and that furthermore, one of the main reasons for the poor quality is that the African mothers had understood little of the formal input during their time at school, because their education was being delivered in an exoglossic language in which they had limited proficiency, whereas this was not the case for the South Americans or South East Asians.

As far as quality in the context of reading and language is concerned, Postlethwaite and Ross (1992), in a huge survey of 9 and 14 year olds in over 4,000 schools in 26 countries (mainly developed ones) concluded, that as far as reading methods are concerned "The more effective school is one where the teachers emphasise, above all the understanding of what is read" (1992: 46). Given that reading is conducted in most sub-Saharan primary schools, as we saw in Chapter 2, through rote repetition with little attention to meaning, in a language, furthermore which the children have little understanding of, then the implications for the lack of effectiveness in reading are clear. Since most children have little exposure to English outside the school, and since the schools are largely ineffective in teaching English, then a policy which makes English the sole medium of instruction (as in Zambia), or the sole medium after year 4 (as in Malawi) is certain to contribute towards the low quality of education. Indeed, one might suggest that as long as language is neglected as a factor in educational effectiveness, then amelioration in other areas, such as physical infrastructure, teaching materials, or school management (c.f. Hawes *et al*, 1986: 41-43), is likely to have little effect.

The majority of primary school pupils who fail to acquire adequate skills in English continue with an English-medium education with little linguistic comprehension, as is demonstrated in the test results and individual reading sessions: in the absence of comprehension the development of academic concepts or skills is negligible. Reading, which is intended to play a major role in formal teaching and learning, is too often simply unable to play that role, primarily because, for the vast majority of children, it is short-circuited by lack of language competence. There is a considerable risk in such cases that the school experience may be a stultifying, rather than an enlightening one[7], calling into question the goal of "education for all". The poor quality of education in Malawian primary schools described in this book has almost certainly deteriorated further as a result of the rapid increase in enrolments since the mid-1990s, which has resulted in a larger proportion of unqualified teachers (16% in 1993/ 94 but over half in 1997: Kadzamira et al, 2003: 514). Furthermore, the same authors claim that: "the evidence from Malawi indicates that the achievement of poverty alleviation goals through increased access to primary schools is unlikely. While [free primary education] has increased enrolment in primary schools, poor quality, particularly at the lower level to which the poor have most access, is apparent" (Kadzamira et al, 2003: 514).

Although there is little consensus on the magnitude of the effects, and although the relative importance of precise pathways of operation is difficult to establish – in brief, although there is no theory – the weight of evidence suggests the following: literacy skills are more easily acquired and deployed in a language with which learners are familiar; proficiency in literacy skills leads to more effective education; effective education can contribute to development. Crucially, however, it is *effective* education that enables individuals to acquire knowledge and skills, which in turn can facilitate development. The simple and obvious point is that education is unlikely to be effective for the majority when an unfamiliar language is introduced prematurely as a medium of instruction. Education in a familiar African language is clearly not a folkloric matter of emphasizing lifestyles, but a crucial matter of enhancing life chances, to borrow a distinction from May (2001: 174).

One must not, of course, overstate the case for the use of local languages as media of education, or indeed for language policy as the answer to deep-rooted educational problems (cf. Treffgarne, 1986: 162). As we

---

[7] In similar vein the cultural interpretation of the African Renaissance sees the assertion of African values as the antidote to Western dominance (see Vale and Maseko, 1998).

saw in Chapter 1 there is no agreement in either Malawi or Zambia on the number of indigenous languages for either country, no money for educational material to be produced in all of them, and no certainty that all local communities would be enthusiastic for their "language rights" to be available in schools. Heugh (1999: 309) claims that "There have been no examples in Africa of the successful implementation of a rights based language policy [...] there have to be instrumental or functional reasons to support the rights based approach", and points out that in the relative absence of demand from the communities themselves little will be achieved. (Hornberger [1987] notes similar community resistance to the use of Quechua in rural Peru.) Local communities and politicians converge in their view that English is "the language of power": it remains the language of global commerce and diplomacy, and no country is prepared to dispense entirely with it.

9.3 Politics, conditions, capitals and agencies

Political will in the matter of local languages is crucial; in both Zambia and Malawi a lack of political will is bound up with politicians' concerns that promoting local languages will hinder national unity, and economic development. Further, their perception of the voters is that the latter see English as the language of personal progress, and are not unduly concerned about local languages. Thus in 1996, which was not only the year when the Zambian policy document *Educating our future* was being drafted, but also a general election year in the country, politicians were worried that to promote Zambian languages as media of instruction at the expense of English would be a potential vote-loser. "[I]t proved not possible, for political reasons, to go as far as changing the medium of instruction to a local language" (Linehan, 2004: 7). Ruling politicians "made clear to senior education officials that unless a non-contentious formula could be found, the political preference would be for maintenance of the status quo, with English remaining in the same position as it had done from 1965" (Linehan, 2004: 7). The compromise position was, as reported in Chapter Two, that initial literacy in year one, should be in one of the seven "educationally approved" Zambian languages, while English continued officially to be the medium of instruction. Even so, some Zambian Members of Parliament protested that the "new language policy [...] forces children to learn in a foreign language" (Linehan, 2004: 8). A "foreign language" here refers to a Zambian language, rather than English! Thanks to the compromise position adopted by *Educating our future*, the protesting politicians were eventually persuaded that the language policy was unchanged – indeed, in main essentials, it was not.

Zambia is not alone in lacking political will in the matter of promoting African languages, which doubtless explains why a succession of reports by educationalists in the past century (from the United Missionary Conference in Kenya in 1909, to the Intergovernmental Conference on African Language Policies in Africa, 1997[8]), all of which advocated a central role for African languages in primary education, were largely ignored. More recently Webb (2002) sees lack of political will demonstrated through lack of implementation and strategic planning with respect to languages in South Africa. Likewise Brock-Utne et al (2003) who adduce evidence from South Africa and Tanzania in favour of local languages, see lack of political commitment as the reason for the continued dominance of English. At the heart of the issue is the problem of how to integrate successful learning of English into the educational system of countries such as Malawi and Zambia, while preventing the debilitating effect which its use as a medium of instruction currently seems to exercise over African languages and learning generally (cf. Serpell, 1989).

One of the many effects of the increase in democratization in Africa with the demise of authoritarian regimes since 1989, is that language education problems have become more salient. The solutions will require informed and sympathetic local negotiation, and will need to take account of educational aims, of evolving literacy practices within society, and of overall political aims. A degree of realism is also necessary: conflicting social and economic pressures, and a teaching base which has many weaknesses, mean that solutions to language education problems are likely to be piecemeal and slow.

Moreover, just as one should not overstate the case for local languages in education, so one should not overstate the case for education in development. Appropriate language policies are not the entire answer to poor quality education, and effective education is not the entire answer to human and economic development. Hawes *et al.* (1986: 13) writing in the context of educational priorities and aid for sub-Saharan Africa, point out that "it would be foolish to make exaggerated claims for the power of education to solve such profound problems". For many African countries,

---

[8] Others include: The Phelps-Stokes Commission of 1922 (West Africa) and of 1924 (East Africa); UNESCO's Report on the Use of the Vernacular Languages in Education, 1953; the Lagos Conference of Education Ministers of African Member States, 1976; the Harare Declaration of Ministers of Education of African Member States, 1982; the OAU's Language Plan of Action for Africa, 1986; the Pan African Colloquium on Educational Innovation in Post Colonial Africa, 1994.

there are a host of inhibiting domestic factors, including corruption, administrative inefficiency, and armed conflict within or between countries. In the 10 years from 1994 to 2003 well over 9 million people are estimated to have died in conflicts in sub-Saharan Africa (UN, 2005: 9), although interests from outside Africa have often been implicated. Likewise climatic disasters in the form of floods, droughts or pests, frequently blight agricultural production, while the high incidence of HIV/AIDS is particularly debilitating at every level of society: the extent to which an effective state education system can operate within a malfunctioning state is debatable. Here we should note that Malawi and Zambia are by no means among the most "malfunctioning" states in Africa, and their people have not indulged in any significant internal armed conflict for the last century.

In sum, although there is no grand theory for sustainable human development, we know that if poor countries are to provide better lives for their people in the modern world, then:

- global economic conditions should not be a barrier to countries acquiring economic capital;
- commitment to the polity by a critical mass of citizens is necessary to ensure social capital;
- provision of effective education is crucial in contributing to human capital.

In a spirit of self-criticism we might grant that these are fine sentiments but are idealizations, not only in the lay sense of being "lofty aspirations", but also in that they do not identify material human agents to implement them. Attempting to identify potential agents reveals the contradictions between the sentiments on the one hand, and on the other, the general view (expressed, for example, by the Commission for Africa, 2005: 14), that Africans rather than outsiders should assume roles of agency, as a consideration of the three capitals suggests.

(i)   Economic capital

In Africa, the framework of global economic structures within which countries have to operate renders economic growth extremely problematic. Internationally, the industrialised countries have built up a technical advantage in manufacture which, without protectionism or massive technology transfer, is not likely to be bridged.

With the failure of economic growth through structural adjustment programmes of the early 1990s in poor countries such as Malawi and

Zambia (*The Economist*, 21st Oct., 1995: 48), the developed world has since been seeking answers to poverty alleviation in policies oriented more to human needs (DFID, 1997: 1.7), while the World Bank "is defining a new role for itself as a global welfare agency and is placing education firmly at the centre of its strategy" (Ilon, 1997: 414), although this strategy seems to address effects rather than causes.

The G7 countries agreed in 2005 to cancel the debts which the 33 most impoverished sub-Saharan African countries owed to three institutions – the World Bank, the International Monetary Fund, and the African Development Bank. Immediate debt relief was agreed for 15 countries (including Zambia), and deferred debt relief, conditional on improved governance, to 9 countries (including Malawi). However, debts owed to financial institutions other than the above three would not be cancelled: thus Zambia would get debt relief on £600 million of a total debt of £3.53 billion, while Malawi (subject to meeting the governance conditions) could get relief on £520 million of £1.72 billion. Whether such partial debt relief is sufficient to turn around African economies is open to question. Significant additional injections of aid are needed to build up infrastructures and help kick start African economies, and much could be achieved if rich countries lived up to the UN target to provide 0.7% of their gross national product as official development assistance. This, as pointed out in Chapter One, is not likely to occur in the near future. Similarly, adverse conditions of trade (e.g. rich countries imposing tariffs on imports from developing countries, while subsidizing their own exports) although showing signs of ameliorating (UN, 2005: 38-39), are not likely to undergo the kind of changes that will bring about significant benefits in Africa. In short, as far as economic capital is concerned, outside agency lacks the will to help Africa, while African agency lacks the ability. For the children of Malawi or Zambia, the "level playing field" will continue to look decidedly uphill: poor quality education is both a cause and an outcome of poverty, at household and national levels (cf. Kadzamira et al, 2003; Colclough et al., 2000).

(ii) *Social capital*
A number of observers of the African scene (e.g. Edwards, 1999; Pakenham, 1991; Reader, 1997) claim that experience suggests it is not through outside intervention that African countries will develop, but rather through transforming themselves into "polities" – a "polity" being a cohesive and functioning state (Edwards, 1999: 68). What polities need to function successfully is "social capital" defined as a critical mass of trust, reciprocity, and a sense of obligation between members of the polity at all

levels, with governments and individuals committed to the welfare of all their fellow citizens. Africa's crisis in this analysis is largely, although not entirely, brought about through a lack of social capital. Edwards (1999: 66) claims that "development needs stability, stability requires a legiti-mate state, and legitimacy rests on [...] a level of political participation that is meaningful in local terms". Many development specialists claim that it is "the polity" that distinguishes the East Asian experience from that of most of Africa[9] (e.g. Sachs, 1996, cited in Edwards, 1999: 68). Similar comments had been made before the term "polity" had entered development discourse. The importance of the social and political ele-ments are stressed by Robinson (1996a: 170-171), who writes of:

> ... the growing appreciation in development circles that development is certainly not only about economics, and may not even be primarily about economics [...] social and political development are seen as the underpinnings of economic development at least as much as the other way around (and probably more).

Likewise over two decades ago President Kaunda of Zambia was wont to draw attention to the lack of "civic responsibility" in his country, while Bamgbose (1991: 44) claims "the primary causes of poverty are deficien-cies in education, organization and discipline". In such analyses such as these, the lack of social capital is seen as brought about by corrupt indi-vidual performances, which can be remedied in the short term when honest individuals take over. Bayart (1993), however, has a different take on the nature of political power in the African state – that of "the politics of the belly", where the expectation is that "big men" generally, and state lead-ers in particular, will amass and redistribute wealth. Bayart is at pains to point out that this is not "similar to a more or less erratic, 'political cul-ture' for which it might be possible to substitute 'good governance'; rather it is a system of historic action whose origins must if possible be sought in the Braudelian *longue durée*." (Bayart, 1993: ix). And again:

> Anyone seeking to dismiss this form of politics as no more than a symptom of corruption or of the decadence of the state is making a grave mistake. These representations can be institutional. The authors of Nigeria's draft constitution in 1976, for example, defined political power as 'the opportunity to acquire riches and prestige, to be in a

---

[9] Botswana, is an exception, where according to Edwards (1999) good govern-ance, social cohesion and mineral wealth all played a role.

position to hand out benefits in the form of jobs, contracts, gifts of money etc. to relations and political allies. (Bayart, 1993: xvii)

If Bayart's disquieting analysis of "doing power" in Africa is correct, then the accumulation within African countries of social capital (at least as envisaged by such as Edwards) is problematic, since it suggests that leaders at all social levels will continue to amass at the expense of the population generally, but will redistribute to a group of "relations and political allies" who may well be numerous, but who will be small relative to the total population. True, individual leaders may be deposed by violence or the ballot box, but the system will continue[10]. If Bayart's analysis is wrong, and the many cases of autocracy and corruption by African leaders are a matter of one-off deviancies which may in principle be halted, then the accumulation of social capital may be a more feasible eventuality. In either case, it is not clear that this mode of exercizing political power, whether it is rooted in "tradition" (for want of a better term), or simply the result of a sequence of rapacious leaders, can itself generate the agency for its own demise.

(iii) *Human capital*
What is crucial in human capital is *effective* education. Although there is no simple causal connection from the language through which education is conducted, to the well-being of the state, the weight of evidence suggests that literacy skills are more easily acquired in a language with which learners are familiar, leading to more effective education; in turn, effective education can contribute to poverty alleviation and development. It is abundantly clear that education in a language that few learners, and not all teachers, have mastery of, detracts from quality, and compounds the other problems arising from economically impoverished contexts. Robinson (2005: 186) concludes from his review of Ouane (2003) that such "patterns of language use in education systems continue to contribute to failure, alienation and waste", while Kelly (1995: 6) delivers a harsher judgement on the compounding effect of the Zambian language policy:

[T]he colossal neglect of education during the years of economic collapse, droughts and sickness are among other adverse factors. But

---

[10] Thus Finlayson (2005: 48) notes that although Bakili Muluzi, who took over democratically as President of Malawi from Kamuzu Banda, claimed to be a reformer, in due course "Bad habits cultivated under the dictatorship of Kamuzu Banda started to reassert themselves … the slide into autocracy and corruption became inexorable".

> [...] *were it not for the language policy, we would have had better*
> *educated people who would have known better how to cope with the*
> *economic problem, and even with those arising from drought, AIDS*
> *and other extrinsic factors.* (my emphasis)

The pessimistic perspective on Africa is that schools are destined to re-main sites of mystification, and that their prime role is that of screening to identify the very small number of the most apt, whom the powerful will then recruit to their cause. The dominance of English as a medium of instruction offers a most convenient screening method, and one, more-over, of which its victims and their parents thoroughly approve. The optimistic perspective on African education, on the other hand, is that the current weaknesses attributable to the dominance of English are the unin-tended consequences of an over-ambitious policy. Furthermore, there is latent agency for correcting these unintended consequences, and bringing about more effective education: Ministries of Education (albeit under stress), schools (although under-resourced), teachers (despite harrowing conditions), and tertiary education institutions (although qualitatively rav-aged: King, K. 2005b: 51) are in place. There is therefore the possibility, and one which is not financially unrealistic, but which does require politi-cal will[11], of educating children in languages that they can understand, which will lead to more fulfilled individuals. Certainly few would claim that the current educational experiences and outcomes for Malawian and Zambian schoolchildren are as positive as they could – and should – be.

The goal of appropriate language policy for effective education must therefore be worth pursuing. Although one may speculate that our three capitals – economic, social and human – are multiplicative in the sense that if the value of one of them is close to zero, then the other two cannot operate, everyday human realities do not proceed on such deterministic lines. Indeed McGinn (2005: 23) maintains that education can contribute directly to social capital, claiming that the reason Japan and Korea recov-ered from post-war impoverishment "was not because they began by slavishly copying the 20th century education models from the US or Great Britain. Instead they provided an education *to rebuild the social fabric* of their societies" (my italics). It is surely misguided to believe that this could have been achieved in any languages other than Japanese or Korean. The

---

[11] Kadzamira et al (2005: 50) in fact question the political will in Malawi for reform "in the face of strong internal pressure within government to pay lip-service to donor-driven agendas whilst maintaining the *status quo* [...] who will be the drivers of change?"

dominant role assigned to English in the primary schools in Malawi and Zambia has proved to be a barrier, rather than a bridge, to effective education, and an obstacle to the development of these states, of their communities, and of the individual children. If the Ministries of Education realise that their current English-dominated language policies generate ineffective education, then the policy contradictions can be addressed, and furthermore, addressed by agents that already exist. However, a necessary first step for all those who would wish to be agents in improving education in Malawi and Zambia is to take cognisance themselves of the present realities in their classrooms – which is, after all, the point of delivery for education – and to consider what is happening in their classrooms, and, more importantly, what is not happening and why.

Envois

You claim that the whites will help me to organise my country. But I find my country good just as it is. [...] Go away now, and above all, never come back.
Wobogo, Paramount Chief of the Mossi, addressing French colonial forces, Burkina Faso, 1895.

Although English is the national language, it is not a familiar language to the overwhelming majority of Zambian schoolchildren when they enter Grade 1. For them, communication through the medium of English at that stage is far from easy. In fact it is impossible.
"Education for Development: Draft Statement on Educational Reform", Paragraph 46, Ministry of Education, Zambia, 1976.

Do the white men teach their children to speak Nsenga?
"The Chosen Bud", John Luangala, 1991.

The dead of all the tribes and nations go there, and live in perfect harmony.
There is but one tongue, which each person acquires immediately he is greeted by the king; no distinction is made between the persons of chiefs, commoners or slaves. Even the persons of witches go there, for their witcheries have been left behind them.
"The Lambas of Northern Rhodesia" C. M. Doke, 1931.

(describing the Lamba *ichiyawafu* 'the great place of levelling')

Appendix 1: Map of Africa

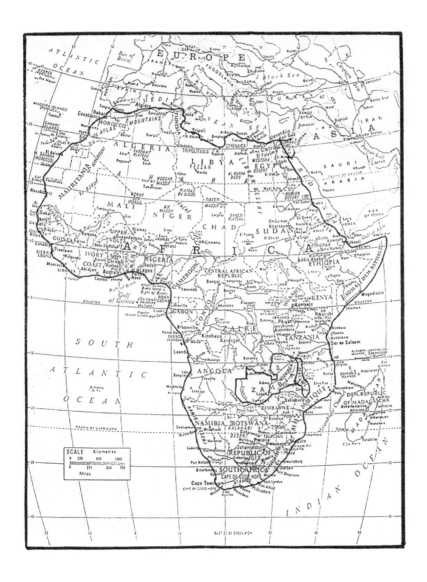

Appendix 2: Text and Transcript for English Lesson, Malawi

Extract from "English in Malawi": Revised Edition, Pupils Book 2, Page 46

Timve and Tsala are inside the store.
They are buying things for mother.

Are they buying matches?
No, they are not.
They are not buying matches.

Are they buying bottles?
No, they are not.
They are not buying bottles.

Are they buying tins?
No, they are not.
They are not buying tins.

They are buying sugar.
They are buying tea.
They are buying sugar and tea.
They are buying things for mother.

Transcript of English lesson
Malawi: Rural School
Year 2 Class. Number of Pupils: 128
Utterances in italics indicate translations from ChiChewa.

Teacher:	Now it's time for English. Class, who can remember to read this word? ... Yes?
Pupil:	Any
Teacher:	Any. Very good. Clap hands for him. (Pupils clapping)
Teacher:	What about this word. What does it say?
Pupil:	Tins.
Teacher:	Very good. Clap hands for ... her. (Pupils clapping) and everybody say "tins".
Class:	Tins.
Teacher:	Tins.
Class:	Tins.
Teacher:	Who can read this word? ... Yes?
Pupil:	Bottle.
Teacher:	Bottles. Very good. Clap hands for her. (Pupils clapping)
Teacher:	Now everybody read.
Class:	Bottles.
Teacher:	Again.
Class:	Bottles.
Teacher:	What does this say? Yes, Danzani?
D:	Matches.
Y:	Matches. Very good. Clap hands for him. (Pupils clapping)
Teacher:	Everybody, say after Danzani.
Class:	Matches.
Teacher:	Again.
Class:	Matches.
Teacher:	Now look here. Look on page 46. Everybody can see it? *Everybody can see it?*
Class:	*Yes*
Teacher:	*Right.* Now, what can you see? What can you see? Yes, Kenneth?
K:	I can see Timve.
Teacher:	You can see Timve. Yes. Noah, where is Timve? Where is Timve? Yes, Makanso?
M:	(indistinct)
Teacher:	No, no. Yes, you.
Pupil:	Timve is wearing a shirt and shoes.
Teacher:	I said, I said, where is Timve? *Where is Timve?* Where is Timve? Yes?

Pupil:	Timve is in the store.
Teacher:	Yes, Timve is in the store. Clap hands for her. (Pupils clapping)
Pupil:	Now everybody say after her.
Class:	Timve is in the store.
Teacher:	Again.
Class:	Timve is in the store.
Teacher:	Now, who is that man? Who is this man? He's a .. He's ... finish it ...Yes?
Pupil:	That is a storekeeper.
Teacher:	Yes. That is a store keeper. Very good. Now this is a storekeeper. Now, what is his name? What is his name? Yes?
Pupil:	(indistinct)
Teacher:	Speak loudly.
Pupil:	(indistinct)
Teacher:	Speak loudly.
Pupil:	Can you hear her?
Class:	His name is ...
Teacher:	*Did you hear what she said?*
Class:	*Yes.*
Teacher:	Say it loudly. Yes, speak it loudly. *Say it loudly.*
Pupil:	His name is Mr Gondwe.
Teacher:	Very good. Say after him.
Class:	His name is Mr Gondwe.
Teacher:	Now here I have written some words. Now the first words reads. "Buying, buying, buying. No, no no. Buying buying. No. Now class, read after me "Buying".
Class:	Buying.
Teacher:	Again.
Class:	Buying.
Teacher:	Again.
Class:	Buying.
Teacher:	Now Botolan read it.
BL:	Buying.
Teacher:	Stand up and read it.
B:	Buying.
Teacher:	Very good. You stand up. Read it.
Pupil:	Buying.
Teacher:	Everybody read it.
Class:	Buying.
Teacher:	Here. Read after me. No.
Class:	No.
Teacher:	No.

Class:	No
Teacher:	No.
Class:	No.
Teacher:	Now, who can read it. Kanyada.
Pupil:	No.
Teacher:	Speak loudly.
Pupil:	No.
Teacher:	Yes. (indistinct)
E:	No.
Teacher:	No. Very good. (Writes on board) What does it say? Yes?
Pupil:	No.
Teacher:	Very good. Clap hands for him. (Pupils clapping) Yes. Juvis?
J:	Buying.
Teacher:	Buying. Yes. Very good. Now you listen, I am going to read. *I am going to read.* "Timve and Tsala are inside the store.

They are buying things for mother.

Are they buying matches?

No, they are not.

They are not buying matches.

Are they buying bottles?

No, they are not.

They are not buying bottles.

They are buying sugar.

They are buying tea.

They are buying sugar and tea.

They are buying things for mother."

Now class, read after me.

Teacher:	Timve and Tsala are inside the store.
Class:	Timve and Tsala are inside the store.

(Class continue repeating text after the teacher, as far as: "They are buying things for mother.")

Teacher:	Now I would like boys to read after me. Girls, keep quiet.

Timve and Tsala are inside the store.

(Boys repeat the text after the teacher.)

Now I would like that line at the back. Stand up. Quickly. Now read after me. And that one. *That one.* Mmhmm.

Line:	Timve and Tsala are inside the store.
Teacher:	No. Timve and Tsala are inside the store.
Line:	Timve and Tsala are inside the store.

(The line read the whole text after the teacher.)

Good, sit down. Now, everybody read. I would like you to read alone (indistinct). Start.

Class:	Timve -
Teacher:	Everybody, girls and boys. Start reading.
Class:	(Read the text, as far as "Are they buying bottles?")
Teacher:	Listen, "Are they buying bottles?"
C:	Are they buying bottles?
Teacher:	Are they buying bottles?
C:	Are they buying bottles? (Class continue to end)
Teacher:	Children, now who can read for me? Yes, Konda.
K:	Timve and Tsala are inside the store. They are buying things
Teacher:	Things.
K:	Things.
Teacher:	Things.
K:	Things. (Continues text to "They are buying matches.")
Teacher:	Very good. Clap hands for ... him.
Now girls.	Yes. Start from here.
G:	Are they buying bottles. No they are not. They are not buying bottles.
Teacher:	Very good. Clap hands for her. (Pupils clapping)
Teacher:	Next. Yes.
Pupil:	They are buying sugar. They are buying tea. They are buying sugar and tea. They are buying things for mother.
Teacher:	Very good. Clap hands for him. (Pupils clapping)
Teacher:	Now. Questions. What is Timve and Tsala buying? What is Timve and Tsala buying? Yes.
Pupil:	Timve and Tsala are inside the store.
Teacher:	Wrong, no. What are they buying? Or let me ask you this way. What are they buying? What are they buying? Yes?
Pupil:	They are buying some tea and sugar.
Teacher:	They are buying sugar and tea. Say it again.
Pupil:	They are buying sugar and tea.
Teacher:	Very good. Say it again.
Teacher:	Now, say after him. They are buying sugar and tea. Say it.
Class:	They are buying sugar and tea.
Teacher:	Now, are they buying bottles? Are they buying bottles. Yes?
Pupil:	No, they are not.
Teacher:	Very good. Clap hands for her. (Pupils clapping)
Teacher:	Are they buying matches? Are they buying matches? Yes?
Pupil:	No they are not.
Teacher:	Very good. Clap hands for her. (Pupils clapping)
Teacher:	Now, who can come and write the word "buying"? Who can come and write the word on the chalk board. Violet. Yes, you? Take a piece of chalk.

Pupil:	(Writes)
Teacher:	Is he correct?
Class:	No.
Teacher:	Now, who can come and correct it? Who can come and correct it? Yes? Come in. Yes, come in front. You. Write "buying". Is she correct?
Class:	Yes.
Teacher:	Clap hands for her. (Pupils clapping)
Teacher:	Now, who can come and write "No, no, no". Yes? Dan Freda. Write "No". Is he correct?
Class:	Yes.
Teacher:	Clap hands for him. (Pupils clapping)

End of lesson.

Appendix 3: Text and Transcript for English Lesson, Zambia

Rural School (some 25 kilometres from Lusaka, and 10 from tarred road)
Year 3. Number in class = 45

The following text from the Year 3 coursebook, the New Zambia Primary English Course, was copied onto the board by the Grade 3 Teacher at the beginning of the lesson:

3. *"Look at that hippo's mouth, Father. It is very big isn't it?" said Chuma.*
    "Yes, hippos have very big mouths," said his father. "Crocodiles have very big mouths too."

4. *Chuma and his father walked away from the river. They walked away from the crocodiles. They walked away from the hippos. Now they were walking between the trees. They walked slowly and quietly between the trees. They were walking slowly and quietly when they saw a very big rhino. The rhino was near a tree and he was eating grass.*

Transcript

Teacher:	English reading. We are going to read the story that is Chuma and the Rhino. That is paragraph three and four, which has been written on the board. Who can read the first sentence in paragraph four? Yes?
Pupil:	Look at that hippo's mouth father
Teacher:	Read aloud.
Pupil:	Look at that hippo's mouth father.
Teacher:	Once more.
Pupil:	Look at that hippo's mouth father.
Teacher:	Yes. The sentence is "Look at that hippo's mouth father".
Class:	Look at that hippo's mouth father.
Teacher:	Look at that hippo's mouth father.
Class:	Look at that hippo's mouth father.
Teacher:	Yes. (Points) What is that sentence? Who can read the next sentence? Simon?
Pupil:	It is very big isn't ... isn't it, said Chuma.
Teacher:	Again.

Pupil:	It is very big isn't it, said Chuma.
Teacher:	Thank you. The sentence is: It is very big isn't it, said Chuma. Read.
Class:	It is very big isn't it, said Chuma.
Teacher:	It is very big isn't it, said Chuma.
Class:	It is very big isn't it, said Chuma.
Teacher:	Big.
Class:	Big.
Teacher:	Big.
Class:	Big.
Teacher:	It is very big isn't it, said Chuma.
Class:	It is very big isn't it, said Chuma.
Teacher:	OK. (Pause) Who can read the next sentence? Navis?
Pupil:	Now, hippos have very -
Teacher:	Is this word "now"?
Pupil:	Now -
Teacher:	No, no, no, no ...
Pupil:	Yes, hippo have very big ... Yes, hippos have very big mouths, said his mother.
Teacher:	Thank you. Uh, what's that word?
Pupil:	Father.
Teacher:	OK. Yes, hippos have very big mouths said his father. Read.
Class:	Yes, hippos have very big mouths, said his father.
Teacher:	Yes, hippos have very big mouths, said his father.
Class:	Yes, hippos have very big mouths said his father.
Teacher:	Say mouths.
Class:	Mouths.
Teacher:	Don't say "mouths", say "mouths".
Pupil:	Mouths.
Teacher:	Yes, hippos have very big mouths, said his father.
Class:	Yes, hippos have very big mouths, said his father.
Teacher:	The next sentence. Musa.
Pupil:	Crocodiles have very big mouths too.
Teacher:	Again.
Pupil:	Crocodiles have very big mouth too.
Teacher:	Mmm. Who can - who can help him? ?
Pupil:	Crocodiles have very big mouths too.
Teacher:	Thank you. Crocodiles have very big mouths too. Read. Crocodiles have very big mouths too.
Class:	Crocodiles have very big mouths too.
Teacher:	Crocodiles.
Class:	Crocodiles.
Teacher:	Crocodiles.

Class:	Crocodiles.
Teacher:	Crocodiles have very big mouths too.
Class:	Crocodiles have very big mouths too.
Teacher:	OK. Paragraph four. The first sentence.
Pupil:	Chuma and his father walked away from the river.
Teacher:	Again.
Pupil:	Chuma and his father walked away from the river.
Teacher:	Yes, that is the sentence. Chuma and his father walked away from the river. Read.
Class:	Chuma and his father walked away from the river.
Teacher:	Walked.
Class:	Walked.
Teacher:	Walked.
Class:	Walked.
Teacher:	Read the sentence.
Class:	Chuma and his father walked away from the river.
Teacher:	Next sentence? Then ...
Pupil:	They ... they walked away from the crocodiles.
Teacher:	Yes. They walked away from the crocodiles. Read.
Class:	They walked away from the crocodiles.
Teacher:	Read this word as "walked." Say "walked."
Class:	Walked.
Teacher:	Now read the sentence.
Class:	They walked away from the crocodiles.
Teacher:	Now this.
Pupil:	They walked away from the hippos.
Teacher:	Again.
Pupil:	They walked away from the hippos.
Teacher:	They walked away from the hippos. Read.
Class:	They walked away from thc hippos.
Teacher:	Next sentence.
Pupil:	(Indistinct) Now they .. now they ... now they were walking between the trees.
Teacher:	Again.
Class:	Now they were walking between the trees.
Teacher:	OK, that is correct. Now they were walking between the trees. Read.
Class:	Now they were walking between the trees.
Teacher:	Now they were walking between the trees.
Class:	Now they were walking between the trees.
Teacher:	Next sentence. *Don't look at the white man.* Look at the board. Look at the board. Look at the board.
Pupil:	(Indistinct)
Teacher:	*Look at the board.*
Teacher:	Yes.

Pupil:	Chuma likes to walk between the trees.
Teacher:	Again.
Pupil:	Chuma liked to walk between the trees.
Teacher:	Thank you. Chuma liked to walk between the trees.
Class:	Chuma liked to walk between the trees.
Teacher:	Chuma liked to walk between the trees.
Class:	Chuma liked to walk between the trees.
Teacher:	Liked
Class:	Liked
Teacher:	Liked
Class:	Liked
Teacher:	Chuma liked to walk between the trees.
Class:	Chuma liked to walk between the trees.
Teacher:	Liked, liked, You're still saying "liked" Say "liked". Read the word as "liked". Chuma liked to walk between the trees.
Class:	Chuma liked to walk between the trees.
Teacher: Next sentence. What are they doing?	
Pupil:	They walked ..they walked slowly and quietly between the trees.
Teacher:	No.
Pupil:	They walked slowly and quietly between the trees.
Teacher:	Again. They-
Pupil:	They walked slowly and quietly between the trees.
Teacher:	OK. They walked slowly and quietly between the trees. Read.
Class:	They walked slowly and quietly between the trees.
Teacher:	Again.
Class:	They walked slowly and quietly between the trees.
Teacher:	Yes.
Pupil:	They were walking slowly and quietly when they saw a very big rhino.
Teacher:	(Indistinct) Read the sentence.
Pupil:	They were walking slowly and quietly when they saw a very big rhino.
Teacher:	Yes. They were walking slowly and quietly when they saw a very big rhino. Read.
Class:	They were walking slowly and quietly when they saw a very big rhino.
Teacher:	They. Say they.
Class:	They.
Teacher:	They.
Class:	They.
Teacher:	Now read the sentence once more.
Class:	They were walking slowly and quietly when they saw a very big rhino.
Teacher:	Yes. Segono. (Indistinct) The last sentence.
S:	(Indistinct)

Teacher:	(*Right.*)
Pupil:	The rhino was near a tree and he was eating grass.
Teacher:	Thank you. The rhino was near a tree and he was eating grass. Read.
Class:	The rhino was near a tree and he was eating grass.
Teacher:	The rhino was near a tree and he was eating grass.
Class:	The rhino was near a tree and he was eating grass.
Teacher:	OK. Now who can read paragraph three? Paragraph three. Ben.
Pupil:	Look at ..Look at that...that...that...that hippo mouth Father.
Teacher:	Hippo's. Hippo's.
Pupil:	Hippo's mouth father. It is very big .. it .. it ... isn't it?
Teacher:	Isn't it?
Pupil:	Isn't it said Chuma.
Teacher:	Start again. Start again.
Pupil:	Look at ... look at that hippo's mouth father. It is very big isn't it, said Chuma. Said hippos....
Teacher:	No, no, no. What's the word. Not said.
Pupil:	Yes
Pupil:	Yes, hippos ... hippos have very big mouth .. mouths said his father. Crocodiles have very big mouths too.
Teacher:	OK, that's alright. It's alright. Let's see, yes, Samuel.
S:	Look at that hippo's mouth, Father. It is very big ... it ... it is very big isn't it, said Chuma. Yes ... yes ... hippos very big ...
Teacher:	Have
Pupil:	Yes hippos very very big mouth said his father. Yes hippos very ...
Teacher:	Have very big mouths.
Pupil:	Yes, hippos have very big mouths. said his father. Crocodiles, crocodiles have very big mouths too.
Teacher:	Thank you. OK. Look at that hippo's mouth father. It is very big isn't it? said Chuma. Yes, hippos have very big mouths, said his father. Crocodiles have very big mouths too. Together read that paragraph.
Class:	Look at that hippo's mouth father. It is very big isn't it? said Chuma. Yes, hippos have very big mouths, said his father. Crocodiles have very big mouths too.
Teacher:	OK. The fourth paragraph. You.
Pupil:	Chuma and his father walked away from the river. They walked away from the crocodiles. They walked away from the hippos. Now they were walking between the trees. Chuma liked to walk between the trees.
Y:	OK that's very nice. Another one? (Indistinct) Musa.
Pupil:	Chuma and his father walked away from the river. They walked away.
Teacher:	They walked.
Pupil:	They walked away from the river, and they walked away from the crocodiles. They walked away from the hippos. Now they were walking between the trees. Chuma liked to walk between the trees.

Teacher:	Thank you. Chuma and his father walked away from the river. They walked away from the crocodiles. They walked away from the hippos. Now they were walking between the trees. Read the sentences.
Class:	Chuma and his father walked away from the river. They walked away from the crocodiles.
Teacher:	They walked away from the crocodiles.
Class:	They walked away from the crocodiles. They walked away from the hippos.
Teacher:	They walked away from the hippos.
Class:	They walked away from the hippos.
Teacher:	You mustn't say "walked", "walked". Say "walked".
Class:	Walked.
Teacher:	Walked.
Class:	Walked.
Teacher:	They walked away from the hippos.
Class:	They walked away from the hippos.
Teacher:	The next sentence.
Class:	Now they were walking between the trees.
Teacher:	Thank you. The next sentences. (writes) Try.
Pupil:	They walked slowly and quietly between the trees.
Teacher:	*Read.* Read.
Pupil:	They ...
Teacher:	They walked slowly.
Pupil:	They walked slowly between the trees.
Teacher:	Come in. Come in.
Pupil:	... the trees.
Teacher:	Sit down. Sit down. Sit down. Sit down. Sit down. Yes. (Indistinct)
Pupil:	(Indistinct) They walked slowly and quietly between the trees. They were walking slowly and quietly when they saw a very big rhino. The rhino was near a tree and he was eating grass.
Teacher:	OK. Thank you. Now ... They were ... Sorry. They walked slowly and quietly between the trees. They walked slowly and quietly between the trees. They were walking slowly and quietly when they saw a very big rhino. The rhino was near a tree and he was eating grass. Read the sentences.
Class:	They walked slowly and quietly between the trees. They walked slowly and quietly between the trees. They were walking slowly and quietly when they saw a very big rhino. The rhino was near a tree and he was eating grass.
Teacher:	OK.

End of lesson

Appendix 4: Test Type Exercises from Course Books

From "English in Malawi: Revised Edition, Pupils' Book 4 (pp 26 and 65)

B Put each of these words into the right place in the story.

someone   no-one   something   anything   Everything

_____ was dark in the room. Wamba could not see _____ . Then _____ moved. "Who is it?" Wamba asked, but _____ answered. "There's _____ there," Wamba said, "Who is it?"

Page 26

B Put each of these words into the right sentence:

excited   young   good   lazy   hard.

1 Mrs Kapezi's best dress was too _____ to wear every day.
2 Before the wedding, Tsala was too _____ to sleep.
3 Old bread is sometimes too _____ to eat.
4 Songiso's friends were too _____ to work.
5 Baby Ulemu was too _____ to go to school.

Page 65

Appendix 5

Year of Introduction of Lexical Items from English Test

ITEM	Zambia Year	Malawi Year	ITEM	Zambia Year	Malaw Year
bad	3	3	lot	3	3
ball	1	1	make-V	2	2
bicyle	2	2	middle	3	3
brother	1	2	morning	2	2
build-V	4	3	mother	1	1
car	1	3	mountain	5	5
carry-V	2	3	now	1	2
catch-V	3	3	old	1	1
cook-V	1	3	people	3	2
come-V	2	2	place	5	4
corner	4	4	quickly	3	2
cut-V	3	2	quietly	2	3
day	1	3	rain	4	3
driver	2	3	ride-V	3	2
eat-V	1	2	river	2	2
eight	1	2	road	2	3
everybody	3	3	root	4	5
fall-V	3	4	run-V	1	2
fat	3	2	say	2	2
father	1	1	school	1	2
fire	1	2	see-V	1	2
fish	1	3	side	2	2
fish-V	1	3	sister	1	1
get out-V	2	2	soil	3	5
girl	2	1	soon	4	3
go-V/went	2	3	stay-V	3	4
good	2	2	stone	4	3
ground	3	4	stop-V	3	3
grow-V	4	2	suddenly	5	4
hand	2	2	take-V	2	3
help	4	3	teacher	1	2
hill	3	3	thin	3	2
hit-V	2	2	three	1	2

hold-V	2	2	together	2	3
home	3	2	tomato	3	2
hospital	2	3	tree	1	1
hungry	3	3	use-V	4	4
hurt-V	2	4	useful	5	4
important	5	5	walk-V	3	2
know-V	3	3	wash-V	1	2
lion	2	3	water	3	2
little	2	2	wood	2	2
live-V	1	2	year	1	3
look-V	1	2			

Note: Verbs are indicated as -V

Appendix 6: Extracts from Reading Tests

Extract 1 (from English Test)

Ruth and her brother

go	ball	old
is	good	home

Ruth Phiri lives with her mother and father and her little
brother, Moses. Ruth is eight years _____, and   1
she goes to school. Moses _____ three years old. 2
He doesn't _____ to school. He stays   3
at _____ with his mother.   4

Extract 2 (from ChiChewa Test): Magule

opsalasula	nyau	ndi
amabvina	mchiuno	chimtali

M'Malawi muli magule osiyana-siyana. Ana, atsikana,
anyamata ndi achikulire, _____ gule amene   11
akonda. Magule ambiri _____ oduka pobvinitsa chiuno. 12
Ena ali ndi _____ chofewa. Pali magule   13
ena _____ miyendo. Gule wotere amachititsa pfumbi   14
kwambiri.

Extract 3 (from Nyanja Test):   Magule

opsalasula	nyau	ndi
abvina	mciuno	cimtali

M'Zambia muli magule osiyana-siyana. Ana, atsikana,
anyamata ndi acikulire, _____ gule amene   11

akonda. Magule ambiri _____ oduka pobvinitsa ciuno.   12
Ena ali ndi _____ kuposa anzao. Pali magule   13
ena _____ miyendo. Gule wotere acita pfumbi   14
kwambiri.

Translation:

In Zambia, [Malawi: for Malawi version] there are different kinds of dances. Children, girls and boys, and adults too, have their favourite dance which they like to do. In many dances you twist from the waist. Some dancers have more supple waists than others. There are some dances where you have to kick your legs and stamp your feet. This kind of dance raises a lot of dust.

Appendix 7: Reliability Results for Tests

1. Discrimination index for English test, Malawi (point biserial)

Number of children = 290, second figure under each item is the significance level (p-value). I = item

I1	I2	I3	I4	I5	I6
0.32549	0.38690	0.19091	0.40023	0.57606	0.46991
0.0001	0.0001	0.0011	0.0001	0.0001	0.0001

I7	I8	I9	I10	I11	I12
0.47387	0.56821	0.60529	0.54681	0.55442	0.57823
0.0001	0.0001	0.0001	0.0001	0.0001	0.0001

I13	I14	I15	I16	I17	I18
0.57675	0.49656	0.34972	0.32128	0.35028	0.49043
0.0001	0.0001	0.0001	0.0001	0.0001	0.0001

I19	I20	I21	I22	I23	I24
0.44606	0.59101	0.46715	0.27074	0.49938	0.45906
0.0001	0.0001	0.0001	0.0001	0.0001	0.0001

I25	I26	I27	I28	I29	I30
0.43040	0.53594	0.42395	0.28651	0.42160	0.18708
0.0001	0.0001	0.0001	0.0001	0.0001	0.0014

2. Discrimination index for English test Zambia (point biserial)

Number of children = 227, second figure under each item is the significance level (p-value). I = item

I1	I2	I3	I4	I5	I6
0.74844	0.75701	0.73200	0.68529	0.76829	0.62454
0.0001	0.0001	0.0001	0.0001	0.0001	0.0001

I7	I8	I9	I10	I11	I12
0.54291	0.71114	0.75258	0.68880	0.73316	0.53897
0.0001	0.0001	0.0001	0.0001	0.0001	0.0001

I13	I14	I15	I16	I17	I18
0.64452	0.78175	0.66224	0.59382	0.72072	0.77762
0.0001	0.0001	0.0001	0.0001	0.0001	0.0001

I19	I20	I21	I22	I23	I24
0.61768	0.72231	0.72709	0.56680	0.59765	0.65100
0.0001	0.0001	0.0001	0.0001	0.0001	0.0001

I25	I26	I27	I28	I29	I30
0.56372	0.51551	0.50766	0.52960	0.52132	0.45677
0.0001	0.0001	0.0001	0.0001	0.0001	0.0001

3.   Reliability Analysis – Scale Alpha

English Test for Malawi and Zambia combined

Item-total Statistics

	Scale Mean if Item Deleted	Scale Variance if Item Deleted	Corrected Item-Total Correlation	Alpha if Item Deleted
Q01	11.5648	57.9866	.5076	.9248
Q02	11.6731	57.4181	.5209	.9246
Q03	11.5841	58.2085	.4553	.9254
Q04	11.6093	57.8315	.4960	.9249
Q05	11.8143	56.5895	.5983	.9235
Q06	12.0039	57.4147	.5114	.9247
Q07	11.9768	57.7708	.4521	.9255
Q08	11.9671	56.6636	.6050	.9234
Q09	11.9323	56.3229	.6432	.9229
Q10	11.9188	56.7453	.5813	.9237
Q11	11.8414	56.9438	.5480	.9242
Q12	11.8008	57.4312	.4840	.9251
Q13	11.8375	56.8960	.5546	.9241

Q14	11.8569	56.5686	.5996	.9235
Q15	12.0484	57.5694	.5095	.9247
Q16	12.1064	58.0681	.4702	.9252
Q17	12.0290	57.3848	.5267	.9245
Q18	11.7776	56.6927	.5893	.9236
Q19	12.1683	57.8379	.5697	.9241
Q20	11.9439	56.3980	.6356	.9230
Q21	11.8433	56.8611	.5593	.9241
Q22	12.1122	58.2471	.4464	.9255
Q23	12.0251	57.3191	.5344	.9244
Q24	12.0135	57.2111	.5448	.9243
Q25	12.1509	57.9888	.5229	.9246
Q26	12.0387	57.5876	.5018	.9248
Q27	12.0851	57.9927	.4674	.9252
Q28	12.1721	58.6777	.4277	.9257
Q29	12.0909	57.9588	.4764	.9251
Q30	12.1663	59.1079	.3480	.9265

Reliability Coefficients

N of Cases =   517   N of Items = 30

Alpha =   .9269

4. Discrimination index for ChiChewa test, Malawi (point biserial)

Number of children = 290, second figure under each item is the significance level (p-value). I = item

I1	I2	I3	I4	I5	I6
0.37073	0.40217	0.32114	0.37881	0.33130	0.45497
0.0001	0.0001	0.0001	0.0001	0.0001	0.0001

I7	I8	I9	I10	I11	I12
0.50830	0.34312	0.38068	0.42620	0.25067	0.41367
0.0001	0.0001	0.0001	0.0001	0.0001	0.0001

I13	I14	I15	I16	I17	I18
0.30048	0.46868	0.49858	0.38487	0.39905	0.44434
0.0001	0.0001	0.0001	0.0001	0.0001	0.0001

I19	I20	I21	I22	I23	I24
0.50799	0.40204	0.30049	0.44712	0.35730	0.42646
0.0001	0.0001	0.0001	0.0001	0.0001	0.0001

I25	I26	I27	I28	I29	I30
0.30580	0.23194	0.39485	0.48163	0.46239	0.50914
0.0001	0.0001	0.0001	0.0001	0.0001	0.0001

5. Discrimination index for Nyanja test, Zambia (point biserial)

Number of children = 227, second figure under each item is the significance level (p-value) I = item

I1	I2	I3	I4	I5	I6
0.52357	0.26977	0.46448	0.45425	0.47425	0.42176
0.0001	0.0001	0.0001	0.0001	0.0001	0.0001

I7	I8	I9	I10	I11	I12
0.36877	0.46444	0.37893	0.44418	0.29156	0.21060
0.0001	0.0001	0.0001	0.0001	0.0001	0.0014

I13	I14	I15	I16	I17	I18
0.26237	0.29354	0.09673	0.32260	0.24622	0.27560
0.0001	0.0001	0.1463	0.0001	0.0002	0.0001

I19	I20	I21	I22	I23	I24
0.18209	0.24224	0.37933	0.20914	0.34638	0.21536
0.0059	0.0002	0.0001	0.0015	0.0001	0.0011

I25	I26	I27	I28	I29	I30
0.09886	0.26019	0.21515	0.23410	0.22704	0.17403
0.1376	0.0001	0.0011	0.0004	0.0006	0.0086

Appendix 8: Test Item Facility Values

1. Facility values for English test: Malawi

Item	N	Facility value
1	290	0.92
2	290	0.75
3	290	0.87
4	290	0.84
5	290	0.53
6	290	0.26
7	290	0.37
8	290	0.36
9	290	0.41
10	290	0.46
11	290	0.44
12	290	0.57
13	290	0.53
14	290	0.55
15	290	0.29
16	290	0.20
17	290	0.27
18	290	0.68
19	290	0.11
20	290	0.42
21	290	0.63
22	290	0.21
23	290	0.37
24	290	0.37
25	290	0.20
26	290	0.36
27	290	0.28
28	290	0.15
29	290	0.24
30	290	0.19

2. Facility values for English test: Zambia

Item	N	Facility value
1	227	0.61
2	227	0.58
3	227	0.63
4	227	0.61
5	227	0.55
6	227	0.46
7	227	0.38
8	227	0.41
9	227	0.42
10	227	0.39
11	227	0.59
12	227	0.52
13	227	0.49
14	227	0.42
15	227	0.32
16	227	0.30
17	227	0.39
18	227	0.44
19	227	0.27
20	227	0.39
21	227	0.34
22	227	0.27
23	227	0.26
24	227	0.29
25	227	0.20
26	227	0.26
27	227	0.25
28	227	0.21
29	227	0.28
30	227	0.17

3. Facility values for Chichewa test, Malawi

Item	N	Facility value
1	290	0.88
2	290	0.86
3	290	0.91
4	290	0.83
5	290	0.83
6	290	0.58
7	290	0.57
8	290	0.90
9	290	0.62
10	290	0.67
11	290	0.79
12	290	0.52
13	290	0.80
14	290	0.56
15	290	0.46
16	290	0.67
17	290	0.73
18	290	0.70
19	290	0.51
20	290	0.61
21	290	0.78
22	290	0.81
23	290	0.52
24	290	0.77
25	290	0.35
26	290	0.59
27	290	0.32
28	290	0.61
29	290	0.46
30	290	0.68

4. Facility values for Nyanja test: Zambia

Item	N	Facility value
1	227	0.25
2	227	0.26
3	227	0.27
4	227	0.18
5	227	0.15
6	227	0.21
7	227	0.10
8	227	0.14
9	227	0.15
10	227	0.14
11	227	0.17
12	227	0.14
13	227	0.19
14	227	0.14
15	227	0.15
16	227	0.15
17	227	0.17
18	227	0.07
19	227	0.05
20	227	0.08
21	227	0.38
22	227	0.11
23	227	0.18
24	227	0.20
25	227	0.07
26	227	0.11
27	227	0.02
28	227	0.05
29	227	0.06
30	227	0.07

References

Afolayan, A. (1999) 'The Alienated Role of the Mother Tongue in Literacy Education for Sustainable National Development: the Western Nigerian Yoruba Example', in S. Manaka (ed.) *Proceedings of the 1ˢᵗ Pan-African Conference on Reading for All*, Pretoria, South Africa: International Reading Association, READ & UNESCO, 70-88

Aikman, S. (2001) 'Literacies, Languages and Developments in Peruvian Amazonia', in B. Street (ed.), *Literacy and Development: ethnographic perspectives*, London: Routledge, 103-120.

Åkesson, G. (1992) *School Books and Buying Power: a study of schools and prescribed books in rural areas of Mozambique*, Education Division Documents, No 59. Stockholm: Swedish International Development Authority.

Alderson, J. C. (2000) *Assessing Reading*, Cambridge: Cambridge University Press.

------ (1984) 'Reading in a Foreign Language: a Reading Problem or a Language problem?', in Alderson and Urquhart (eds.), *Reading in a Foreign Language*, London: Longman, 1-25.

------ (1993) 'The Relationship between Grammar and Reading in an English for Academic Purposes Test Battery', in D. Douglas and C. Chappelle (eds.), *A New decade of Language Testing Research*, Washington: TESOL, 204-214.

------ and A.H. Urquhart (eds.) (1984) *Reading in a Foreign Language*, London: Longman.

Allsop, T. (2005). 'Review of Al-Samarrai, S., & Bennell, P. (eds.) *Where has all the education gone in Africa?*, Brighton: Institute of Development Studies, University of Sussex', *International Journal of Education Development*, 25: 92-93.

Anderson, C. A. (1966) 'Literacy and Schooling on the Development Threshold: Some Historical Cases', in C.A. Anderson and M.J. Bowman (eds.), Anderson, C. A. and Bowman, M. J. (eds.) *Education and Economic Development*. London: Frank Cass, 347-362.

------ and M.J. Bowman (eds.) (1966) *Education and Economic Development*, London: Frank Cass.

Appleton, S. (1996) 'Problems of Measuring Changes in Poverty over Time: the case of Uganda'. *Institute of Development Studies Bulletin, 27/1:* 43-55.

Arcand, J-L., (1995) 'Development Economics and Language: the earnest search for a mirage?', *International Journal of the Sociology of Language,* 121: 119-157.

Association for the Development of African Education. (1996) *A Synopsis of Research Findings on Languages of Instruction and their Policy Implications for Education in Africa,* (mimeo by Working Group on Educational Research and Policy Analysis, for African Ministers of Education Meeting, Accra, 1996).

Azariadis, C. and A. Drazen (1990) 'Threshold Externalities in Economic Development', *The Quarterly Journal of Economics,* May: 501-26.

Bailey, R. (1995) 'The Bantu Language of South Africa: Towards a Socio-historical Perspective', in R. Mesthrie (ed.), *Language and Social History: Studies in South African Sociolinguistics.* Cape Town: David Philip, 19-38.

Baker, V. J. (1998) 'Literacy in Developing Societies: Native Language Versus National Language Literacy', in A.Y. Durngunoglu and L. Verhoeven (eds.) *Literacy Development in a Multilingual Context,* Mahwah, NJ.: Lawrence Erlbaum, 21-36.

Balibar, E. and I. Wallerstein (1991) *Race, Nation, Class: Ambiguous Identities,* New York: Praeger.

Bamgbose, A. (1991) *Language and the Nation,* Edinburgh: Edinburgh University Press for the International African Institute.

Bayart, J.-F. (1993) *The State in Africa: the Politics of the Belly,* London: Longman.

Baynham, M. (1995) *Literacy Practices: Investigating Literacy in Social Contexts,* Harlow: Longman.

Becker, G. S. (1964) *Human Capital: A Theoretical and Empirical Analysis,* New York: National Bureau of Economic Research.

Berman, R. A. (1984) 'Syntactic Components of the Foreign Language Reading Process', in J.C. Alderson and A.H. Urquhart (eds.), *Reading in a Foreign Language,* London: Longman, 139-159.

Bermingham, D. (2005) 'From Commitments to Action: what (2005) will mean for DFID's education programmes', *NORRAG News,* 36: 38-40.

Bernbaum, M., M. Chatsika and E. Chinguo (1998) *Lessons Learned: Evaluation of USAID/Malawi Girls Attainment in Basic Literacy and Education (GABLE) Program,* Academy for Educational Development, Washington, DC.

Bernhardt, E. B. (1991a) *Reading Development in a Second Language: Theoretical, Empirical and Classroom Perspectives,* Norwood, New Jersey: Ablex Publishing.

------ (1991b) 'A Psycholinguistic Perspective on Second Language Literacy', in Hulstijn and Matter (eds.), *Reading in two languages,* AILA Review, 8, Amsterdam, 31-44.

------ and M. L. Kamil (1995) 'Interpreting Relationships between L1 and L2 Reading: consolidating the linguistic threshold and linguistic interdependence hypotheses', *Applied Linguistics* 16(1): 15-34.

Blommaert, J. (2001) 'Ethnography as Counter-hegemony', presentation at 'Literacy and Language in Global Settings' Conference, Cape Town, November, 2001.

------ (ed.) (1999) *Language Ideological Debates,* Berlin: Mouton de Gruyter.

------ (ed.) (1999a) 'The Debate is Open', in Blommaert, J. (ed.), *Language ideological debate,* Berlin: Mouton de Gruyter, 1-38

------ (1999b) 'The Debate is Closed' in Blommaert J. (ed.), *Language ideological debate*, Berlin: Mouton de Gruyter, 1-38 425-438.

Bond, P. (ed.) (2001) *Fanon's Warning: A Civil Society Reader on the New Partnership for Africa's Development,* New Jersey: Africa World Press.

Booth, M. Z. (2004) *Culture and Education: The Social Consequences of Western Schooling in Contemporary Swaziland,* Lanham: University Press of America.

Brainerd, C. J, and M. Pressley (eds.) (1982) *Verbal Processes in Children,* New York: Springer-Verlag.

Bratt-Paulston, C. B. (1992) *Sociolinguistic Perspectives on Bilingual Education,* Clevedon: Multilingual Matters.

Brock-Utne, B., Z. Desai and M. Qorro (eds.) (2003) *Language of Instruction in Tanzania and South Africa,* Tanzania: E & D Limited.

Bunyi, G. (1991) 'Rethinking the Place of African Indigenous Languages in African Education', *International Journal of Educational Development,* 19: 337-350.

Carrell, P. L. (1991) 'Second Language Reading: reading ability or language proficiency?', *Applied Linguistics* 12(2): 159-179.

Carter, R. (1987) *Vocabulary: Applied Linguistics Perspectives,* London: Allen and Unwin.

Carter, T. D. T. (1969) 'The Question of Language in Barotse Primary Schools', *Journal of African Languages,* 8: 141-152.

Central Statistical Office (CSO), Zambia, (1995a) *Census of Population, Housing and Agriculture (Volume 10),* Lusaka: Central Statistical Office.

------ (1995b) *Report on the 1990 Census of Population, Housing and Agriculture: Dissemination Seminar,* Lusaka: Central Statistical Office.

Centre of African Studies, (1986) *Language in Education in Africa,* (proceedings of 1985 seminar), Edinburgh, University of Edinburgh.

Chall, J. (1958) *Readability: an Appraisal of Research and Application,* Ohio State Bureau of Education Research Monographs.

Chall, J. S. (1967) *Learning to Read: the Great Debate,* New York: Mc Graw-Hill.

Cheshire, J. (ed.) (1991) *English around the World,* Cambridge: Cambridge University Press.

Chick, J. K. (1996) 'Safe-talk: Collusion in Apartheid Eucation', in C. Candlin and N. Mercer (eds.) *English Language Teaching in its Social Context,* London: Open University and Routledge, 227-240.

------ (1992) 'English as a Medium and as a Subject in Post-apartheid South Africa', *Southern African Journal of Applied Linguistics,* 1(1): 29-40.

Chifwa, J. T. (n.d.) *Research in Reading Ability in Eastern and Southern Provinces of Zambia,* (1980-92) Zambia: mimeo (no further details available)

Chikalanga I. W. (1990) *Inferencing in the Reading Process,* unpublished Ph.D. Thesis, University of Reading.

Chimombo, M. (1994) 'Early Literacy in Malawi: Problems and Prospects', in Soderbergh R. (ed.) *Lasning och skrivning fore skolaldern* (*Literacy before school start*), Child Language Research Unit, Lund University, 51-65.

Chimombo, S. (1988) *Malawian Oral Literature*, Zomba: University of Malawi.

Clammer, J. (1976) *Literacy and Social Change: A Case Study of Fiji*, Leiden: Brill.

Clarke, M. (1979) 'Reading in Spanish and English: evidence from adult ESL students', *Language Learning*, 29: 121-150.

Cleghorn, A. (1992) 'Sociolinguistic Perspectives on the Quality of Instruction in African Primary Schools', *Southern African Journal of Applied Language Studies*, 1(2): 45-63.

Cochrane, S. H. and S. M. Farid (1989) *Fertility in Sub-Saharan Africa: Analysis and Explanation*, World Bank Discussion Paper No.43, Washington DC: World Bank.

Colclough, C. with K. Lewin. (1993) *Educating All the Children: Strategies for Primary Schooling in the South*, Oxford: Clarendon Press.

------, Rose, P. and M. Tembon, (2000) 'Gender Inequalities in Primary Schooling: the roles of poverty and adverse cultural practice', *International Journal of Educational Development*, 20 (1), 5-29.

Commission for Africa. (2005) *Our Common Interest: Report of the Commission for Africa. www.commissionforafrica.org [accessed January 5th, 2006].*

Connor, U. (1987) *A study of reading skills among English-as-a-second-language learners*, unpublished doctoral dissertation, University of Wisconsin, Madison.

Coulmas, F. (1992) *Language and Economy*, Oxford: Blackwell.

Coxhead, A. (1998) *An Academic Word List*, Wellington, New Zealand: English Language Institute Occasional Publications, No 18.

Criper, C. and W.A. Dodd (1984) *Report on the Teaching of English Language and its Use as a Medium in Education in Tanzania*, Dar es Salaam: The British Council.

Croft, A. (2000) *'Strategies of effective teachers of standard 1 classes in Malawi'*, paper presented at the Applied Linguistics Circle, University of Reading, June.

------ (2002) 'Singing under a Tree: does oral culture help lower primary teachers be learner-centred?', *International Journal of Educational Development*, 22 (3-4): 321-337.

Crooks, T. and G. Crewes (eds.) (1995) *Language and Development*, Bali Indonesia: Australia Language Foundation.

Crystal, D. (1987) *The Cambridge Encyclopedia of Language*, Cambridge: Cambridge University Press.

CSO. *See* Central Statistical Office.

Cummins, J. and M. Swain (1986) *Bilingualism in Education*, London: Longman.

Davies, A. (1996) 'Ironising the Myth of Linguicism', *Journal of Multilingual and Multicultural Development*, 17(6): 485- 496.

------ (1986) Introduction. In Centre of African Studies. pp. 1-18.

de Gaay Fortnum, (1987) 'Oral Competence in Nyanja among Lusaka School-children', in Ohannessian and Kashoki (eds.), *Language in Zambia.* International African Institute, London, 181-206.

de Haan, A. (1999) *Social Exclusion: towards an holistic understanding of deprivation,* http://www.dfid.gov.uk

Denison, E.F. (1962) *The Sources of Economic Growth in the United States and the Alternatives before Us,* New York: Committee for Economic Development.

Devereux, S. (1999) 'Making Less Last Longer: informal safety nets in Malawi', *IDS Discussion Paper* No 373. IDS, Brighton, page numbers?

Devine, J. (1987) 'General Language Competence and Adult Second Language Reading', in Devine, Carrell and Eskey (eds.) title of volume in italics, place of publication: publisher, 73-87.

------, P. Carrell and D.E. Eskey (eds.) (1987) *Research in Reading in English as a Second Language,* Washington: TESOL.

DFID (Department for International Development) (2000) *Poverty Elimination and the Empowerment of Women,* DFID: London.

------ (1997) Eliminating World Poverty: a challenge for the 21st century, UK Government White Paper, November, 1997.

Djité, P. G. (1993). 'Language and Development in Africa', *International Journal of the Sociology of Language,* 100/101: 149-166.

Douglas, D. and C. Chappelle (eds.) (1993) *A New Decade of Language Testing Research,* Washington: TESOL.

Dowden, R. (1996) 'Special Report: The Return of the Kings', *Prospect,* July: 61-64.

Duffy, G. and L. Anderson (1981) *Final Report: Conceptions of Reading Project,* Unpublished report, Institute for Research on teaching, Michigan state University, East Lansing, MI.

Durstan S, (1996) *Increasing Education for All: community schools in Zambia.* UNICEF sponsored report for the Education Sector Integrated Programme, Lusaka, Zambia.

(The) Economist, (1995) (21st October), 'Biting the Hand that Squeezed Them', (*anonymous*).

Edwards, M. (1999) *Future Positive: International Cooperation in the Twenty First Century,* London: Earthscan/Kogan Page Ltd.

Eisemon, T. O., J.Schwille, R. Prouty, F. Ukobizoba, D. Kana and G. Manirabona (1993) 'Providing Quality Education when Resources are Scarce: Strategies for Increasing Primary School Effectiveness in Burundi', in H.M. Levin and M.L. Lockheed (eds.), *Effective Schools in Developing Countries.* London: The Falmer Press, 130-157.

Elkan, W. (1995) (2nd Ed.) *An Introduction to Development Economics,* New York: Prentice Hall.

Ellerman, D. (2005) 'Investing in Development: here we go again!' *NORRAG News,* 36: 24-26.

Elley, W. B. (1994) *The IEA Study of Reading Literacy: Achievement and Instruction in Thirty Two School Systems*, Oxford: Pergamon.

------ (1984) 'Exploring the Reading Difficulties of Second Language Learners in Fiji', in J.C. Alderson and A. Urquhart (eds.), *Reading in a Foreign Language.* London: Longman, 281-297.

English in Malawi (revised edition), (1965-68) Books 1-8. Pupil's Books and Teacher's Books, Blantyre, Malawi: Dzuka Publishing Company Limited/ Longman Malawi.

Engels, L. (1968) 'The Fallacy of Word Counts', *International Review of Applied Linguistics* 6: 213-231.

Eskey, D. E. (1988) 'Holding in the Bottom: an Interactive Approach to the Language Problems of Second Language Readers', in P. Carrell, J. Devine and D. Eskey (eds.), *Interactive Approaches to Second Language Reading.* Cambridge: Cambridge University Press, 93-100.

Etxeberria, F. and J. Arzamendi (eds.) (1992) *Bilingualism and Language Acquisition,* Bilbao: Spanish Association of Applied Linguistics.

Farah, I. (1998) 'Sabaq: Context of Learning Literacy for Girls in Rural Pakistan', in Durngunoglu, A. Y and Verhoeven, L. (eds.) *Literacy Development in a Multilingual Context,* Mahwah, NJ.: Lawrence Erlbaum, 249-266.

Favreau, M. and N. Segalowitz (1982) 'Second Language Reading in Fluent Bilinguals', *Applied Psycholinguistics,* 3: 329-341.

Ferguson, C. (1959) 'Diglossia', *Word* 15: 325-40.

Finlayson, G. (2005) 'Malawi: a suitable case for treatment?', *NORRAG News,* 36: 48-49.

Fishman, J. A. (1971) 'The Impact of Nationalism on Language Planning', in J. Rubin and B.H. Jernudd (eds.), *Can Language be Planned?* Hawaii: University Press of Hawaii, 3-20.

------ (1970) *Sociolinguistics: an Introduction,* Rowley: Newbury House.

Fodor I. and C. Hagege (eds.) (1990) *Language Reform: History and Future, Vol. V,* Hamburg: Helmet Bask Verlag.

Francis, W. N. and H. Kucera (1982) *Frequency Analysis of English Usage,* Boston: Houghton Mifflin Company.

Fries, C. C. (1963) *Linguistics and Reading,* New York: Holt, Reinhart & Winston.

Fry, M. A. (1967) *A Transformational Analysis of the Oral Language Structure used by two Reading Groups at the Second Grade Level,* unpublished PhD dissertation, University of Iowa.

Gadsden, F. (1992) 'Education and Society in Colonial Zambia', in S.N. Chipungu (ed.) *Guardians in their Time: experiences of Zambians under colonial rule, London,* Macmillan, 97-125.

George, S. and F. Sabelli (1994) *Faith and Credit: The World Bank's Secular Empire,* London: Penguin.

Giglioli, P. P. (ed.) (1972) *Language and Social Context,* Harmondsworth: Penguin.

Goldman, S.R. (1976) 'Reading Skill and the Minimum Distance Principle: a comparison of listening and reading comprehension', *Journal of Experimental Child Psychology,* 22: 123-142.

Goodman, K.S, (1967) 'Reading: a psycholinguistic guessing game' *Journal of the Reading Specialist,* 6, 4: 126-135 (reprinted in H. Singer and R.B. Ruddell (eds.) (1994) *Theoretical Models and Processes of Reading* 2nd edn. Newark: International Reading Association. 470-96.

Greaney, V. (1996) 'Reading in Developing Countries: problems and issues', in V. Greaney (ed.) *Promoting Reading in Developing Countries,* Newark, Delaware: International Reading Association, 5-39.

Green, R. and C. Weir (1998) *Statistical Analysis for Language Testing and Evaluation,* Centre for Applied Language Studies: University of Reading.

Gregory, E. and A. Williams (2000) *City Literacies,* London: Routledge.

Grimes, B. F. (ed.) (1992) *Ethnologue: Languages of the World,* Dallas: S.I.L.

Grin, F. (1996) 'Economic Approaches to Language and Language Planning: an introduction', *International Journal of the Sociology of Language,* 121: 1-16.

Gumperz, J. (1968) 'The Speech Community', in *International Encyclopedia of the Social Sciences,* Macmillan. 381-386 (reprinted in Giglioli, P. (ed.) (1972): 219-231.)

Harbison, F. H. and C.J. Myers (1964) *Education, Manpower, and Economic Growth: Strategies of Human Resource Development,* New York: McGraw Hill.

Hardman, J. (1965) *Primary English teaching in Zambia: Report and Recommendations,* (Paper presented to the Zambian Ministry of Education), Lusaka: mimeo.

Hatch, E. and A. Lazaraton (1991) *The Research Manual: Design and Statistics for Applied Linguistics,* New York: Newbury House.

Hawes, H., T. Coombe, C. Coombe and K. Lillis (eds.) (1986) *Education Priorities and Aid Responses in Sub-Saharan Africa,* London: ODA/University of London Institute of Education.

Haynes, M. (1993) 'Patterns and Perils of Guessing in Second Language Reading' in T. Huckin *et al.* (eds.), *Second Language Reading and Vocabulary Learning.* Norwood, New Jersey: Ablex Publishing Corporation, 46-42.

Herbert, P. and C. Robinson (2001) 'Another Language, Another Literacy? Practices in northern Ghana', in B. Street (ed.), *Literacy and Development: ethnographic perspectives.* London: Routledge, 121-136.

Heugh, K. (1999) 'Languages, Development and Reconstructing Education in South Africa', *International Journal of Educational Development,* 19: 301-313.

Heyneman, S. P. and W. A. Loxley (1983) 'The Effect of Primary School Quality on Academic Achievement across Twenty-nine High- and Low-income Countries', *American Journal of Sociology* 88(6): 1162-1194.

Hicks, N. L. (1980) 'Is there a Trade-off between Growth and Basic Needs?', *Finance and Development,* 17(2): 17-20.

Hirsh, D. and P. Nation (1992) 'What Vocabulary Size is Needed to Read Unsimplified Texts for Pleasure?', *Reading in a Foreign Language,* 8(2): 689-686.

Hobcraft, J. (1993) 'Women's Education, Child Welfare and Child Survival: a review of the evidence', *Health Transition Review* 3(2): 159-75.

Hoppers, W. H. M. L. (1981) *Education in a Rural Society: Primary Pupils and School Leavers in Mwinilunga, Zambia,* Centre for the Study of Education in Developing Countries, The Hague, Netherlands and The Institute for African Studies, Lusaka, Zambia.

Hornberger, N. H. (1987) 'Bilingual Education Success, but Policy Failure', *Language in Society,* 16: 205-226.

------ and J.K. Chick (1998) *Co-constructing Safetime in Peruvian and South African Classrooms,* paper delivered at Sociolinguistic Symposium 12, Roehampton, London, 27th March.

Huckin, T. and J. Bloch (1993) 'Strategies for Inferring Word Meaning in Context: a cognitive model', in T. Huckin, M. Haynes and J. Coady (eds.), *Second Language Reading and Vocabulary Learning.* Norwood, New Jersey: Ablex Publishing Corporation, 153-180.

Huckin, T., M. Haynes and J. Coady (eds.) (1993) *Second Language Reading and Vocabulary Learning,* Norwood, New Jersey: Ablex Publishing Corporation, 153-180.

Hudson, T. (1982) 'The Effects of the Short Circuit in L2 Reading Performance', *Language Learning,* 32: 1-30.

Hymes, D. (1972) 'On Communicative Competence', in J.B. Pride and J. Holmes (eds.) *Sociolinguistics.* Harmondsworth: Penguin. 269-293 (first published: D. Hymes (1971) On Communicative Competence. Philadelphia: University of Pennsylvania Press.)

------ (ed.) (1964) *Language in Culture and Society,* New York: Harper and Row.

Ilon, L. (1997) 'The Changing Role of the World Bank: education policy as global welfare', *Policy and Politics,* 24(4): 413- 424.

Jimenez, R. T., G.E. Garcia and P.D. Pearson (1996) 'The Reading Strategies of Bilingual Latino/**a** students who are successful English readers: opportunities and obstacles', *Reading Research Quarterly* 31(1): 90-112.

Johnson, D., J. Hayter and P. Broadfoot (2000) 'The Quality of Learning and Teaching in Developing Countries: assessing literacy and numeracy in Malawi and Sri Lanka', *Education Research* No 41, London: Department for International Development.

Kadzamira, E. and M. Chibwana (2000) *Gender and Primary Schooling in Malawi,* Brighton: Institute of Development Studies.

------ and K. Moleni (2005) 'Investing in Malawi: reflecting whose priorities?', *NORRAG News,* 36: 49-51.

------ and P. Rose (2003) 'Can Free Primary Education Meet the Needs of the Poor? Evidence from Malawi', *International Journal of Educational Development,* 23: 501-516.

------ N. Swainson, D. Maluwa-Banda and A. Kamlongera (2001) *The Impact of HIV/AIDS on Formal Schooling in Malawi,* University of Sussex: Centre for International Education.

Kamil, M. L., J.A. Langer and T. Shanahan (1991) *Understanding Research in Reading and Writing,* Boston, Mass.: Allyn and Bacon.

Kapembwa, R. (1990) *An Analysis of the Reading Problems among Zambian Children in Primary Schools,* MA Dissertation, Centre for ELT, Warwick University.

Kashoki, M. E. (1990) *The Factor of Language in Zambia,* Lusaka: Kenneth Kaunda Foundation.

------ (1987a) 'The Language Situation in Zambia', in S. Ohannessian and M. E. Kashoki (eds.), *Language in Zambia.* International African Institute, London, 9-46.

------ (1987b) 'Between-language Communication in Zambia', in S. Ohannessian and M. E. Kashoki (eds.), *Language in Zambia.* International African Institute, London, 123-143.

Kasonde-Ng'andu, S., N.C. Chilala and N. Imutowana-Katukula (2000) *Gender and Primary Schooling in Zambia,* Research Report 39, Brighton: Institute of Development Studies.

Kaul, I. (1996) *Globalisation and Human Development,* EADI Annual Conference, Vienna, September.

Kayambazinthu, E. (1999) 'The Language Planning Situation in Malawi', in B. Kaplan and R. B. Baldauf (eds.) *Language Planning in Malawi, Mozambique and the Philippines,* Clevedon: Multilingual Matters, 15-85.

Kell, C. (2005) Review of Street (ed.) (2001), *Literacy and Development: ethnographic perspectives.* London: Routledge. *International Journal of Educational Development,* 25: 85-89.

Kelly, M. (1998) 'Primary Education in a Heavily Indebted Poor Country: the case of Zambia', Lusaka: UNICEF, (Background paper prepared for *Education Now* report, (1998) Oxfam, Oxford.)

------ (1995) *Language Policy in Education in Zambia,* (Paper presented at the Zambia National Reading Forum, Lusaka).

Kennedy, C. (ed.) (1989) *Language Planning and English Language Teaching,* London: Prentice Hall.

Kenny, B. and W. Savage (1997) *Language and Development: Teachers in a Changing World,* Harlow: Longman.

Khaila, S. P. and Mvula (1999) *Malawi Consultations with the Poor: Country synthesis report,* World Bank, Washington, DC.

Khor, M. (2002) *Rethinking Globalisation: Critical Issues and Policy Choices,* London: Zed Books.

King, K. (2005a) '2005: The Year of Development that was to Change the World? A review from the angle of education', *NORRAG News,* 36: 13-22

------ (2005b) 'Higher Education and Professional Leadership', *NORRAG News,* 36: 51-53.

------ (ed.) (1998) *NORRAG News,* Edinburgh: Centre for African Studies, Edinburgh University.

------- (1986) 'Problems and Prospects of Aid to Education in sub-Saharan Africa', in H. Hawes, T. Coombe, C. Coombe and K. Lillis (eds.), *Education Priorities and Aid Responses in Sub-Saharan Africa.* London: ODA/University of London Institute of Education, 113-134.

King, P. (2005) 'Where are We Now?', *NORRAG News,* 36: 45-46.

Kinnear, P. R. and C.D. Gray (1994) *SPSS for Windows Made Simple,* Hove: Lawrence Erlbaum Associates.

Kishindo, P. J. (1990) 'An Historical Survey of Spontaneous and Planned Development of Chichewa', in I. Fodor and C. Hagege, (eds.), *Language Reform: History and Future, Vol. V.* Hamburg, Helmet Bask Verlag, 59-82.

Klare, G. R. (1974) 'Assessing Readability', *Reading Research Quarterly* 10: 62-102.

Knight, J. B. and R. H. Sabot (1990) *Education, Productivity and Inequality: The East African Natural Experiment,* Oxford: Oxford University Press for the World Bank.

Kotze, H. and C. Higgins (1999) *Breakthrough to Icibemba Pilot: an evaluation,* (mimeo for the Zambian Ministry of Education).

Krashen, S. (1989) 'We Acquire Vocabulary and Spelling by Reading: additional evidence for the input hypothesis', *Modern Language Journal,* 73(4): 440-464.

Kulpoo, D. (1998) *The Quality of Education: some policy suggestions based on a survey of schools: Mauritius,* (SACMEQ Policy Research: Report No. 1) Paris: International Institute for Educational Planning, UNESCO.

Lambert, W. E. (1977) 'The Effects of Bilingualism on the Individual: Cognitive and Sociocultural Consequences', in P.A. Hornby (ed.) *Bilingualism: Psychological, Social, and Educational Implications,* New York: Academic Press, 15-27.

Laufer, B. (1997) 'What's in a Word that Makes it Hard or Easy: Some Intratextual Factors that Affect the Learning of Words', in N. Schmitt and M. McCarthey (eds.) *Vocabulary: Description, Acquisition, and Pedagogy,* Cambridge: Cambridge University Press, 140-155.

Lee, J-W. and D.L. Schallert (1997) 'The Relative Contribution of L2 Language Proficiency and L2 Reading Ability to L2 Reading Performance: a test of the threshold hypothesis in an EFL context', *TESOL Quarterly,* 31(4): 713-739.

Leki, I. and J. G. Carson, (1994) 'Students' Perception of EAP Writing Instruction and Writing Needs across Disciplines', *TESOL Quarterly,* 28(1): 81-101.

Lehmann, D. A. (1987) 'Languages of the Kafue Basin: Introductory Notes', in S. Ohannessian and M.E. Kashoki (eds.), *Language in Zambia.* International African Institute, London, 102-122.

Levin, H. M. and M.L. Lockheed (1993) (eds.) *Effective Schools in Developing Countries,* London: The Falmer Press.

Lewin, K. M. (1993) *Education and Development: the Issues and the Evidence,* Education Research, Serial No. 6. London: Overseas Development Administration.

Lind, A. and A. Johnson (1990) *Adult Literacy in the Third World,* Stockholm: SIDA.

Linden, I. (1975) 'Chewa Initiation Rites and *Nyau* Societies: the Use of Religious Institutions in Local Politics at Mua' in T.O. Ranger and J. Weller (eds.), *Themes in the Christian History of Central Africa,* Berkeley: University of California Press, 30-44.

Linehan, S. (2004) *Language of Instruction and the Quality of Basic Education in Zambia,* [Paper for UNESCO].

Lockheed, M. E., Jamison D. T. and L. J. Lau (1980) 'Farmer education and farm efficiency: a survey', *Economic Development and Cultural Change* 29: 37-76.

Luangala, J. (1991) *The Chosen Bud,* Lusaka: Kenneth Kaunda Foundation.

Luckett, K. (1994) 'National additive bilingualism: towards a language plan for South African education', *Southern African Journal of Applied Language Studies,* 2(1).

Lungwangwa, G., (1989) *Multigrade Schools in Zambian Primary Education: A Report on the Pilot Schools in Mkushi District,* (SIDA Education Division Documents, No 47), Stockholm, SIDA.

Lunzer, E. and Gardner, K. (eds.) (1979). *The Effective Use of Reading,* London: Heinemann Educational.

Machingaidze, T., P. Pfukani and S. Shumba (1998) *The Quality of Education: some Policy Suggestions Based on a Survey of Schools: Zimbabwe,* (SACMEQ, Policy Research Report No. 3), Paris: International Institute for Educational Planning, UNESCO.

MacDonald, C. (1990) *Crossing the Threshold into Standard Three,* main report of the Threshold Project, Pretoria: HSRC.

Manchisi, P. C. (2004) 'The Status of the Indigenous Languages in Institutions of learning in Zambia: past, resent and future', *The African Symposium,* Vol. 4: 1-8.

Martin-Jones, M. and K. Jones (2000) *Multilingual Literacies.* Amsterdam & Philadelphia: John Benjamins.

May, S. (2001) *Language and Minority Rights: Ethnicity, Nationalism and the Politics of Language,* Essex: Pearson Education.

------ (1994) *Making Multicultural Education Work,* Clevedon: Multilingual Matters.

Mazrui, A. (1996) 'Language Policy and the Foundations of Democracy: an African perspective', *International Journal of the Sociology of Language,* 118:107-124.

Mbeki, M. (2005) 'Eye Witness', *Sunday Times Magazine,* (03/07/05): 31-33.

McAdam, B. (1987) 'The New Zambia Primary Course', in S. Ohannessian and M. Kashoki (eds.), *Language in Zambia,* International African Institute, London, 329-354.

McArthur, T. (1992) *The Oxford Companion to the English Language,* Oxford: Oxford University Press.

McGinn, N. (2005) 'The Sachs' Ideas in the Context of Development History', *NORRAG News,* 36: 22-24.

Mchazime, H. S. (1989) *The Teaching of Reading: developing a perspective for teacher training in southern Africa,* unpublished BPhil Dissertation (Education), Birmingham University.

Melchers, G. and N-L. Johannesson (eds.) (1994) *Non-standard Varieties of Language,* Stockholm: Almqvist & Wiksell International.

Microsoft Excel, Version 5.0a. (1993), Microsoft Corporation.

Milner, G., J. Chimombo, T. Banda and C. Mchikoma (2001) *The Quality of Primary Education in Malawi (an interim report),* (Working document in SACMEQ Reports), Paris: International Institute for Educational Planning, UNESCO.

Mincer, J. (1980) 'Human Capital and Earnings', in A.B. Atkinson (ed.), *Wealth, Income and Inequality: Selected Readings,* Oxford: Oxford University Press.

------ (1976) 'Progress in Human Capital Analyses of the Distribution of Earnings', in A.B. Atkinson (ed.) *The Personal Distribution of Incomes,* London: Allen and Unwin, 136-192.

Ministry of Education [Malawi] (1991) *Malawi Primary School Teaching Syllabus: English, standards 1 – 8,* Zomba: Malawi Institute of Education.

------ (1990) *Primary Teacher Training English Teaching Syllabus (Two Year Course),* (mimeo), Zomba: Malawi Institute of Education.

------ (1980) *New Arithmetic Book,* Blantyre, Malawi: Dzuka Publishing Company.

------ (1965-68) (revised edition), *English in Malawi* Books 1 - 8. Pupil's Books and Teacher's Books, Blantyre, Malawi: Dzuka Publishing Company Limited/Longman Malawi.

------ (n.d.(a)) *Activities with English* (Pupils' Books and Teachers' Guides) Zomba: Malawi Institute of Education.

------ (n.d.(b)) *Teacher Training Programme (One Year),* (mimeo. No place of publication or publisher provided).

------ Teacher Development Unit. (n.d.(c)) *Student Teacher's Handbook, 2,* (mimeo). No place of publication or publisher provided).

Ministry of Education [Zambia] (1996) *Educating Our Future (National Policy on Education)*, Lusaka, Zambia: Ministry of Education.

------ (1992) *Focus on Learning,* Lusaka: Ministry of Education.

------ Curriculum Development Centre (1991) *Primary Teacher Training Colleges: English Syllabus,* Lusaka: mimeo, the Examinations Council of Zambia.

------ (1991-1997) *Zambia Basic Education Course, (English)*, Lusaka: Kenneth Kaunda Foundation.

------ (1988-1992) *Werenga Cinyanja, Geredi 1-5,* [Read Cinyanja, Grades 1-5] Lusaka: Zambia Educational Publishing House.

------ Examinations Council of Zambia, (1986) *The Structure of the New School Curriculum,* Lusaka: Government of Zambia.

------ (1976) *Education for development: Draft statement on educational reform,* Lusaka, Zambia: Ministry of Education.

------ Curriculum Development Centre (1968-71) *Zambia Primary Course (English), Grades 1-7.* (Pupils' books and Teachers' Guides) Lusaka: Kenneth Kaunda Foundation.

------ (n.d.) *Teaching Syllabus: Functional Objectives,* (mimeo).

------ (n.d.) *Writers' Guide: Word List,* (mimeo).

MOE: *see* Ministry of Education.

Moock, P. R. and H. Addou (1994) 'Agricultural Productivity and Education', in *International Encyclopaedia of Education Vol.1.*, Oxford: Pergamon Press, 244-54.

Moon, R. (1997) 'Vocabulary Connections: Multi-word Items in English', in N. Schmitt and M. McCarthey (eds.) *Vocabulary: Description, Acquisition, and Pedagogy,* Cambridge: Cambridge University Press, 40-63.

Mwanakatwe, J. M. (1968) *The Growth of Education in Zambia since Independence,* Lusaka: Oxford University Press.

Myers-Scotton, C. (1990) 'Elite Closure as Boundary Maintenance: the evidence from Africa', in B. Weinstein (ed.) *Language Policy and Political Development,* Norwood, NJ: Ablex, 25-41.

Nassor, S. and K.A. Mohammed (1998) *The Quality of Education: some policy suggestions based on a survey of schools: Zanzibar,* (SACMEQ Policy Research: Report No. 4), Paris: International Institute for Educational Planning, UNESCO.

Nation, I.S.P. (1990) *Teaching and Learning Vocabulary,* New York: Newbury House.

Nation, I.S.P. and R. Waring (1997) 'Vocabulary Size, Text Coverage and Word Lists' in N. Schmitt and M. McCarthy (eds.) *Vocabulary: Description, Acquisition, and Pedagogy,* Cambridge: Cambridge University Press, 6-19.

National Statistics Office (Malawi) (2000) *Malawi Population and Housing Census, 1998,* Zomba: National Statistics Office.

Neville, N.H. and A.K. Pugh (1982) *Towards Independent Reading,* London: Heinemann Educational.

New Zambia Primary Course, English Language (1968-1973). Lusaka: Ministry of Education.

Ninyoles, R. L. (1972) *Idioma y Poder Social.* Madrid: Editorial Tecnos.

Nkamba, M. and J. Kanyika (1998) *The Quality of Education: some policy suggestions based on a survey of schools: Zambia,* (SACMEQ Policy Research: Report No. 5), Paris: International Institute for Educational Planning, UNESCO.

Nuttall, C. (1996) *Teaching Reading Skills in a Foreign Language,* Oxford: Heinemann.

Ohannessian, S. and M.E. Kashoki (eds.) (1987) *Language in Zambia,* International African Institute, London.

Ouane, A. (ed.) (2003) *Towards a Multilingual Culture of Education,* Hamburg: UNESCO Institute for Education.

Oxfam, (1999) *Break the Cycle of Poverty: Education Now,* Oxfam International, Oxford, (preliminary report).

Pakenham, T. (1991) *The Scramble for Africa,* London: George Weidenfield & Nicolson.

Papen, U. (2005) 'Literacy and development: what works for whom? or, how relevant is the social practices view of literacy for literacy education in developing countries?', *International Journal of Educational Development* 25(1): 5-17.

Pearson, B. Z., S.C. Fernandez and D. Kimbrough Oller (1993) 'Lexical Development in Bilingual Infants and Toddlers: comparison to monolingual norms', *Language Learning* 43(1): 93-120.

Pennycuick, D. (1993) *School Effectiveness in Developing Countries: A Summary of the Research Evidence,* Education Research, Serial No. 1, London: ODA.

Perera, K. (1984) *Children's Writing and Reading,* Oxford: Blackwell.

Phillipson, R. and T. Skutnabb-Kangas (1999) 'Linguistic Imperialism, Gobalism and the English Language', in D. Graddol and U. Meinhof (eds.), *English in a Changing World,* Milton Keynes: Catchline for AILA. 19-36.

------ (1994) 'Language Rights in Postcolonial Africa', in T. Skutnabb-Kangas and R. Phillipson (eds.) *Linguistic Human Rights: Overcoming Linguistic Discrimination,* New York: Mouton de Gruyter: 335-345.

Postlethwaite, T. N. and K.N. Ross (1992) *Effective Schools in Learning,* The Hague: International Association for the Evaluation of Educational Achievement.

Puchner, L. D. (1995) 'Literacy Links: issues in the relationship between early childhood development, health, women, families, and literacy', *International Journal of Educational Development* 15(3): 307-19.

Rampton, B. (1998) 'Language Crossing and the Redefinition of Reality', in P. Auer (ed.) *Code-switching in Conversation,* London: Routledge, 290-317.

Ranger, T. O. (1975) 'The *Mwana Lesa* Movement of 1925', in T.O. Ranger and J. Weller (eds.) *Themes in the Christian History of Central Africa*, Berkeley: University of California Press, 45-75.

Rassool, N. (1999) *Literacy for Sustainable Development in the Age of Information*, Clevedon: Multilingual Matters.

Rayner K, and A. Pollatsek (1989) *The Psychology of Reading*, Englewood Cliffs, NJ: Prentice Hall.

Read, J. (1997) 'Vocabulary and Testing', in N. Schmitt and M. McCarthey (eds.) *Vocabulary: Description, Acquisition, and Pedagogy*, Cambridge: Cambridge University Press, 303-320.

------ (1997) *Africa: a Biography of the Continent*, Harmondsworth: Penguin.

Richards, J. (1974) 'Word Lists: problems and principles', *RELC Journal*, 5(2): 69-84.

Robinson, C. D. W. (2005) Review of A. Ouane (ed.) (2003) *International Journal of Educational Development*, 25: 183-186.

------ (1996a) 'Winds of Change in Africa: Fresh Air for African Languages? Some Preliminary Reflections', in H. Coleman and L. Cameron, (eds.), *Change and Language*, Clevedon, British Association for Applied Linguistics and Multilingual Matters, 166-182.

------ (1996b) *Language use in Rural Development: an African Perspective*, The Hague: Mouton de Gruyter.

------- (1992) *Language Choice in Rural Development*, Dallas: Summer Institute of Linguistics.

Rogers, A. (2003) *Literacy, Communication and Development*, Report of a consultancy undertaken for DFID-Malawi, (unpublished mimeo).

------ (2001) 'Afterword: Problematising Literacy and Development', in B.V. Street (ed.) *Literacy and Development*, London: Routledge, 205-222.

------ (1990) 'Background to the Seminar', in B.V. Street (ed.) *Literacy in Development*, London: Education for Development and the Commonwealth Institute. 2-4.

Roller, C. M. (1988) 'Transfer of Cognitive Academic Competence and L2 Reading in a Rural Zimbabwean Primary School', *TESOL Quarterly* 22: 303-328.

Rosenbaum, P. S. (1967) *The Grammar of English Predicate Construction*, (Research Monograph No 47), Cambridge, Mass: MIT Press.

Rubagumya, C. M. (ed.) (1991) *Language in Education in Africa*, Clevedon: Multilingual Matters.

Rubin, J. R. and B.H. Jernudd (1971) *Can Language be Planned?*, Hawaii: University Press of Hawaii.

Sachs, J. (2005) 'How Africa Lit up the World', in *Sunday Times Magazine (Special Africa Issue)* (03.07.05): 20-24.

------ (1996) 'Growth in Africa', *The Economist* (29.06.96): 19-21

SAS, (1985) *SAS Users Guide: Statistics, Version 5*, Cary, NC: SAS Institute Inc.

Saville-Troike, M. (1984) 'What really matters in second language learning for academic achievement?' *TESOL Quarterly,* 18(2): 199-219.

Schlesinger, I. M. (1968) *Sentence Structure and the Reading Process,* The Hague: Mouton (Janua Linguarum), (1969).

Schmied, J. (1991) *English in Africa,* London: Longman.

Schulte, C. (1967) *A Study of the Relationship between Oral Language and Reading Achievement in Second Graders,* unpublished PhD dissertation, University of Iowa.

Schumann, J. H. (1976) 'Social Distance as a Factor in Second Language Acquisition', *Language Learning,* 26: 135-143.

Seashore, R. H. and L.D. Eckerson (1940) 'The Measurement of Individual Differences in General English Vocabularies', *Journal of Educational Psychology,* 31: 14-38.

Segalowitz, N., C. Poulsen and M. Komoda (1991) 'Lower level Components of Reading Skill in Higher Level Bilinguals: Implications for Reading Instruction', in J.H. Hulstijn and J.F. Matter (eds.), *Reading in Two Languages,* AILA Review, 8, Amsterdam: 15-30.

Serpell, R. (1996) 'Cultural Models of Childhood in Indigenous Socialization and Formal Schooling in Zambia', in C.P. Hwang, M.E. Lamb and I.E. Sigel (eds) (1996) *Images of Childhood,* Mahwah, New Jersey: Lawrence Erlbaum:129-142.

------ (1993) *The Significance of Schooling: Life-journeys in an African Society,* Cambridge: Cambridge University Press.

------ (1989) 'The Cultural Context of Language Learning: Problems Confronting English Teachers in Zambia', in C. Kennedy (ed.), *Language Planning and English Language Teaching.* London: Prentice Hall, 92-109.

------ (1987) 'Some Developments in Zambia since 1971', in S. Ohannessian and M.E. Kashoki (eds.), *Language in Zambia.* International African Institute, London, 424-447.

------ (1978) 'Comprehension of Nyanja by Lusaka Schoolchildren', in Ohannessian, S. and Kashoki, M. E. (eds.), *Language in Zambia.* International African Institute, London. pp. 144-181.

Sharma, R. (1973) *The Reading Skills of Grade 3 Children,* (mimeo), Psychological Service Report 2/(1973), Ministry of Education, Lusaka.

Siachitema, A. K. (1991) 'The Social Significance of Language use and Language Choice in a Zambian Urban Setting: an Empirical Study of Three Neighbourhoods in Lusaka', in J. Cheshire (ed..): *English around the World.* Cambridge: Cambridge University Press, 474-490.

Sichinga, W. K. (1994) *Language Statistics in Malawi* (unpublished mimeo), Office of Statistics, Zomba.

Simons, H. D. (1971) 'Reading comprehension: the need for a new perspective', *Reading Research Quarterly* 6: 340-363.

Smith, D. (2005) 'The mountain to climb', *Sunday Times (Special Africa Issue*

03.07.05): 29-31.

Smith F, (1988) *Joining the Literacy Club: Further Essays into Education,* London: Heinemann.

Spencer, J. (1985) 'Language and Development: the Unequal Equation', in N. Wolfson and J. Manes (eds.) *Language of Inequality,* Berlin: Mouton, 387-397.

SPSS (Statistical Package for the Social Sciences), (1989-94) *SPSS for Windows,* Release 6.1.

Steffensen, M. S. and C. Joag Dev (1984) 'Cultural Knowledge and Reading', in J.C. Alderson and A.H. Urquhart (eds.), *Reading in a Foreign Language.* London: Longman, 48-61.

Street, B. V. (2003) 'The Implications of the "New Literacy Studies" for Literacy Education' in S. Goodman, T. Lillis, J. Maybin and N. Mercer (eds.) *Language, Literacy and Education: a Reader,* Stoke on Trent and Sterling: Trentham Books and the Open University, 77-101.

------ (ed.) (2001) *Literacy and Development: Ethnographic Perspectives,* London: Routledge.

------ (1995) *Social Literacies: Critical Approaches to Literacy in Development, Ethnography, and Education,* Harlow: Addison Wesley Longman.

------ (1984) *Literacy in Theory and Practice,* Cambridge: Cambridge University Press.

Strother, J. B. and J.A. Ulijn (1987) 'Does Syntactic Rewriting affect ESL for Science and Technology (EST) Text Comprehension?', in J. Devine, P. Carrell and D.E. Eskey (eds.) *Research in Reading in English as a Second Language,* Washington: TESOL, 89-101.

Stroud, C. (1999) 'Portuguese as Ideology and Politics in Mozambique: semiotic (re)constructions of a postcolony', in Blommaert (ed.), *Language ideological debates.* Berlin: Mouton de Gruyter, 342-380.

Subbarao, K. and L. Raney (1993) *Social Gains from Female Education: a Cross-National Study,* World Bank Discussion Paper no.194, Washington DC: World Bank.

Summers, L.H (1994) *Investing in All the People,* Washington DC: World Bank.

Swain, J. (2005) 'Eye Witness', *Sunday Times Magazine (Special Africa Issue). (03.07.05)*: 24-25.

Tabatabai, H. (1995). 'Poverty and Inequality in Developing Countries: a Review of Evidence', in G. Rodgers and R. van der Hoeven (eds) *New Approaches to Poverty Analysis and Poverty - III.* Geneva: ILO : 13-35.

Thomas, H. (1997) *The Slave Trade,* Basingstoke: Picador.

Thomas, A. and D. Potter (1992) 'Development, Capitalism, and the Nation State', in T. Allen and A. Thomas (eds.) *Poverty and Development in the 1990s,* Oxford: Oxford University Press/The Open University, 116-141.

Thompson, G. B., W.E. Tunmer and T. Nicholson (eds) (1993) *Reading Acquisition Processes,* Clevedon: Multilingual Matters.

Thorndike, E.L. (1971) 'Reading as Reasoning: a study of mistakes in para-
    graph reading', *Journal of Educational Psychology*, 8: 323-332.

Tikly, L (2003) 'The African Renaissance, NEPAD and Skills Formation: an
    identification of key policy tensions', *International Journal of Education
    Development*, 25/3: 543-564.

Torrey, J. W. (1973) 'Illiteracy in the Ghetto', in F. Smith (ed.), *Psycho-linguis-
    tics and Reading*, New York: Holt, Rinehart, and Winston, 131-137.

Trappes-Lomax, H. R. (1991) 'Can a Foreign Language be a National Medium?',
    in C.M. Rubagumaya (ed.), *Language in Education in Africa.* Clevedon:
    Multilingual Matters, 94-104.

Treffgarne, C. (1986) 'Language Policy in Francophone Africa: scapegoat or
    panacea?', in Centre of African Studies: 141-170.

Trudell, B. (2005) 'Language Choice, Education and Community Identity', *In-
    ternational Journal of Educational Development*, 25: 237-251.

Tunmer, W. E. and W.A. Hoover (1993) 'Language Related Factors as Sources
    of Individual Differences in the Development of Word Recognition Skills',
    in G.B. Thompson, W.E. Tunmer and T. Nicholson (eds.), *Reading acquisi-
    tion processes.* Clevedon: Multilingual Matters, 123-147.

UN: see United Nations

UNESCO, (1964) *Report of the UNESCO Planning Mission: education in
    Northern Rhodesia,* Lusaka: Government Printer.

------ (1953) United Nations Educational, Scientific and Cultural Organisation.
    The use of the vernacular languages in education, (Monograph on Fun-
    damental Education VIII; Paris: UNESCO).

United Nations (2005) *The Millennium Development Goals,* New York: United
    Nations Department of Public Information.

Urquhart, A. H. (1987) 'Comprehensions and Interpretations', *Reading in a
    Foreign Language,* 3(4): 387-409.

    and C.J. Weir (1998) *Reading in a Second Language: Process, Product
    and Practice,* London: New York.

Vale, P. and S. Maseko (1998) 'South Africa and the African Renaissance',
    International Affairs, 74/2: 271-285.

Vellutino, F. R. and D.M. Scanlon (1982) 'Verbal Processing in Poor and Normal
    Readers', in C.J. Brainerd and M. Pressley (eds.), *Verbal Processes in Chil-
    dren.* New York: Springer-Verlag, 189-264.

Verhoeven, L. (1990) 'Acquisition of Reading in a Second Language', *Reading
    Research Quarterly,* 25: 90-114.

------ (1991) 'Acquisition of Biliteracy', in J.H. Hulstijn and J. F. Matter. (eds.),
    Reading in two languages. AILA Review, 8, Amsterdam. 61-74

------ and R. Aarts, (1998) 'Attaining Functional Biliteracy in the Netherlands',
    in A.Y. Durngunoglu and L. Verhoeven (eds.) *Literacy Development in a
    Multilingual Context,* Mahwah, NJ.: Lawrence Erlbaum, 111-134.

Vihman, M. M. and B. McLaughlin (1982) 'Bilingualism and Second Language

Acquisition in Preschool Children', in C.J. Brainerd and M. Pressley (eds.) *Verbal Processes in Children,* New York: Springer-Verlag: 35-58.

Voigts, F. (1998) *The quality of Education: some policy suggestions based on a survey of schools: Namibia,* (SACMEQ Policy Research: Report No. 2), Paris: International Institute for Educational Planning, UNESCO.

Wagner, D. A. (1995) 'Literacy and Development: rationales, myths, innovations, and future directions', *International Journal of Educational Development* 15(4): 341-62.

------ (1998) 'Putting Second Language First: Language and Literacy Learning in Morocco', in A.Y. Durngunoglu and L. Verhoeven (eds.) *Literacy Development in a Multilingual Context,* Mahwah, NJ: Lawrence Erlbaum, 169-184.

------, J.E. Spratt and A. Ezzaki (1989) 'Does Learning to Read in a Second Language always put the Child at a Disadvantage? Some counter-evidence from Morocco', *Applied Psycholinguistics,* 10(1): 31- 48.

Wallace, C. (1988) *Learning to Read in a Multicultural Society: the Social Context of Second Language Literacy,* New York: Prentice-Hall.

------ (1992) *Reading,* Oxford: Oxford University Press.

Watkins, K. (2000) *The Oxfam Education Report,* Oxford: Oxfam Publishing.

Watson, K. (1999) 'Language, Power, Development and Geopolitical Changes: conflicting pressures facing plurilingual societies', *Compare,* 29: 5-22.

Webb, V. (1999) 'Multilingualism in Democratic South Africa: the overestimation of language policy', *International Journal of Educational Development,* 19: 351-366.

------ (2002) *Language in South Africa: the Role of Language in National Transformation, Reconstruction and Development,* Amsterdam & Philadelphia: John Benjamins.

Werenga Cinyanja, Geredi 1-5 (1988-1992) Lusaka: Zambia Educational Publishing House.

Wheeler, D. (1980) *Human Resources Development and Economic Growth in Developing Countries: a Simultaneous Model,* World Bank Staff Working Paper, No. 407.

Wickstead, M. (2005) 'Has 2005 been the Year of Africa?', *NORRAG News,* 36: 37-38.

Widdowson, H. G. (1984) *Explorations in Applied Linguistics, 2,* Oxford: Oxford University Press.

Williams, A. (1989) *The Influence of a non-standard Dialect on Children's School Writing,* unpublished PhD Dissertation, Birkbeck College, University of London.

Williams, E. (1998) *Investigating Bilingual Literacy: Evidence from Malawi and Zambia.* (Education Research Report, No 24), London: Department for International Development.

------ (1996) 'Reading in Two Languages at Year 5 in African Primary Schools', *Applied Linguistics* 17(2): 182-209.

------ (1993a) *Report on Reading in English in Primary Schools in Malawi,* (Education Research Report, Serial Number 4), London: Overseas Development Administration.

------ (1993b) *Report on Reading in English in Primary Schools in Zambia.* (Education Research Report, No 5), London: Overseas Development Administration.

------ (1992) 'Consensus and Conflict Perspective on Language use in Bilingual Contexts', in F. Etxeberria and J. Arzamendi (eds.), *Elebitisuna eta Hizkuntz Jabekuntza / Bilingüismo y Adquisicion de Lenguas (Bilingualism and Language Acquisition),* Bilbao, Spanish Association of Applied Linguistics, 87-96.

------, P. Thompson, G. Varela and A. Makocho (2001a) 'Again! Kawarinso! Repetition in English and Chichewa in Malawi Classroom Discourse', in *Working Papers in Linguistics,* Vol. 5, School of Linguistics and Applied Language Studies, University of Reading: 67-83.

------, P. Thompson, G. Varela and A. Makocho (2001b) 'Repetition in Malawi Classrooms: the "discoursification" of text', presentation at 'Literacy and Language in Global Settings' Conference, Cape Town, November, (2001).

Williams, P. (1986) African Education under Siege, in H. Hawes, T. Coombe, C. Coombe and K. Lillis (eds.), *Education Priorities and Aid Responses in Sub-Saharan Africa.* London: ODA/University of London Institute of Education, 91-105.

Williams, T. D. (1978) *Malawi: the Politics of Despair,* Ithaca and London: Cornell University Press.

Wolff, H. (1964) 'Intelligibility and Inter-ethnic Attitudes', in D. Hymes (ed.), *Language in Culture and Society.* New York: Harper and Row, 440-445.

Woodhall, M. (1987) 'Earnings and Education', in G. Psacharopoulos (ed.) *Economics of Education: Research and Studies*, Oxford: Pergamon Press, 209-17.

Woods, A., P. Fletcher and A. Hughes (1986) *Statistics in Language Studies,* Cambridge: Cambridge University Press.

World Bank (1996) *Malawi: Human Resources and Poverty,* Report No 15437-MAI, The World Bank: Southern Africa Department.

------ (1995a) *Priorities and Strategies for Education: a World Bank Sector Review,* Washington: The World Bank.

------ (1995b) *The Use of First and Second Languages in Education: a Review of International Experience,* Washington: The World Bank.

------ (1990) *Poverty: World Development Report 1990,* Washington DC: World Bank.

World Factbook, http://www.odci.cia/publications/factbook/za.html accessed 10th January 2006.

Wright, M. W. (2001) 'More than just chanting: Multilingual Literacies, Ideology and Teaching Methodologies in Rural Eritrea', in B. Street (ed.), *Literacy and Development: ethnographic perspectives.* London: Routledge, 61-77.

Yahya-Othman, S. 1991. 'When international languages clash: the possible detrimental effects on development of conflict between English and Kiswahili in Tanzania', in Rubagumya, C. (ed.) *Language in Education in Africa*, Clevedon: Multilingual Matters, 42-53.

Zambezi Mission, (1986) *The Student's English-Chichewa Dictionary*, Blantyre: CLAIM. [first published in 1972 by the Zambezi Mission as the *English-Nyanja Dictionary*].

Zentella, A. C. (1997) *Growing up Bilingual*, Blackwell: Oxford.

Index

A

Aikman, 8
Anderson, 14
Appleton, 10
Arcand, 7, 8
Azariadis, 14
absenteeism, 22, 29, 100, 185
additive bilingualism, 66, 131
African Renaissance, 1, 195
African Union, 2, 5
aid, 4, 25, 197, 199
Arab War, 24

B

Bamgbose, 15
Bayart, 5
Baynham, 30, 49
Becker, 11
Berman, 56
Bermingham, 12
Bernbaum, 25
Bernhardt, 40, 61, 66, 82, 169
Blommaert, 50, 188, 189
Bond, 2, 5, 183
Bratt-Paulston, 66, 67
Brock-Utne, 197
Bunyi, 8, 15, 179
Banda, 24, 27, 190, 201, 204
Bantu language, 18, 20, 21, 29, 30,
    77, 86
Barotseland, 21
behaviorist, 15, 32, 35
Bemba, 17, 20
Berber, 177, 185
Botswana, 13, 21, 191, 200

C

Carrell, 62, 66, 169
Carter, 21, 57
Chall, 57
Chick, 39, 64, 176
Chifwa, 44
Chikalanga, 44, 63, 176
Chimombo, M, 45
Chimombo, S, 42
Clammer, 49
Clarke, 61
Cleghorn, 188
Cochrane, 13
Colclough, 11, 12, 25, 199
Connor, 61
Coulmas, 186, 187
Coxhead, 58
Criper, 63
Croft, 40
Crooks, 7
Crystal, 20
Cummins, 8, 65, 66, 179
Cameroon, 9, 179
Canada, 65, 66
Census, 21, 25, 26, 27, 190,
Chewa, 17, 20, 22, 25, 27, 42, 168,
    170, 183, 190
ChiChewa, 17, 18, 20, 27, 29-33,
    35, 41, 45, 46, 67-69, 71, 76,
    77, 79, 81-86, 90, 106, 109, 110,
    118-128, 130-134, 139, 141,
    142, 145, 148, 154-157, 162-
    164, 166-170, 172, 173, 189,
    190
Chilomwe, 27
Chimuthali, 22
ChiNyanja, 27
ChiTumbuka, 27, 29
ChiYao, 27
choral repetition, 41, 42, 43, 173
Cloze, 44, 45, 79-83, 87, 115

colonisation, 187
Commission for Africa, 2, 6, 7, 198
Communicative, 30, 36, 43, 48
community schools, 22
competence, 52, 54, 55-57, 64, 66, 77, 82, 83, 86, 118, 127, 130, 155, 164, 169-174, 182, 184, 191, 195
Comprehensive Development Framework, 4
Congo, 24, 187
conjunctive orthography, 86
corruption, 5, 198, 200, 201

D

Davies, 54
De Gaay Fortnum, 164, 165
De Haan, 10
Denison, 6, 7
Devereux, 29
Devine, 61
Djité, 190, 191
Dowden, 188
Durstan, 21
debt, 3, 5, 6, 199
development, 5, 6-10, 12-15, 32, 37, 57, 63, 186, 187, 189-193, 195-201, 203
diglossia, 52, 53
drop-out, 22, 25, 28, 102

E

Edwards, 188, 199, 200, 201
Eisemon, 63
Elkan, 7
Ellerman, 6
Elley, 56, 62
economic capital, 198, 199
enrolment, 22, 28, 195
environmental, 2, 9, 10, 13, 193

exoglossic languages, 1, 194
Experimental World Literacy programme, 14
externalities, 12

F

Farah, 49
Favreau, 61
Ferguson, 52, 53
Finlayson, 25
Fishman, 53, 192
Francis, 58
Fries, 55
Fry, 57
first language, 1, 7, 18, 19, 27, 61, 62, 64, 66, 138, 186, 189

G

Gadsden, 67
George, 9
Goldman, 53
Goodman, 137
Greaney, 62
Green, 89
Gregory, 51
Grimes, 18, 26
Grin, 8
GDP, 4, 10, 11, 16, 17, 25, 188, 192, 193
gender, 2, 45, 115
Ghana, 13, 15
Girls' Attainment in Basic Literacy and Education, 45
globalization, 1, 5
grammar, 54-56, 58, 80, 140, 166

H

Harbison, 13

Hardman, 22
Hatch,88
Hawes, 194, 197
Haynes, 55, 60, 61, 150
Herbert, 8, 50
Heugh, 8, 15, 172, 184, 185, 191, 196
Heyneman, 67
Hicks, 11, 13
Hirsh, 61
Hobcraft, 13, 194
Hoppers, 81
Hornberger, 39, 196
Huckin, 61
Hudson, 61
Hymes, 48
health, 2, 9, 13, 15, 192, 193
HIV/AIDS, 192, 193, 198
Hukwe, 21
human capital, 193, 198, 201
human needs, 9, 10, 12, 192, 199

I

Ilon, 199
inference questions, 142-146, 153, 155, 160
initial literacy, 23, 45, 178, 179, 181, 183, 196
Integrated Framework for Least Developed Countries, 4
International Institute for Educational Planning, 45
International Monetary Fund, 3, 4, 199

J

Jimenez, 153
Johnson, 45, 46

K

Kadzamira, 12, 28, 29, 31, 32, 45, 46, 79180, 193, 195, 199, 202
Kamil, 62, 66, 71, 169
Kapembwa, 35, 44
Kashoki, 17, 18, 19, 20, 21, 55, 86, 164, 166, 179
Kasonde-Ng'andu, 17, 21, 22, 36, 45, 183
Kaul, 194
Kayambazinthu, 17, 20, 24, 26, 27, 29, 154, 190, 191
Kell, 50, 51
Kelly, 21, 201
Kenny, 7
Khaila, 193
Khor, 5
King, K, 8, 25, 183, 202
King, P, 6
Kinnear, 92
Klare, 57
Knight, 12, 194
Krashen, 60
Kulpoo, 15
Kenya, 13, 15, 63, 188, 197
Khoisan, 21
Kwengo, 21

L

Lambert, 66
Laufer, 58
Lee, 62, 66, 169
Leki, 57
Lehmann, 20
Lewin, 7, 10, 11, 13
Lind, 14
Linden, 22, 25
Linehan, 23, 166, 183, 196
Lockheed, 12
Luangala, 204

Luckett, 63
Lungwangwa, 71, 76
language policies, 1, 2, 67, 68, 104, 178, 197, 201, 202, 203
language rights, 196
lexis, 20, 58, 83, 154
lingua franca, 20, 27, 186, 191
literacy, 7-12, 14, 15, 23, 25, 41, 45, 48-51, 63-65, 67, 70, 81, 166, 167, 170, 177-179, 183, 185, 186, 187, 195-197, 201
Live, 83
look and say, 30, 31, 35, 37, 169, 170, 172
Lozi, 17, 21, 42

M

Machingaidze, 8, 15, 63
Macdonald, 172
Manchisis, 23
Martin-Jones, 51
May, 43, 187, 195
Mazrui, 187
Mbeki, 1, 5, 10
McAdam, 25
McArthur, 59
McGinn, 202
Mchazime, 29, 45
Milner, 28, 46, 175
Mincer, 11
Moock, 12
Moon, 58
Mwanakatwe, 188, 189
Myers-Scotton, 191
Make Poverty History, 2
Mali, 13, 63
maternal education, 13, 194
Mauritius, 15
medium of instruction, 15, 22, 23, 29, 41, 47, 63, 67, 90, 106, 132, 172, 179-181, 183, 184, 194-197, 202
Millennium Development Goals, 2, 4, 7
modernisation, 188, 192
Morocco, 64, 66, 177
mother tongue, 23, 29, 52, 54, 62-64, 173, 178, 185, 189
Mwana Lesa, 17

N

Nassor, 15
Nation, 58, 59, 60
Ninyoles, 53,
Nkamba, 15, 19, 45, 63, 175
Nuttall, 49, 182
Namibia, 15
neo-liberal, 9
New Partnership for Africa's Development, 2, 8
Nigeria, 10, 63, 200
non-standard (language variety), 27, 52, 53, 164-167, 170
Northern Rhodesia, 16, 21
numeracy, 11, 12
Nyanja, 20, 27, 30, 44, 69, 71, 76-86, 109, 111-118, 120, 130-135, 139, 141-143, 154, 155, 157-159, 161-168, 170-172, 174, 177
Nyasaland, 24
Nyau, 22

O

Ouane, 201
Organisation of African Unity, 2

P

Papen, 51
Pakenham, 24, 200

Pearson, 53
Pennycuick, 8
Phillipson, 187
Postlethwaite, 8, 194
Puchner, 13
phonics, 35
polity, 198-200
poverty, 1-7, 9,10, 13, 14, 25, 36,
    170, 180, 185
Poverty Reduction Strategy Paper,
    4
productivity, 11, 12

Q

qualified teachers, 28, 195

R

Rampton, 245
Ranger, 17
Rassool, 8, 14, 49
Rayner, 55
Richards, 59
Robinson, 7, 8, 9, 50, 200, 201
Rogers, 9, 14, 25, 52
Roller, 64
Rubin, 192
reading aloud, 31, 32, 35, 36, 39,
    40, 86, 137, 140, 145, 153,
    168, 172, 184
reading strategies, 70, 136, 137
religious affiliation, 17
repetition, 28, 30, 32, 35, 39-43,
    50, 172, 173, 194
rural schools, 28, 69, 71, 81, 87,
    92-95, 100, 105, 109, 134, 135

S

Sachs, 5, 200
Saville-Troike, 57

Schlesinger, 55
Schmied, 15
Schulte, 57
Schumann, 177
Seashore, 60
Segalowitz, 61, 172
Serpell, 15, 41, 53, 63, 66, 117, 164,
    171, 173, 183, 189, 197
Sharma, 43, 44
Siachitema, 117
Sichinga, 26
Simons, 138
Smith D, 3, 4
Smith F, 81
Spencer, 187
Steffensen, 138
Street, 8, 14, 29, 49, 50, 51
Strother, 56
Stroud, 189
Subbarao, 13
Summers, 13
Swain, 5, 8, 65, 66, 179
safetalk, 39, 177
scramble for Africa, 186
screening theory, 11
second language, 8, 18, 19, 34, 52-
    54, 56-58, 60-66, 138, 150,
    162, 170, 177, 181, 183, 184
sex, 75, 76, 87, 90, 93-95, 97-99,
    101, 102, 104-106, 108, 111,
    114-116, 122-125, 127, 130,
    134
slaves, 24
social capital, 198-202
social exclusion, 10
South Africa, 1, 15, 63, 64, 172,
    176, 180, 181, 184, 185, 191,
    197
Southern African Consortium for
    Measuring Educational Quality,
    45
standard (language variety), 20, 52,

53, 80, 166, 167, 186, 187
Structural Adjustment Programme 17, 198
subsidies, 5, 199
subtractive bilingualism, 66, 131
syllabic approach (to teaching reading), 30, 31, 169, 170
syncretism, 17, 25
syntax, 54-58, 165

T

Tabatabai, 1
Thomas, A, 9
Thomas, H, 24
Tikly, 1, 6, 8
Treffgarne, 8, 195
Trudell, 176, 179
teacher training, 32, 36, 37
Town Nyanja, 20, 165, 166
trade, 5-7, 24, 199

U

Urquhart, 49, 51, 55, 56, 57
Uganda, 10, 13
UNESCO, 14, 23, 197
unification, 23, 188, 189, 192
urban schools, 28, 69, 71, 87, 92, 96, 103, 105, 108, 109, 117, 125-127, 134, 135

V

Vale, 195
Vellutino, 55, 56, 57
Verhoeven, 167
Vihman, 53
Voigts, 15
vocabulary, 54, 55, 57-60, 146,
147, 166, 170-172, 176, 181
voice, 9

W

Wagner, 8, 49, 64, 177
Wallace, 49, 81, 153
Watkins, 8, 14, 194
Watson, 8
Webb, 8, 15, 174, 181, 191, 197
Wheeler, 10, 13
Wickstead, 3, 4
Widdowson, 48
Williams, A., 166
Williams, E, 44, 45, 46, 102, 175
Williams, P., 37
Williams, 24
Wolff, 20
Woodhall, 11
Woods, 148
Wright, 40
World Bank, 3, 4, 6, 17, 25, 193, 199
world knowledge, 142, 144, 147, 153, 155
World Trade Organisation, 4, 5

Y

Yahya-Othman, 63
Yao, 24
Year of Africa, 2

Z

Zentella, 53
Zambia Basic Education Course, 36
Zambia Primary Course, 35, 44
Zanzibar, 15
Zimbabwe, 8, 13, 15, 63, 64